To: Grandma & Grandpa
Thanks for helping me → (encouraghs)
to dream
     Ben

www.EuropeBackpack.com

To Mary and Leslie,
I hope you enjoy these real
stories from Europe.

cheers,

Europe FROM A Backpack

Real Stories from Young Travelers Abroad

Edited by
Mark Pearson and Martin Westerman

PEARSON VENTURE GROUP
SEATTLE, WASHINGTON U.S.A.
WWW.EUROPEBACKPACK.COM

Europe From a Backpack: Real Stories from Young Travelers Abroad
First Edition

Pearson Venture Group
P.O. Box 70525
Seattle, WA 98127-0525
U.S.A.
www.EuropeBackpack.com

Library of Congress Cataloging-in-Publication Data:

Europe From a Backpack: Real Stories from Young Travelers Abroad / edited by Mark Pearson and Martin Westerman. –1st ed. Pearson Venture Group.
p.   Cm.

Does not include index
ISBN 0-9743552-0-8
1.   Anthology—Travel Book. 2. Travel—Essays
Library of Congress Control Number: 2003095329

Cover design by Greg Pearson (www.gregpearsondesign.com)
Coliseum photo, 3rd and 4th from left on back: Copyright © Nicolay Thomassen
Top left cover photo: Copyright © Andrew Schein
Top right and bottom left on cover, 1st on back cover: Copyright © Katie Brown
5th from left on back cover: Copyright © Kiersten Throndsen

Printed in the United States of America

10 9 8 7 6 5 4 3 2 1

To my Grandfather and fellow traveler, Waldemar E. Pearson

The world is a book, and those who do not travel, read only a page.

Saint Augustine

The whole object of travel is not to set foot on foreign land; it is at last to set foot on one's own country as a foreign land.

G.K. Chesterton

CONTENTS

Chapter 5: GERMANY

Chapter 6: CZECH REPUBLIC

Chapter 7: HUNGARY

Chapter 8: AUSTRIA

Chapter 9: SWITZERLAND

Chapter 10: ITALY

Chapter 11: GREECE

Chapter 12: OFF THE BEATEN PATH

INTRODUCTION

When I returned home from studying art history in Rome and backpacking, my friends asked, "How was your time in Europe?" I didn't even know where to begin summarizing the four-months of stories and reflections that left a lasting impression on me. Since most of my friends were not interested in viewing all 2,200 of my digital photos, I ultimately chose a few must-tell stories: the Tuscan family who took me in when I got stranded in their hill town; camping overnight in the queue for the Wimbledon tennis tournament; my private tour of the Sistine Chapel; visiting the Dachau Concentration Camp; and hiking in the Swiss Alps. These life-shaping experiences helped communicate the larger story of my time abroad.

Every year, Europe draws 1.7 million Americans between ages 18 and 29, as well as hundreds of thousands of Canadians, Australians, and Britons. Whether it's an obligatory one or two-month backpacking tour, or studying or working abroad, young people are flocking to the continent. Despite the power struggle between the European Union and the United States, Europe's old-world charm, rich history and natural beauty still draw young adults across the political spectrum.

Europe From a Backpack collects these must-tell stories of young adults backpacking on shoestring budgets. The contributors capture life abroad: engaging in the culture, sleeping in streets and hostels, living with a host family, train-travel debacles, romance, and an outlook of taking each day as if it were the last.

This book is organized to reflect the countries most visited by young travelers: United Kingdom, Spain, France, Italy, Germany, Netherlands, Switzerland, Greece and so on. Stories range from a harrowing attack in Morocco to bribery on the Moldovan border; bicycling through Austria to running with the bulls in Spain; painting the Eiffel Tower to an awkward proposition on the train from Budapest to Vienna. Reflections on each city attempt to draw out the themes of the major cities in Europe. From a night at the Hofbräuhaus in Munich to a whirlwind tour through Berlin, one is able to recall a prior trip or get a foretaste of the adventure that awaits.

Why are so many young people going abroad? Dr. James Clowes, director of the University of Washington's Comparative History of Ideas program, compares traveling abroad to one's first childhood sleepover at a friend's house. In many ways, it's sensory overload. Not only does the sleepover family have a different set of rules (your friend can watch PG-13 movies) and values (they pray before meals), they eat strange food, the house smells funny, and they have four dogs. All that your senses recorded became clear when you returned home to what you consider "normal." The same is true for Europe. From the absence of ice cubes to the presence of ancient ruins in the midst of modern cities, the sound of the language, the taste of the food, the smell of the hostel and the sight of a sunset will make an indelible mark on your life.

I invite the reader to travel vicariously through these stories and see how the ordinary becomes extraordinary. Travel always places one at a new *point*; and the result is quite often a new *view*. May they motivate and inspire you to travel abroad.

Mark Pearson
Seattle, Washington

All during the fiesta you had the feeling, even when it was quiet, that you had to shout any remark to make it heard. It was the same feeling about any action.

ERNEST HEMINGWAY, *The Sun Also Rises*

Spain

The Running of the Bulls:
He who hesitates is lunch

Pamplona, Spain

BILLY ANDERSON

"WHY AM I HERE?" THIS IS THE THOUGHT GOING THROUGH MY mind as I prepare for the *encierro*, the famous Running of the Bulls in Pamplona, Spain. *Los Sanfermines*, as the festival is known by the local Pamplonicos, has been famous ever since Ernest Hemingway described it in *The Sun Also Rises*. If you don't run fast, I am told, your sun will never rise again.

For four weeks I had been backpacking around Europe, hearing stories of the infamous Running of the Bulls: a week-long extravaganza of drinking, dancing and partying, highlighted by the bull run itself — a mass of lunatics chased by six extremely large and unhappy bulls. Thus far, my European adventure had gone smoothly. I hadn't been mugged, maimed or laid waste, and I was feeling the need for a little excitement. That cute town in the Austrian Alps suddenly seemed stale. At that moment came something I don't normally have a surplus of: courage. I thought to myself: "I'm a pretty fast runner. I could outrun a bull or two. What the hell, let's give it a go."

So now, three days later on a sunny July morning, I'm standing on Santo Domingo Road in Pamplona for what could very well be the last day of my life. I wait impatiently with a few hundred adrenaline seekers, listening anxiously for the rockets signaling that the gates have opened and the bulls have been turned loose. The night before, I'd been cruising Pamplona's bars, full of sangria-induced bravado, boasting of my upcoming adventure. Now my knees are shaking and my mouth is parched. The guy

18

beside me in the crowd leans over to me with a look of panic and says, "I don't think my travel insurance covers this."

Boom! The rockets sound and I have one sudden wish: "Beam me up Scotty!" But Scotty is obviously asleep at the Transporter switch, because I'm still standing in the cobblestone street as the crowd begins running like men possessed. I have a sudden flash of complete sobriety. Every ounce of machismo drains from my body. People are yelling and hollering; it seems I'm one of them. As I start into a full-out sprint, I have a horrifying realization: I can run only as fast as the people in front of me. At this moment, self-preservation takes over, and I switch from a running-in-sheer-terror tactic to a run-push, run-push strategy.

The buildings lining the street overflow at every orifice with spectators who are smart enough to just watch. Side streets are barricaded with fences — and the remainder of the Spanish spectators, who kindly push you back into the running throng should you attempt a quick exit. The end of the run empties into the *Plaza de Toros*, or bull ring. It is at this bottleneck where most of the accidents usually take place. A fatal goring is not uncommon. I dash into the ring, the bulls' hooves pounding toward me. I'm convinced that, out of all these people, the only target they see is my plump rear end. The red shorts might have been a bad idea.

Some of the spectators in the stands boo us as we enter the ring. We're near the front of the running crowd, which is apparently for the wimps. It seems it's more "honorable" if you're at the back of the crowd, with a better chance of getting trampled. In my opinion, the wimps are the people sitting in the stands. Shouldn't I be booing them?

The bulls charge in behind us as we position ourselves around the perimeter of the ring, simultaneously catching our breath and thanking the Lord for sparing our lives. I'd been told that once the bulls were ushered out of the ring, mid-size bulls would be let in and we would spend the next half-hour horsing around with them, trying to keep a healthy distance. It is at this point that I get a little confused about which bulls are which. Maybe it's the adrenaline of the run or perhaps the sleepless night and crate of sangria coursing through my veins, but I peel myself from the crowd and run up to the lead bull. Suddenly I'm not so confused anymore. I am downright petrified. I am in something like a Bugs Bunny cartoon as I stare level-eyed at this behemoth with steam pumping out his nostrils. From out of nowhere come two locals with bamboo sticks. Their job is smacking the bulls on the behind to keep them in line. But instead of hitting the bulls, they wind up like Babe Ruth and whack me in the head.

As they walk away, their sticks broken, I reach up to discover blood streaming down my face. A young Spanish boy takes me by the arm and ushers me to the infirmary under the bull ring, where I am cleaned up. I either don't need stitches or they're too busy to give me any, but I don't care — I just want to get back to the ring and the excitement I had traveled three days to experience. And if my head wound turns into a scar that I can show off for the rest of my life, all the better.

Back in the ring, the crowd tries to stay away from the bulls. With so many people blocking the view, you have to watch the movement of the crowd to determine where the bulls are. If you get too focused on one bull, another can charge up from behind and flatten you like a tortilla. Suddenly the crowd parts, and there, much to my chagrin, is a bull bearing down on me. My brain is yelling, "RUN!" — but from head to toe I am frozen with fear. The bull's head crashes into my paella-stuffed stomach, sending me through the air to land in a heap of 100% terrified tourists. Luckily it doesn't come after me to attempt a disemboweling. I don't feel any pain. I may have lost a few brain cells, but I'm so scared and my heart pounding is so fast that all I can think is, "I've been trampled! I can't wait to tell my friends!"

Back home, long after the event, I fondly remember my brush with death. *Los Sanfermines* is still as popular as ever with Spaniards and tourists alike, and when I see it on TV or in the newspaper I proudly say to those around me, "I was there, man! I did that." I often contemplate a return to Pamplona, but … in the end, the desire to live until my mid-life crisis prevails.

Billy Anderson's head wound turned into a scar that now adds zest to his storytelling. In pursuit of a similar shot of adrenaline, Billy has tried bungee jumping and is a licensed skydiver. Adventures like the Running of the Bulls convinced him to leave his job in the corporate world to pursue a career in guiding trips and freelance writing. When not on the road, he lives on a lake in northern Ontario, Canada.

Camino de Santiago

Northern Spain

HEATHER NEALE

WE WERE STANDING ON THE SIDE OF A DUSKY HILL IN NORTHERN Spain, about to sleep in the same tiny cabin with a handful of other international strangers. My boyfriend, Dave, and I were stopped here along an ancient pilgrim's route we had been following for a solid two weeks. We still had roughly two more weeks to go before reaching the proverbial "pot of gold" at the end of this journey — the legendary bones of St. James, mythical or real brother of Jesus, depending who tells you the story, allegedly buried on the west coast of the country in the first century A.D.

We had chosen to walk there over a span of 30 days, give or take a few for sore feet, because it would enhance our relationship, test our strength, give us a chance to commune with the Spanish countryside and cost next to nothing. After spending some time in London, anything cheaper looked good. A lot of work to check out some bones, you say? Ah, but the destination lies in the journey.

The world-famous trek is named El Camino de Santiago, or "the way of James." It follows the route James' bones were carried to their burial location, and a wide cross-section of people from Europe, Australia, North and South America have been making this symbolic and prolific trip since the poor man died. Along the walk, signs mark significant points of interest, such as the stone bridge where King Ferdinand engaged in a gallant sword fight with a villainous foe, or the ornate castle fashioned out of love in Astorga by world renowned Spanish architect Antoni

Gaudi.

Seven hundred years ago, Templar Knights took it upon themselves to look out for travelers making this trip from the south of France, over the Pyrenees Mountain range out to Spain's west coast. Now it has become a collective effort. Hospitals along the way offer free treatment to all those pilgrims suffering from tendonitis in their legs or stiffness in their lower backs. Locals set up massage tables at the higher geographical points so that after a long hill climb, one can rest and relax in the sun, and ease the pain a little.

We smiled as elderly folks in berets or aprons shouted their best wishes from small stone-village sidewalks. We inhaled freshly brewed coffee made for us by warm and friendly restaurateurs while we sat for an hour or so at a time to rest our feet. The people we passed and met along the way had great appreciation for the strength of body and mind required to complete this journey, and their support is part of what gives travelers the energy to finish. It's a long journey by foot, but we were determined to do it. It would be a measure of our ability to endure in all aspects of our lives. So here we were, two weeks in, at a cabin in the small ruined town of Manjarin with our swollen feet.

The moment we showed up at the hostel's small wooden door, Dave was accosted by a mammoth white goose with anger-management issues. The hostel matron, Maura, was quick to jump in, grabbing the poor web-footed foe by the neck and scolding it. We were grateful. She smiled a toothy grin and said, 'Welcome, my friends; take off your shoes and make yourselves at home.' Her breathy melodic voice vibrated in the room like the soothing song of a siren after a stormy battle at sea. And stormy it was. By ten in the morning, Dave and I had already reached our kilometer quota for the day and he was content to stay put and drink beer with a handful of rowdy Spaniard men in some small roadside pub. It was me that got restless.

"It's only ten, Dave. We can get at least another twenty clicks behind us today and then go easier tomorrow — even sleep in past five a.m. for a change!" He was reluctant. I was determined. He was a compromiser, I was a totalitarian dictator. Our relationship didn't always work this way, but this time he could see the fire in my eyes. I would jump out of my skin hanging out there all day. We continued.

Almost exactly halfway into our walk to the next hostel, the rain clouds moved in. Clad in lightweight Northface shorts and tank tops, sporting backpacks that had not yet been waterproofed, we hurriedly transformed from happy-go-lucky hikers to drowned rats with marathon-length faces. Turning the bend, I spotted a little roadside restaurant, and we ran for it.

The owner, a lone man living in a village full of broken, abandoned houses and ghosts from years past, gave us a warning. "You are planning on going to Manjarin tonight?" He smirked.

"What?" I asked him, in my best Spanish accent.

"It's a pretty shady place you are headed for. They have no light, no water, no food, no bathrooms, and no showers, but they certainly have cucarachas…." (Cucarachas are cockroaches … I have trouble just saying it out loud.)

The man stuffed our bags full of day-old bread and *chorizo*, lemon Fanta drink and chocolate sugar cookies, informing us that there would be no sign of food for at least another twenty-five kilometers.

We rested for a while in the empty stone tavern, regrouping, recharging and speculating about whose turn it was to carry the heavy pack, and when we'd arrive at the hostel.

Just hours before, we had been cuddled into a cozy restaurant booth, tossing back cervezas and telling dirty jokes in broken Spanish. What the hell had I been thinking, making us plod on ahead?

The moment we exited the restaurant, I started to cry. Dave frowned.

"What are you crying about? This was your idea."

"I ... knnnoooooooow," I wailed like a big baby. I felt horrible that I had made such a poor decision and was forcing Dave to face its consequences too. Just then, like something out of a Hollywood film, a huge sheet of lightning split the sky and thunder cracked simultaneously.

He rolled his eyes. I looked at the ground. He stormed on ahead. I blubbered and wiped my eyes on my shirt. For the first time in our lives, we were miles from the nearest amenities, unprepared in shorts and T-shirts, and scared of what the day and the weather would bring. We kept moving forward.

When we reached the hostel in Manjarin and were introduced to Maura and the goose, and later to owner Tomas, the self-proclaimed Templar Knight, both Dave and I decided that camping out in this dark hut-like hostel with fairytale-esque characters was a great alternative to freezing out in the rain all night.

We stayed. Despite my misgivings about the place, we really enjoyed ourselves. Tomas cooked a candlelight dinner for us with the food he had carried in the week before. Maura poured the wine.

"Salud," Tomas cried from the end of the table as he raised his wine mug high. He then muttered to himself under his breath something about God and protection and salvation. I missed the jist of it due to my limited Spanish, but it sounded very sweet.

"Salud," we chirped in response. I love the warmth of that expression.

As it turns out, this hostel was the best experience of the whole trip. We stayed up late conversing with Tomas about the history of the Templar Knights, how they were the protectors of

Christ and his followers. When we got stuck behind language barriers, a shy blonde guy from Finland would pipe up from the darkest corner of the hut and offer us a translation. It's as though he was mute save for the dictionary filed conveniently in his brain.

We slept in the loft, cozy in our down sleeping bags, looking down on a crackling fire pit. Cows mooed all night long in the field outside, assuring me of my safety, lulling me into a dream state. The next morning, after rolling up our sleeping bags and washing our faces in a water bowl outside, we walked off down the gravel trail. We descended through clouds onto the next small ruined village below, mildly desperate for a bathroom, having had nothing but the great outdoors to fall back on for over a day. But we were well rested and ready to take on the world. And that's what we did.

Heather Neale is a Vancouver-based freelance writer with a love for travel. She has visited sixteen countries over the past ten years and is already planning her next trip. Heather received a Bachelor of Arts degree in English and Spanish literature and has now been published in Toronto's The Globe and Mail, The Georgia Straight, The Times Colonist, The Icelandic Canadian *and* The Edmonton Journal. *She is currently working on a novel and several anthologies. In her spare time, she can be spotted dancing salsa.*

Madrid at Midnight

Madrid, Spain

Cara Nissman

I SPIED THE YOUNG BARTENDER *MADRILEÑO* THROUGH THE window, fascinated by the motions of his rippling arms as he wiped down a countertop. Then and there I decided to seek refuge from the chafing January wind.

I walked in, grabbed a stool and ordered a *café con leche*. He was 19 years old, his name was Borja, and he invited me to have a drink with him after he finished his shift – at 12:30 a.m. In the endless nightlife of Madrid, people generally stay out past dawn. While I never would have agreed to a date that late back home, I was studying and backpacking abroad for a year. I decided to let down my guard, accept his offer, and see where the hypnotic power of the interminable night would lead me. The bartender turned out to offer more warmth than my coffee.

When we met outside the *cervecería* later on, I could smell the sweet scents of *chorizo* and coffee in the air. Borja laid his hand on my shoulder and led me to his favorite hangout.

If ever arose the question "Where would Jesus drink?," I have the answer:

Borja brought me to a shadowy bar decked out in red lighting and religious paraphernalia. Seated in a pew topped off with a large cross and surrounded by paintings of the man with heavenly connections, I decided to ignore the irony of getting smashed in front of Jesus — hey, I'm Jewish, so it didn't matter, right? — and chatted with my date about favorite sports, pop-culture icons, including Robert DeNiro and Penelope Cruz, and spots in Madrid.

I remarked on my infatuation with the *Museo del Prado*, revealing that I had spent countless hours trolling the art museum's halls to bask in the brilliance of painters Francisco de Goya and Diego Velásquez. I expressed my appreciation of the regal *Parque del Retiro*, where I often picnicked while watching *niños* play tag around the fountains. And I described my fondness for aimlessly wandering alone around the narrow, medieval streets of Madrid, discovering antique bookshops, quaint clothing boutiques and irresistible *pastelerías*, brimming with the aromas of fresh pastries.

He told me about his obsession with his *moto* and other Spanish youths' love of speeding on their motorcycles, explaining why I had seen so many of Madrid's young adults with crutches and casts. We shared a love of movies, including the film "Abre los ojos" (which unfortunately became "Vanilla Sky" in the United States). Acknowledging our spiritual setting, we talked about our values. I found it interesting that he didn't consider himself a particularly religious person, yet he favored this bar above countless others clustered in the area of northern Madrid, saying he enjoyed talking with the other regulars there. And Borja told me that he, among many other Spaniards in their early 20's, lived at home with no eagerness to leave until he married. Madrid's high cost of living and shortage of living spaces, he said, are partly to blame, but he also acknowledged a strong sense of tradition and familial ties.

As Borja walked me back to my apartment, he took my hand and asked if we could be *novios*. I laughed, considering that we had just met. He seemed sincere, so I diplomatically said that I thought we needed to know each other a little bit longer before we committed ourselves. Yet, his innocence was endearing. He hugged me and gallantly asked me for a *beso* goodnight. He kissed me on the cheek! After watching me struggle with my front door's old lock and making sure I got into my apartment, he waved goodbye.

I never went out with Borja again, but stored that night deep within my heart as one of my only encounters with a genuinely sweet young man from Madrid, recognizing after traveling the city alone for nearly a year that Borja's chivalry was the exception rather than the rule.

Indeed, a few months later, I suffered a serious wake-up call amid the shadows of Madrid's seemingly utopian nightlife.

I had spent the last four hours *saliendo de la marcha,* going clubbing, with my friend Judy one night in the part of downtown Madrid known as the *Puerta del Sol.* This area teems with youths, who like to meet at *Kilometro Cero,* a symbol on the ground that marks the center of Spain's road network, and disperse to various bars under the Great Gatsby-esque glow of the enormous neon sign for *Tío Pepe* sherry.

We sucked down *vodka y limón* (vodka mixed with lemon Fanta) and *Cuba libre* (rum and Coke) while swaying to Shakira, experiencing little drama, save a sneer from a bearded guy twice our age. We had been living in Madrid for five months, studying the city's culture and customs as much as the subjects introduced in our art history and theater classes. We claimed the night as our public playground, knowing that if we didn't take part, we would be missing the pulse of Madrid.

Parts of Madrid, we had learned, betray a struggle between tradition and modernity. Austere Internet cafes buzzing with activity share the same streets with tiny fabric shops boasting dusty bolts of lace and silk. The intellectual dramas presented at the historic *Teatro Español* compete with bawdy drag-queen shows down the block. And the spots where you can find trendy threads and popular music during the day often degrade into dangerous haunts for heroin addicts and raucous drunks at night. But we had grown confident about exploring the city's hot spots on our own, feeling as if we were impervious to any evil that might have lingered in the shadows.

Before my friend and I parted ways that night, we decided to share *churros*, or plain doughnuts, and *chocolate*, hot chocolate as thick as hot fudge (the typical Spanish post-partying indulgence) at the venerable *Chocolatería San Ginés*. We mooned over the muscular *camarero* who served us. After dancing for hours, ignoring sore feet, strained eyes and impending headaches, savoring these treats fortified us for our long walks home.

Having strolled back solo to my apartment dozens of times before without difficulty, I began my trek feeling as safe as I would walking from the laundry room to my dorm in Boston. Passing the *panaderías* that would soon emit scents of sourdough, I hummed a Chayanne song and turned aimlessly on to my street. At 12:30 a.m., the street was silent, save for one *cervecería*, at which a couple of men and women chatted casually in the cool spring breeze.

As I passed them, a gangly guy in a gray suit shouted a greeting and asked me if I'd fancy sharing a *copa* with him, holding up his wineglass as if he were toasting a ghostly dinner party in the dead of night.

Exhausted from dancing downtown, I acknowledged him with a tepid "Hola," shook my head and continued on my way, feeling the warming effects of the chocolate wearing off and my eyelids drooping toward sleep with every step.

As I neared my apartment, which was then about half a mile away, I heard footsteps and turned to see the boisterous man grinning mischievously at me.

His voice stilted and hair mussed, the strange man asked me why I didn't want to have a drink with him and implored me to accompany him back to the bar for a beer.

I chuckled nervously and again declined politely as I quickened my pace, but he continued to shadow me until he suddenly caught up with me and grabbed my right arm and purse, now shouting about the damn drink. I swung around in shock at how rapidly everything had escalated, struggled and wrenched myself free, running and screaming in vain. There was nobody but my pursuer to hear my pleas.

Fortunately I had sobered up by that point and dashed with a fervor I would have killed for during my junior high track meets. Whizzing past my favorite coffee shop and grocery store, with colorful signs advertising comforting items such as milk and crackers, I ran past my apartment, fearing that he would catch me at the door. As I ran around the block to try to lose him, I noticed that the man's energy persisted while my faith dwindled. I started imagining the worst scenario and tightened my grip around my keys.

Without warning, the guy tripped and a last burst of hope shot through me and carried me to my door. I fumbled with the latch as he collected himself and sprinted towards me. I leapt through the open door and locked it behind me as if a ravenous pit bull were lunging at me. Watching him wail and bang on the door, I defiantly stepped into the elevator and reclaimed the night.

Cara Nissman lived in Madrid and backpacked alone around Western Europe for about a year, thanks to the Boston University Madrid Internship Program and a Pamela Posen Endowed Memorial Scholarship. She is now a features reporter at The Boston Herald. *She travels and writes about her experiences every chance she gets, and hopes to return to Europe soon.*

My First Day in Spain

Madrid, Spain

Peter Malcolm

It began as the most exciting day of my life. It ended as the most terrifying.

On the morning of August 28th, I arrived in Madrid, Spain, from Seattle, wide-eyed and giddy with excitement, not knowing that in 14 hours my life would be in danger.

For the moment, life was great.

I was 19 years old with a pocket full of traveler's checks and nothing but good things on the horizon. It was the first day of four months I was to spend in Spain.

My final destination was the coastal city of Alicante, where I was going to live with a host family and attend the local university. Accompanying me on my voyage were John and Javi — my best friends from my stateside school, Western Washington University.

We weren't due to arrive in Alicante for three days, so we had time to kill in the Spanish capital. Luckily, we had a place to go. Javi is originally from Spain, and a substantial part of his family tree is still rooted there. The plan was to find our way to his grandparents' apartment to set up our center of operations for the next few days. We hauled our mountain of luggage through the massive *Barajas* terminal and found a taxi driver willing to accommodate us for a minimal extra fee.

The drive through the city was magnificent and filled with spectacular sights — the classic Spanish bull ring, the legendary Real Madrid soccer stadium and — of course — the golden arches of McDonald's.

32

After a 20-minute drive we arrived at Javi's grandparents' house, nestled deep in a crowded residential district somewhere in the sprawling metropolis of Madrid. We received a warm greeting from the elderly Spanish couple, highlighted by the customary *dos besos*, two kisses, and a barrage of seemingly friendly words I woefully didn't understand.

After we lugged our godforsaken luggage up the five flights of stairs in the sweltering Spanish heat, we retreated into the spare room to discuss our plan for the evening.

"You guys have no idea what it's like," said Javi, as he went into his formulaic yet enthralling stories of Spanish nightlife. "Everybody parties till at least 7 in the morning, the music is unbelievable and the girls are out of this world."

By now John and I were getting worked into a frenzy and we almost lost it when Javi told us that Spanish women *love* American guys (a statement I later found to be grossly inaccurate).

Around 8:30 p.m. the three of us hopped in a cab. Unbeknownst to us, the seemingly insignificant ride set into motion the wheels of fate, putting us on course for an encounter we would never forget.

"Can you believe 24 hours ago we were back home?" John asked me as we drove past the Spanish parliament buildings.

"Well, actually, we were on a plane, but I know what you mean," I said, trying not to take anything away from the surreal feeling I knew we were experiencing. Soon we were let loose in the heart of the city and proceeded directly to the nearest bar.

After 30 minutes of guzzling *cervezas* and ogling the 50th Penelope Cruz look-alike, I decided to make a toast and raised my pint of Heineken. "To good friends and to the first of many great nights we'll have on this trip."

Javi and John echoed my sentiments as we clinked our glasses. Next on our agenda was to make our way to Club Joy, a Javi-described "dance club utopia," and a place where we could get in for half-price with the coupon we ripped out of some "Explore Europe" book.

We pressed our way through the densely populated Plaza del Sol, unsuccessfully searching for the club and taking in all the things that endlessly flooded our senses. The enticing smell of paella wafting out of a cafe, the obnoxious sound of mopeds careening through traffic and the awe-inspiring sight of the city skyline set against a vivid orange sunset.

Just when we thought we were lost and Javi was prepared to ask a local to point us in the right direction, a skinny, middle-aged man approached John and struck up a conversation in Dutch-accented English.

"Hey, how are you guys doing tonight?" he asked John in a friendly, interested tone.

"Not too bad, thanks," John said. "We're just trying to find our way to Club Joy so we can party like rock stars."

The friendly Dutch stranger said he was headed to the same club and offered to lead us to the sacred palace of music, beer and women. We were more than happy to follow and I welcomed the chance to speak English with someone other than my travel mates.

The man, who told us his name was Carl, was friendly, no question there, but after a few blocks his topics of discussion shifted from praising Americans and congratulating us on our arrival to inner-city violence and drug dealing. Eventually I noticed we were getting farther and farther from the crowds of people and began to get leery of our guide's intentions.

Javi and John had noticed too. Every few moments we shot looks at one another as if to say, "This guy is really sketchy. We need to get the hell out of here."

A shadow of fear crept over me. Suddenly, a group of eight

or nine Moroccan thugs greeted our guide with high-fives. They joked and laughed at us while conversing in a foreign tongue. I noticed a patch of angry-red needle marks dotting Carl's arm as he lead us down the increasingly isolated back roads. With each additional sign, the chances of our safe passage to the club seemed to diminish.

"We need to get our asses outta here," John whispered, as Carl urged us along.

I noticed Carl surveying the surroundings; his scruffy, gaunt face was looking from side to side, deciding if this spot was removed enough from the bustle of the Plaza.

Suddenly, Javi decided it was time to take action.

"What the hell do you want with us?" he asked as I held my breath for fear of Carl's response.

"To take you to the club," he responded automatically, though the assurance with which he answered was wavering.

After a few more uneasy blocks of walking, Javi spoke again.

"Hey bro," he stammered, "Thanks for taking us along and everything, but we really gotta go back and meet our grandparents."

Carl must have sensed the fear and desperation in Javi's plea, because at that moment he dropped the friendly tour-guide façade.

"I don't give a fuck about your grandparents!" he yelled. A wave of fear coursed through my body.

Around me, everything seemed to stop. I felt as if I was in a dream — or, rather, a nightmare. The seconds passed like hours, and it wasn't until Carl spoke again that I realized the magnitude of our situation.

"I'm not here to fuckin' play games with you; I'm here to rob you."

At that moment the three of us saw a ray of hope approaching in the form of five men in their 20s, talking jovially and heading straight for us. I flashed Javi a desperate look and he courageously took action.

"*Ayuda me, ayuda me*, help me, help me," he pleaded as the entourage marched past us. But his calls for help were ignored, and they only managed to aggravate our already-angry acquaintance.

"That was very stupid of you; do it again and one of your friends will die."

I was stunned. How could these people not try to help us? Our only chance of escaping the ordeal with our money had vanished; now I was concerned about escaping with my life. Carl opened his black leather fanny pack and pulled out a syringe half-filled with blood.

"This needle is filled with my own AIDS-infected blood. Give me your money or I'll stab one of you."

The syringe was pointed directly at my face. My back was to the brick wall of a rundown apartment complex. John was to my right and Javi to my left. Carl was directly in front of me, his eyes cold and ruthless. I was at his mercy. I thought I was going to lose control of my bladder.

"Give me everything you've got."

Automatically, I reached into my pocket and pulled out my remaining 2,000 pesetas (roughly $15) and prayed that he would just take the money and leave. John and Javi did the same, handing over their wads of bills as submissively as possible.

Carl seemed extremely disappointed.

"What the fuck is this?" he asked furiously. "Where is the rest of it?"

"I'm sorry sir, that's all we brought out with us. I'm sorry," I stammered in a feeble attempt to pacify him.

"Do you want this," I asked frantically, fumbling to undo the silver Swiss Army watch on my left wrist.

But Carl wasn't interested. He didn't take my watch, nor did he ask for John's $5,000 Rolex, or any of the silver chains dangling from our necks. He had our money in his pocket and our lives in his hands.

Just then, Carl let out a laugh, threw the needle to the pavement and crushed it under his boot.

"You think I'm stupid enough to walk around with an AIDS needle?" he asked.

We were duped. He robbed us with a very convincing bluff. I was at a loss.

"If you want to fight, let's go," he said. "I'll take on all three of you."

I just wanted to get out of there, so I signaled John and Javi not to try any of the ideas that were undoubtedly circulating in their heads, and we began to head down the way we came — toward safety.

We hadn't gone 20 feet before Carl called after me.

"Hey you, come here for a second."

Every part of me said not to walk toward him, but I did. I couldn't help it. John and Javi shot me looks that said, "What the hell are you doing?"

"Listen to me carefully," Carl said when I was next to him, his eyes flashing dangerously. "You seem like the calm one, so tell your friends not to try anything or those Moroccans you saw will kill all of you."

I promised I would make sure nobody would start anything and waited, praying that he would let me leave.

"One more thing," Carl said as I turned to leave. "Can I bum a smoke?"

It was so unexpected, I was happy to comply. I gave him a cigarette from my pack of Camels and provided him with a lighter as well. What I did next still amazes me to this day. I extended my hand to the man who had only moments ago threatened my life and robbed me. Carl grabbed it and shook it firmly for a second, then turned and fled into the night.

I'm not sure why I shook Carl's hand, but my theory is that I was so relieved to be free that I shook it out of gratitude — thanking him for not killing me.

Whenever I tell this story to friends, their response is the same: "Why couldn't the three of you take him on? He was only an old skinny dude with a needle that turned out to contain no life-threatening diseases."

I respond by saying that you don't know how to react in situations like that when pure adrenaline and fear are guiding your every decision. Yes, it is true we could have taken him in a fight, but I don't think that would have been the smartest decision.

When we returned to Javi's grandparent's place and told them our account, they praised our handling of the situation and told us about a similar mugging that took place two weeks before. In that instance the Americans being mugged put up resistance and were killed — by a group of Moroccans who were lurking in the shadows.

Peter Malcolm is a 21-year-old journalism major at Western Washington University who is having Europe withdrawals. Traveling abroad was a great experience for him and he was ecstatic to be able to contribute a story to the readers of this collection. What he hopes people take away from this is a desire to live it up in the great cities around the world — and to come out in one piece. This is his first submission to a narrative publication. He has previously been published in his school paper and magazine.

24 Hours in Ibiza

Ibiza, Spain

Avi Vichniac

You know how it is when you go to a party and the place is bumping, but around 1 or 2 a.m., the party fades. A few people in the crowd are still energized, but that's not enough to keep you going. Soon you find yourself tired and ready to call it a night. Now picture yourself in a place where everyone is that upper-echelon partier, no one wants to quit, and the music is so intense that you feel like you could keep going forever. Welcome to the Spanish island of Ibiza, a destination filled with white sandy beaches, immaculate architecture and a nightlife that never ends. If one party draws to a close, you just simply move on to the next. Take this 24-hour cycle for example:

It was Monday night, and I started off at the bars much like I would on a normal night out. The place of choice was called Base Bar, a chic spot overlooking the marina of Ibiza Town. I began the night relaxing, sipping on vodka Red Bulls along with two college buddies. We couldn't wait for the anything-goes atmosphere of the "White Isle" to begin, and soon enough it did. By midnight, the marina air turned electric from the swarms of supermodels, disco moguls, and high-rolling backpackers, and we had prime seats. It didn't take long to realize that in just one short hour, we had encountered a full year's worth of beautiful women in the U.S. This is no exaggeration. Ibiza is filled with girls that no one from home would believe exist, women that put our American models and actresses to shame. If we tried to describe this scene to our friends, we know they wouldn't believe us, because hey, we wouldn't have either. At around 2 a.m., we couldn't take it anymore and it was time to hit a club called Privilege.

We rode to the club in style via the Disco Bus. Only in Ibiza would the public transportation system be fully equipped with blaring house music and route its buses specifically to the mega-clubs. They really thought of everything on this island. At about 2:30 a.m., we made it into Privilege. Look it up in the *Guinness Book of World Records*, this is the world's largest club. We couldn't believe our eyes when we walked in and saw thousands of people going mental on the dance floor. This mind-blowing complex is host to a colossal main room, giant pool, stage setup, energetic side room, chill-out dome and first-rate outdoor patio. I even found a DJ spinning in the bathroom.

Now, we knew Mondays in Ibiza were synonymous with Manumission, the craziest club night of the week, but we didn't know exactly what that entailed. At about 4 a.m. we realized we were in a place where unconventional and outlandish behavior was the norm. On the dance floor we witnessed everything from acrobats and fire-breathers to midgets on stilts and dancers performing kinky sex acts. All around us partygoers danced the night away to the bumping beats of the famous international DJs that Ibiza always attracts. That night, it was UK legend John Kelly and Fat Boy Slim. At 6:30 a.m., the club was not dying down but was intensifying. As daylight slowly seeped in through the club, the energy of the crowd built higher and higher, and I felt like I was on top of the world. It was unbelievable. And no drugs for me — just pure adrenaline, the love of a good time, and, OK, a few sangrias and vodka tonics.

We left Privilege at 8 a.m. and the club was still going. My friends and I were left completely speechless, still in shock and disbelief about what had just occurred. Nowhere in the U.S. could one experience a venue of such unbridled debauchery! We returned to the hotel after a long bus ride, but it wasn't time to sleep yet — it was time to go to the Manumission after-hour party at club Space. I quickly showered up, changed into more beachy attire, refueled on a sandwich and water, and was ready to go. Unfortunately, my friends were out cold and had no shot at awakening in the near future. The rational thing would have been for me to do the same, but then again, how often is one in Ibiza, right?

Walking into this legendary after-hours club at 10 a.m., I knew I was in for an all-new sort of experience. After all, Space was an Ibiza must, and everything I heard about it attested to the fact that it had reached cult status on the global dance circuit. The entrance of the club led me right into a beautiful sunny outdoor terrace. There I felt like I was at a funky beach party as I danced to the blissful Balearic grooves. I also soon discovered that the club was situated in close proximity to the airport runway, so that the sight and sound of low-flying planes were built into the musical sets. The crowd at Space was so happy and the atmosphere was so alive, it is hard to put into words. Even though I came by myself, it was easy to mingle with the eclectic group of clubgoers that surrounded me. After about an hour, the staff started handing out random costumes to the crowd. I received giant funky sunglasses and a cool hat and soon the mass of people transformed into everything from cats and sea creatures to devils and angels. The sudden change of atmosphere really sparked the crowd, and it didn't even occur to me that I had been partying for half a day straight now.

What made Space truly unique was that it offered two widely different dance arenas. Entering into the inner part of the club, I felt like I was in outer space, with its dark deep house music and starry indoor skyline. Once inside this black hypnotic main room, it was easy to lose track of everything else, like the time of day or the fact that I would eventually have to leave this amazing island. At the bar, the guy next to me was handing out shots, and since there were extras, I was included. When I took a closer look at the man giving me the shot of Sambuca, I realized that it was none other then Mike Manumission himself, the main man responsible for this marathon of a fiesta that I was enduring. I thanked him for the drink and told him that I came all the way from Boston to experience Manumission. He was pleased and greeted me with open arms. A half-hour later I said basically the same thing to Fat Boy Slim, as he was trolling around the terrace.

At 3 p.m. the music came to a close and the promoters thanked everyone who was daring enough to complete the full Manumission experience. They also welcomed anyone who wanted to come into the backroom of the club for free drinks. It turned out that Garlands, a famed British club, was throwing a party that night and the cocktails were a promotion to start us off. I was so close to bailing out that last hour, but suddenly it was all worth it. In the room itself, I found two beautiful girls handing out drinks from two giant vats of alcohol. One tub contained sangria and the other Champagne and vodka, a winning combination. After downing a few of each I started chatting it up with the only other English speakers in the room, who happened to be club promoters from Dallas. I tried to tell them that it might be time to get some much-needed sleep but they persuaded me to check out the scene at the beach, and I wasn't about to argue.

Just a short walk from club Space was the crowded beach of Playa d'en Bossa, which is the longest beach on the isle, as well as an afternoon party place. Right away I found myself at Bora Bora, the famous beach bar. Once again, I was now at a wild beach party. It was not difficult to keep going as I fed off the energy of the up-for-it crowd. And despite having its own legendary DJ, DJ Gee, the experience was free! At the beach itself, I saw more nudity than in all of the Porky's movies combined. The only problem was the view of German and Italian tourists in Speedos!

At around 5 p.m., it was time for a quick break, and I hit the water. Swimming in the picturesque, turquoise-colored water of the Mediterranean after countless hours of partying was perhaps the most euphoric sensation I've ever felt. Back at Bora Bora, the foam machines were on, so I promptly jumped into the action. The day continued to roll on and I kept telling myself that it was time to go, but I just couldn't leave. A couple of times I started walking away toward the road, but then found myself walking right back into the mix. I saw Mike M. again and said, "It never ends." He smiled back in agreement. At 7:30 p.m., I finally left the beach.

On the road back, I waited for a bus that never seemed to come. I heard two more Americans asking around for directions to the Sunset bars. Oh man, I thought, what better way to complete the day than Sunset Strip! It wasn't a sane decision, but then again, not much of the day was. I decided to take them under my wing and hit one last stop before sleep. After all, they were willing to split a cab with me and the bus was nowhere in sight.

We arrived at the illustrious Sunset cafes on time. Picture four beach bars and thousands of people just relaxing in anticipation of a breathtaking sunset, all to the tunes of the soft, ambient tracks that the DJs would provide. It was the ultimate chill-out. We somehow managed to acquire seats at Café Mambo, perhaps the liveliest spot on Sunset Strip. I soon learned that my two new friends had just arrived from Miami and both happened to be recently divorced, ready to live it up for the week. It didn't take us too long to lure two young, attractive females to our table.

After all, once again, we had prime seats. The girls were recent college graduates from the New York City area and were also new to the island. We spent the next hour conversing about life and our travels. I told the group about my past day's events and soon enough I had them all foaming at the mouth in awe of what they just heard. It's times like these that make traveling so unique — the ease of making new friends and the instant bond you have with these people. It keeps me feeling young and alive.

It was now over an hour past sunset and the group was ready to move on to the next spot. The last discussion was about what was ahead for the night. The debate was between Pacha, the oldest and most authentically Spanish club on the isle, or Amnesia, another super-club known for its two distinctively captivating dance floors. Not me, I said, I am going to sleep. And soon enough, I finally did just that.

Avi Vichniac is a 2000 graduate from the University of Wisconsin - Madison, where he received a degree in economics and played lacrosse. Currently he lives in Boston and works in finance. Avi has backpacked around Europe for the past four summers and does not plan on stopping anytime soon.

Pushing the Limit

Majorca, Spain

Tyler Toby

I was upside down, thinking "Wow, I could die, but maybe not" — and then the car landed on all fours. Here we were, around 6 a.m., coming back from BCM, pinnacle of the club circuit on the big island of Majorca. Khan and I were enjoying life, sweating the summer away on the dance floors of Europe, always looking for action — decadence at its finest. Now, we were almost getting killed for the third time on this trip.

That was it, putting yourself on the edge of life, tempting fate, winning and making it through your twenties. Khan and I had been backpacking all over southern Europe for the past two months, with the primary goal of hitting dance club after dance club until we reached the point of exhaustion. We had become vampires of the dance floor, in search of good times and beautiful women.

BCM was a massive club situated smack dab in the middle of the British overrun town of Magaluf. Everywhere you looked you saw the British flag flying and heard the British accent floating through the air. Inside the club, fascinating laser-light shows made it look as if all three stories of the building were rocking back and forth. Our mission was to booze up on the way there and then dance all night with women from all over Europe. The music was fantastic and the good times were there for the taking. By 5 a.m., we had sweated out our last cocktail and were out of luck on the lady ticket. Though not a completely successful night, we ventured back out into the morning twilight, with visions of sleep in our heads.

We had almost made it back to the condo when our rental car decided to take a wrong turn. Actually, I was the one behind the wheel and in retrospect, the corner didn't seem that bad at all. In fact, it was a simple curve, but my mind was still on the dance floor rather than the road. The funny thing is that I can remember every moment of the crash. I can remember missing the corner and then putting my foot on the brake just before we barreled into a very large tree. The braking saved us from the tree, but caused the car to go into a roll. It seemed like a very delicate roll; the car appeared to glide over the bushes on the side of the road. The great thing was that the rolling stopped after one turn and we landed on all four tires. The only downside was that the windshield popped out from the force of my buddy's head slamming in to it. Once the car stopped, I looked around and realized that at first glance all was still intact. Khan had a slight bump on his head and his knee was a bit scraped up. Other than that, we were good. We jumped out of the car and started doing a dance around the car. We had tested the odds and won. We then proceeded to grab two beers out of the dumped cooler and made the toast of our lives. Little did we know that a farmer in the distance was watching our every move.

After toasting our new lease on life, we climbed back into the car and passed out. There was no way to drive away from the scene. Next thing we knew, two Spanish police officers were knocking on the roof of the car, trying to determine if we could be awakened or if we had expired. Once awake, we tried to explain to them that the turn was very sharp and we had misjudged it. They looked around for any evidence of alcohol and then took us down to the local station. In our previous moment of triumph, I had decided that stashing any evidence of booze was probably in our best interest. I had quickly collected all beer cans and the cooler and stashed them under a large rock. Thus our butts were saved for the time being.

At the police station, we were mildly interrogated about the details of the incident. We pleaded guilty to bad driving only. The subject of alcohol was quickly passed over. With no reason to hold us, we were sent on our merry way. But in order to stay out of trouble, we had to go on a recon mission: go back to the scene of the crime and snatch our cooler. If the damn thing was found, it would unravel our whole story to the local police, and we would be up a creek without a new rental car. So as soon as we finished, we headed straight back to the spot, in our new rental. As we pulled up, we saw our old car being towed away, but no farmer. He must have been on his lunch break or enjoying siesta. We managed to dig up the cooler without anyone spotting us.

Over the next few days, we passed that very large, fateful tree, and thought about how lucky we had been that night. The fact is we were damn lucky. We could have easily rammed right into that tree, and I wouldn't be here to write this story. I wouldn't be here to meet my future wife, or to do anything worthwhile. I had once again escaped the dangers of my 20s, and if you can make it through your 20s, you have a good shot at making it the rest of the way. It is great to live life to the fullest, but sometimes the fullest can catch up with you when you least expect it. Luckily, it didn't catch me that day.

Tyler Toby is an adjunct history professor at Emmanuel College and a marketing director for an Internet start up. Previously, he was a Boston public school teacher for four years, lived in Ireland for a year and traveled all over Europe. Toby is working on a book called Visions From A Treadmill.

Soy Escritora, Soy Pintor

Barcelona, Spain

ROSE SKELTON

"SOY ESCRITORA," I SIGHED, ANSWERING THE MAN WHO HAD TAKEN the empty chair next to mine. I sat drinking mojitos at a wobbly table, the only table left in the wee hours of an early Spanish morning at this crowded little Barcelona jazz club. I figured him for just another red-blooded Latino male, interested in listening to a female for only long as it took to get his real work with her done. So I was focused more on my distressing writer's block than on his delicious eyes.

"Tell me," he asked, "what are you writing now?"

This question surprised me. To a writer, it is either music or murder. Just then, I needed a sympathetic ear, and he looked ready to supply some attention. Not that that meant he really was interested, of course. I knew he wasn't really. But I decided to tell him anyway, as a sort of punishment for his asking.

"I'm writing a love story, a story I've been needing to tell for three years, and I can't finish it because I can't find the ending," I said. "The story is true, about lost love across continents. I thought I could make up an ending once I got there, but it still means too much to me to mess it up with fantasy. So here I am, in Barcelona in the middle of the night, getting drunk on mojitos, talking to you."

I looked up then and found that this man was looking right into me. A tingling rose from my neck up over my jawbone, and my face flushed. I'd fixed a smile on my face to pretend this was just another story, and to divert his attention from me. But when our eyes connected, I couldn't fool myself about the story or him.

Something about him was astonishingly beautiful: He seemed to understand and care, and in that instant, I felt that somehow things were set right.

I had been suffering over this story for some time when, in early March, I decided on a whim that I'd head for Barcelona with just the clothes I was wearing. Shortly after I arrived, I took a late-evening walk to the high arches of the Plaza Real. There, crowding voices bounced at me off the stone walls and flimsy metal chairs and tables as marauding French schoolchildren with dyed green hair hurried among waiters and tourists and large white Englishmen eating chips and calling loudly for beer. In the midst of all this, I saw a single palm tree growing out of the cracked stones. That oddly incongruous element lifted my spirits, as if I had just noticed the arrival of spring.

In my hand, I carried the address of a club that was upstairs from the plaza's arcade. A friend had passed it to me, telling me it was too good to miss and cautioning me to keep it quiet, so that the tourists wouldn't "discover" and ruin it. Because of that, I expected to find hundreds of people like me there, each believing they were the lucky one to have found out about this treasure.

I looked up. I could see the surrounding buildings rose another two stories above the arcade. Lights shone there in high-ceilinged rooms, and curtains blew in the breeze. It looked quiet up there; surely, eyes were meeting across those rooms, dances were being danced in dazzling dresses and starched white suits, and people were falling in love. I could hear gentle strains of music, see the black-and-white tiled floors, breathe in the jazz of those warm, human spaces.

My friend had explained that the door to the club stood next to a kebab shop off the plaza. Ringing the doorbell, I waited, and eventually a woman opened the door. Offering my thanks, I slipped through, not into the club, but into a stone hallway. I instantly felt I was intruding, but I wasn't going to stop now that I had begun. I climbed the stairs, nervous that I was entering someone's private home, not a club. I had visions of bursting into a Spanish supper: a madre grande, at the head of a heaving table of guests, stopping her ladle mid-dip in the tureen, as everyone turns, conversation instantly dead, to look silently at me.

The steps were stone, and shallow wells had been worn into them by centuries of climbing and descending feet. The wooden banister along the wall was broken in places, and only bare bulbs lit my way. At a door at the top of the second flight of stairs, I knocked. A man opened it, releasing an cloud of cigarette smoke. He greeted me and asked what I wanted to drink. The place looked like his apartment, but he didn't seem the least bit surprised to see me, and instead of rooms filed with home furnishings, I found a small club where Spaniards were drinking and chatting gently, gathered around small, low-lit, round tables, while lazy jazz played on a sound system. The music was subdued, mingling with the patrons' murmuring. For a woman coming from England, a place famous for the drunken debauchery of its small hours clubs, I found this jazz club utterly civilized and marveled at how the Spaniards do it.

This was exactly the kind of place I had pictured from the plaza below. The low music, the couples at small tables — even the floor tiles were checkered black and white. With a mojito in hand, I made my way through the rooms, and, finding no seats free, I settled on the edge of a long table. It tipped as I put weight on it, so I adjusted myself and leaned back. Finally resting comfortably, I felt strangely and suddenly soothed.

That's when the astonishing man joined me, and our eyes met.

"Soy pintor (I am a painter)," he told me. His name was Abel, a short form of his Moroccan name, which he had given up as a child when his family had moved to Barcelona. He looked young, his wondrous skin dark and lucid. His black eyes, sparkling even in the dim light of the club, seemed to me like cool, clear pools of water. I felt something so profound burning inside him, I longed to touch it, and I imagined that he must be an extraordinary artist.

"I know what it feels like, Rosa; you're not alone. You feel as if you're the only one who understands what you're trying to do." Abel laughed, his head tilted backwards, and he settled back with a broad, sweet smile that remained until I was charmed out of my self-indulgent gloom. As we drank more potent mixes, I gave him a synopsis of my story, telling it much better than I had written it. He asked if, when it was finally completed, I might send it to him so that he could illustrate it with his own work. He had a studio on the other side of the Plaza, and he took me to the window so that I could see it across the gray light of the stone square. It had started to rain. We turned toward each other, standing like two dancers poised to hold one another and move, and he said, no longer smiling his perfect smile, "There is something in you, Rosa, which shines. Your story is going to be perfect."

Outside, with day breaking, we walked in the rain to the middle of the square. "It's my birthday today," I told him. I had meant to spend it alone, perhaps forget it altogether, and only remembered then that it was the fifth of March. All around us were the imposing stone arcades; and above them, the secret rooms and clubs and homes in which people surely were falling in love.

"Well, señorita, in that case, you must dance. Every girl must have at least one dance on her birthday." Abel took my hand and placed his arm around my waist. He held me to him so that our hips were touching lightly and we moved to music that he hummed softly into my ear, my cheeks sensing the warm damp skin of his neck, as the rain fell upon us both.

I did not complete my story; Abel was never able to do illustrations for it. I stopped work on it, glad to have written as much as I had, and happy to lay it to rest. I have found a new place to write now, where I spend the odd weekend when I want to feel I am at the center of a romantic reverie. It looks down on a solitary palm tree and beer-guzzling Englishmen, and across at high-ceilinged rooms where couples dance and are surely falling in love. As the sounds of the Plaza Real drift through the open wooden shutters and into the studio, I write as Abel paints. I find my inspiration here, now.

Based in her hometown of London, Rose's one constant is that of being a writer. Her work has been published in The London Sunday Times *and* The Independent, *and she has worked in the past for* Lonely Planet *travel guidebooks. She is also a student of African religious culture, a specialist in Senegalese music, a bread baker, salsa dancer and cyclist. Future adventures include farming in Spain and environmental education in Guatemala, with always half an eye on the trans-Saharan route from Southern Spain to Senegal where she hopes she will finish her novel.*

Hostels: The only way to stay

Gandia, Spain

JASPER LIAO

BEFORE I HAD DONE ANY CONSISTENT TRAVELING, I HAD THOUGHT that youth hostels were just run-down hotels. They loom precariously beneath even the shadiest one-star hotel in any travel book, and offer suspiciously cheap prices for room and board. I remember having visions of roach motels, with a heavy emphasis on the roaches.

So that was the impression that stood out in my mind as my childhood friend Orion and I sat at the Gandia bus station, trying to figure out where to stay that night. We had flown into Madrid a week ago, managing to find reasonable *pensiones* in Madrid, Sevilla, and Granada. I was getting edgy, though, as my travel budget seemed to be thinning and the only hotels with vacancies in Gandia were out of my price range. Which left the dreaded youth hostel.

We decided to bite the bullet and got into a cab. With my limited Spanish capabilities, I had a short conversation with the driver, who said that the hostel was actually in a nearby town called Piles. We didn't have much choice, and as he drove us through remote rows of citrus and olive trees my disappointment grew. I heard Orion grumbling in the back seat about staying in an abandoned farm house.

After about twenty minutes, we rolled into a ghost town. Spare, whitewashed houses lined the deserted streets, softening the sun's glare but barren of life. Storefronts were obscured by locked sheet-metal gates, and restaurant signs lazily swayed in the sea breeze. Empty driveways lacked cars, empty sidewalks lacked pedestrians, even empty trees lacked birds. The charm of the town hadn't left with its inhabitants though, and its relaxed, winding alleys mellowed our minds.

A concrete driveway ramped up from the street, and our taxi driver told me that the blocky white building behind it was the hostel. Large stenciled stick figures on its walls engaged in various sports, an indication of what lay within. Orion and I collected our bags, paid the driver, and hustled up the walk.

The scent of sunscreen was the first thing I noticed upon stepping through the French doors, followed by the inevitable whiff of bathroom cleanser. A receptionist perched reading behind a white formica counter, while two flickering security monitors gave split angles of the lounge's lone ceiling fan.

The receptionist slowly looked up with a visibly irritated glance and said curtly, "Yes?"

After digging out our money belts to pay, we were shown up to the spacious and sunny second floor, through the vacant lounge and to our shared dorm room. Wooden framed bunks were pushed up against the walls, and a few occupants were still snoring off their hangovers in the mid-afternoon doldrums. One of the chubbier lumps stirred, sat up and grinned at us groggily.

He introduced himself as Peter while sliding on a pair of rimmed glasses. He had arrived a few days ago and was on his way up the coast to Barcelona. But as he talked in his thick Austrian accent, my attention was fully drawn to the five-pronged white mark spanning his right breast.

"What the hell is that?" I blurted, tactful as ever.

I had caught him in mid-sentence, and he jerked his head around to see what I was referring to. Orion laughed and pointed at Peter's chest, and he covered it in mock embarrassment. Then he began:

"I vas lying on ze beach when I fell asleep viss my hand on my chest," he recalled, fitting his right hand perfectly over the blotch.

"Didn't you wear sunscreen?" Orion asked.

"It doesn't really matta afta three houas."

After taking an obligatory picture with Peter and his badge, we walked downstairs, through a set of oversized glass doors — and on to one of the most beautiful expanses of shoreline I had ever seen. Sugary sand compressed under my feet and between my toes, subdued waves gently licked at the beach's edge, and bits of sun sparkled across the sea's heaving spine. The ambient splash and hiss of the breaking tides drowned out all other sound, except for occasional wind-carried murmurs from the few sun-baked hostelers.

We sat and talked to the diverse group for a while, trading stories of the road.

Jed was a hippie kid from Northern California who had a broken wire in his braces. He had made the mistake of play-fighting with a group of models one night at the beach in Barcelona. One of the especially attractive ones, he explained, was a female kickboxing champ. His lip was almost fully healed, but the damage to his braces was permanent. It was painful for him to smile, but he couldn't help but laugh with us.

Then there was Sadie, a spunky blond girl from Canada. I had always pictured Canada as a snow-covered wasteland with Mounties and some decent hockey players, but Sadie made a hard case about the wildness of Canucks and their parties, and furiously cooked up more stories to one-up anyone else's offerings.

As we sat on the stone seawall and talked, I found myself surprised at how interesting, intelligent, and open these people were. We were all in the same situation, and related to each other fully about the range of ludicrous experiences we had. As varied as our personalities were, a sturdy concept threaded us together: our love of travel and discovery.

Some discoveries were more grotesque than others. Ben was an Australian who had spent the last few months knee-deep in Southeast Asia. Apart from the expected sightseeing, he had been brought to a shooting range in Vietnam. He had spent ten U.S. dollars to fire an assault rifle at a target, an extravagant price in those parts. Then the range owners offered to up the ante.

"It sounds brutal," said Ben, "but how many times in your life do you get the chance to fire a grenade launcher at a live cow?"

The conversation continued like this for hours, as shadows lengthened and dimmed. Hostel transients ducked in and out of our circle, tossing in morsels about other hostels, cities, restaurants, and sights. We segued to dinner, the upstairs lounge, and finally back on the sand.

Eventually it was only Jed, Sadie, Orion, and me chatting, our volume rising as bottles of sangria were passed around.

At a lull in our talk, Sadie suggested that we go for a night swim. The deserted beach was dimly lit by the lights inside the hostel, and the waves offered relief from the day's humidity that lingered still. The four of us changed into bathing suits, and reconvened on the shore.

Sadie was an attractive, charismatic girl, and through our splashings and other flirtations in the radiant moonlight, she carefully found ways to make each one of us melt for her. I was fascinated by both her silhouette and her boisterousness, and I could tell by Jed and Orion's glinty eyes that they were captivated, too.

When Sadie ran inside to use the bathroom, the three of us jabbered about how amazing she was and tottered in and out of the surf, tipsily throwing a frisbee. The moon hung bright and full over our heads, and we whooped in its luminous glory.

Half an hour later, the primal spirit was fading, and we wondered why Sadie was taking so long. We stumbled up the beach, through the glass doors, up the stairs, and mischievously pushed open her door.

She was gone.

It wasn't until the following morning that Orion realized his Platinum credit card was missing from his wallet, left in his cargo shorts during our swim. We had buried our money belts in with our filthy clothes, and in those hurried 40 minutes Sadie either hadn't had enough time to dig, or was too repulsed.

It was a small matter to cancel the card, and after a few more days of sopping up sunrays, Orion and I made on our way up the coast to Valencia, Jed tagging along to see if he could find an English-speaking dentist. We spent the train ride laughing about the characters we had met in Piles, a bit disappointed at leaving that melting pot but anxious to see what the rest of our trip would produce. My first hostel experience had been educational, to put it mildly, and I was sure I would never think about youth hostels the same way again. Or beautiful travelers.

A recent graduate from Rutgers University, Jasper Liao is an aspiring writer with a degree in journalism. Increasingly nomadic, he has lived in Europe and South America, and recently taught ESL in China. Jasper plans to establish a base in Boston, but will never stop long enough for his passport to get dusty.

The Bullfight

Seville, Spain

SARAH SPRADLING

I FOUND SEVILLE VERY MUCH LIKE MADRID. IT DIDN'T HAVE THE hilltop charm of Toledo; it lacked the heavy Moorish influence of Cordoba. It was a city of traffic and nightclubs. The modern world had taken over; the city oozed university students and seeped elderly tourists.

My alarm woke me early to a dreary morning that day, where scattered gray clouds ever so often sprinkled rain. The one thing that made today different was that today, I was going to witness an exciting event, a tradition of which only Spain could profess ownership: a bullfight.

My friends and I consumed our "continental" breakfast of coffee, jam and bread, and trooped out into the city's intertwining streets. Those of us attending the fight retrieved our maps and began to study them. The bullring was — as every city attraction in Spain — hidden deep within a maze of avenues and alleys, so as each of us deciphered a route, we announced conflicting directions, yet miraculously managed to find it. The ring was a round building among square block buildings, a symbol of tradition in a world of modernization.

By the time we reached our destination, the clouds had been whisked away and the sun was beating down on our backs. I began to wonder if the sunscreen I'd slathered on that morning would be enough to hold me over throughout the day.

Looking up at the towering ring before me, I realized how beautiful it was. It called to mind ladies drowning in lace, with great decorative combs on their heads, parading under the arched walkways. The ever-present vendors were posted at various spots around the ring, offering posters and dolls, refreshments and trinkets. Women selling flowers forced them into our hands, then demanded pay. It was tiring.

After we had purchased our tickets, killed a few hours, and endured lunch at a TexMex restaurant where the guacamole was certainly nothing I recognized as guacamole, we returned to the bullring, enthusiastic and impatient. We immediately joined the forming crowd.

Once inside the ring, I was reminded of Rome's Coliseum. There were no plastic chairs, only stone benches. In the center, below the slanted rows of seats, was the grand circle of earth on which the performance would take place. The dirt was wide, smooth, and a glorious orange color. I felt exhilarated just looking at it and wondering what sort of show lay ahead, and we sat and waited in hyper-anticipation. The sun was bearing down in all its merciless strength, and I was momentarily worried about my skin burning once again.

Then it began.

A cluster of brass instruments burst into the traditional Spanish fanfare recognized worldwide as the introduction to a bullfight. They announced the entrance of several staunch looking, costumed men riding brightly decorated horses, who all paraded around and around the ring, glittering like jewels under the sun. After they made several circuits around the ring, it was time for the matador to march out, dressed in satiny, pale blue pants and top, covered in gold fringes and buttons. His trousers were tight and ended at his knees; his calves were covered in white silk stockings tucked into shiny leather shoes. The wide black hat on his head resembled mouse ears. I was intrigued and thrilled to see this living definition of Spain right before my eyes.

As the horses cleared the ring, the crowds around us cheered.

They had made way for the other star of this cultural show: the bull. He bounded out, kicking up the dirt, and his sleek, dark coat shimmered. He was a beautiful animal, full of energy and animation. The matador addressed the bull then, but not alone. Other costumed men stood waiting at different stations around the ring. I discovered their purpose after the bull had charged and the matador had swept his classic red cloak before the fuming animal several times. I wasn't able to tell what their cue was, but throughout the fight, the men would rush into the ring with flowery spears in their hands. One by one, they stabbed their weapons deep into the bull's back. Soon the beast was dripping blood along with his sweat.

Never had I seen an animal more tireless. With as much pain as he must have been in, the bull kept trying, kept charging, kept attacking. The matador was young. Glancing at my program, I realized he was only 17. More than once, he was close to being gored or trampled. I feared for him. He was too young to be taunting such a beast. Not only was the matador in danger, but the animal was suffering right before my eyes. There was some irony about it. I was no animal activist, but to see such a beautiful creature teased into his death by so inexperienced a boy was no longer enticing – it was revolting.

The oddity of what was happening sank into me. Throughout the bullring, onlookers were cheering at each gain, gasping at each loss. They were a mass of emotion, writhing with every twist of the matador's cape. Enveloped in this blanket of "ole's" and "oohs" and "aahs," I thought of the bullring itself – a leftover of times past amidst all the angular, up-to-date structures of modern-day Seville. It occurred to me that I, along with my group (who were likely feeling the same things I was) did not belong in the ring. We were the square blocks thrown in with the circular ones. We would have been more comfortable in our angled restaurants, watching our angled programs, attending our angled sporting events.

As the bull began to grow tired, his effect on the crowds wore thin. He was no longer a massive animal filled with fiery rage and life; he was a tired old creature. He had aged in minutes, and I felt as though I had too. Withdrawing a blade, the matador gave the beast before him one final blow. The bull fell to the ground and dusty orange clouds billowed around him. His body baked in the sun. With a resounding cheer, the ring burst back to life. Flowers fell onto the dirt as the matador took his bows. Horses came out, hooked the bull to them, and dragged him around the ring several times before finally taking the humiliated thing away. I didn't want to look at it.

When we left the ring that afternoon, I heard that the bull's ears were cut off and given to the matador as a trophy. I found myself wondering what they did with the ears after they began to pile up in the display case. Although I hadn't noticed my appetite previously, I found myself suddenly hungry as we passed a tapas bar. Upon entering the restaurant, I noticed under the lights that my skin was bright pink. During our meal, I could only complain about the burn I'd tried so hard to protect myself from that day.

Sarah Spradling is a 2003 graduate from the University of Missouri in St. Louis. She received a degree in middle-school education and is currently teaching 6th-grade communication arts at a school in St. Louis. She has been to numerous parts of Europe, including the British Isles, the Iberian Peninsula, and the majority of the mainland, and she plans on heading back as soon as time allows.

Twenty years from now you will be more disappointed by the things that you didn't do than by the ones you did do. So throw off the bowlines. Sail away from the safe harbor. Catch the trade winds in your sails. Explore. Dream. Discover.

MARK TWAIN

United Kingdom and Ireland

Belfast by Accident

Belfast, Northern Ireland

Arin Greenwood

"Swear to me you won't go to Northern Ireland," my mother begged when I told her of my plan to visit Ireland after my British work permit expired. I said I would avoid it at all costs, as I had no desire to be there then, just after the Unionist march season was underway and violence in that region was at a post-ceasefire high. When I bought my ferry ticket a day later, I didn't call home to tell anyone that my ferry landed in Belfast; I had a ticket for the new, high-speed hover craft crossing between Scotland and Belfast that would get me in with only a half-hour between arrival and my train to Dublin. "What could happen in a half-hour?" I reasoned. Surely not enough to warrant worrying anyone about.

As weather would have it, the sea was choppy enough, the service new enough, that we who were convinced to pay the extra fifteen pounds for our quicker ride to Eire were held up first in Scotland, then in the sea, for over three hours — as long as the "slow" ferry would have taken and just long enough to miss the last train to Dublin. Stena Ferry Line, monopoly as they were, suggested we hire taxis to Dublin, the cost of which would be refunded at some vague future time, if we were really in such hurries to get out of Belfast or into Dublin, as the case may have been.

My ticket, bought at a special cheap rate, was good only during week days, and this was already Friday. So I could have used the little money I had to get to a supposedly safer city and then starved once I got there, or stayed in Belfast for the weekend. With no tent for protection against the inevitable rain (and anyway, as lore had it a German couple had been murdered while camping on the greens of Trinity College) I decided that I would be better off in a hostel in Belfast than I would be on the streets of Dublin.

Belfast had an exaggerated sense of darkness, what with the rain and my fatigue; crumbled brick buildings were topped by barbed wire and covered with graffiti in a strangely appealing way. A bus driver brought me to the city-center hostel, whose glass and asymmetrical architecture looked anomalous on the dingy back road it inhabited. The attitude of those behind the desk, too, seemed anomalous (where was the Irish friendliness I'd heard so much about?); they would not let me stay since the hostel was fully booked, claiming that the sitting room in which the couch I thought I might sleep on was locked after eleven. My pleas to consider the inherent flexibility in hostelling brought me no reprieve, and neither did my tears. I was directed to another hostel, not far away and renowned for fitting in stragglers.

I found "Wilf's" on a trendy-looking side street lined with small student-y brick houses. An Australian bloke invited me in, and told me he'd be sure to find me a room, or at least a bed (there was that friendliness). He introduced me to the other residents, all Australians, all long-termers working in Belfast.

At a fast-food cafe a block from our hostel, I asked the Australians if they liked living in Belfast. They did, they said, because the wages at the pork processing plant where they all worked were high enough that they could periodically quit for a pub binge, then get rehired a few days later. (It is worth noting that they were fired during my stay, and I believe that their sketchy attendance records precluded further employment at this particular establishment.) Did they feel safe?, I asked. "Oh yeah," they agreed, "We've been here one month, two months, six months, and haven't seen any trouble." This was only a week or so after the Orangemen, Loyalist Protestants who want Belfast to stay part of the U.K., had finished their highly confrontational and controversial march through predominantly Catholic areas, much to the ire and spite of the Catholic Republicans, who are bitterly opposed to the U.K.'s presence in Northern Ireland and who want Belfast to be part of Ireland proper. I began to feel less wary, assured that the news reports were exaggerated and did not describe what the majority of people, and therefore myself as well, would witness in their daily lives. I had experienced something similar in Tel Aviv when I was a student there in the spring of 1994. In Tel Aviv I had to watch CNN to see any of the violence I heard and read was everywhere there, so I saw no reason to doubt the Australians' Belfast story.

Back at the hostel, I met Wilf, a lovely, self-declared A-Political Being from Northern Ireland, and his assistant Andrew, who was from a city in England and immediately proclaimed membership to Sinn Fein. Andrew offered to take me on a tour of Shankill Street, Belfast's most Catholic neighborhood, famous for its pro-Ireland, anti-Britain murals on the sides of houses, then to a Sinn Fein pub (he bristled and motioned "shush" when I asked if it was an IRA venue). I declined, still not convinced that Belfast was really that safe, let alone in a neighborhood so heated up by recent events. That night on the news was a debate about whether the Derry Boys should be allowed to march a week later, and how much violence it might cause if they were, and how much violence there would be if they weren't.

I spent the next day wandering about Belfast's many malls, looking at its huge, white, heavily guarded town hall, walking down long tree-lined streets by Queen's University, looking at a photography show at a modern art gallery in converted warehouse space along the river, and browsing in a wonderful, disorganized, used bookstore/cafe, just like the one I hoped to open one day. I planned to go back to the hostel to relax before going out that night to see *Apocalypse Now* at the university cinema. En route home, I followed my duplicitous sense of direction, and found myself on a street with shabby-looking duplexes, many of which had huge brightly painted murals on their outside walls. The murals looked like they might well be political, and I staved off a strong feeling of apprehension as I walked, paying as much attention as I could to the art without allowing myself an excess of fear. There were depictions of soldiers raising Irish flags, Union Jacks crossed out, and messages written in what I assume is Gaelic all the way to the end of the road; still, though, not much was happening on the street, except for some people playing with their kids in the duplexes' tiny yards.

I checked my pocket map to see if I could figure out how to get home, and as I made several turns I heard the sound of parade music — loud horns, marching-band drums, that sort of thing. I followed the noise until I reached the main square, two blocks from Wilf's and across the street from where the Hari Krishnas set up their free vegetarian meal cart. In the street were troops of musicians, many dressed in Orange, marching.

Each group had several drummers, but the outstanding thing was the ubiquitous enormous vertical drum, invariably painted with some town name, preceded by the word ULSTER. One man held a sign that read "ULSTER SHARPSHOOTERS." I watched, entranced, frightened out of my wits, snapping pictures with my just-purchased disposable camera for posterity and possibly the AP wire. Next to me were a bunch of men drinking from cans of beer. I wondered how long it would be before someone started throwing rocks, or worse.

The crowd stayed peaceful, though, and it wasn't long before the music became tedious and the crowd started to drift away.

I thought, "So *this* is what these marches are like; boring and loud."
A guy I worked with in Edinburgh was from Bangor, a seaside
town not far from Belfast, and he'd said exactly that: "The marches
go right by my house, and my only complaint is the racket." Still,
I watched the uniformed musicians until I was too tired to stay
any longer, for the sake of having been there. Just before I left, I
turned to one of the beer drinkers at my side and asked him what
this procession was about; I expected some heated political rheto-
ric.

"It's the yearly marching band competition," he said, "Fierce
battle, it is." He turned back to his mates for another beer, and I
went back to Wilf's, where the Australians were watching rugby
on an old color television, which they had turned up to full blast
to drown out the sound of the procession.

*After living in Europe for almost two years, Arin Greenwood moved
to New York City to attend (and graduate from) Columbia University Law
School. Arin now lives on Saipan - an island in Micronesia - where she
writes and works as a lawyer at the Commonwealth of the Northern
Mariana Islands Supreme Court. She still thinks of opening up a cafe/
book store, but only if the health department will overlook her dog Barky's
constant presence.*

Dublin: Just for the Craic

Dublin, Ireland

MARTIN ASHPLANT

THE RAIN HAMMERS DOWN ON TEMPLE BAR. IT'S THE SORT OF heavy dark rain that soaks your soul as well as your skin. The clouds loom eerily above the city and show no signs of being in any hurry to leave. They quite clearly like the Dublin skies, and have grown quite accustomed to being here.

But it will take more than a few dark clouds to dampen the spirits of Dubliners today, or mine for that matter. As rain, or no rain, — and in Dublin it is usually the former — today is the day when all the family trees come out as proof of one's Irish heritage, regardless of what part of the world you happen to be displaced in. Today is the day when from New York to Nairobi people suddenly develop an affinity for little green folk with funny hats, and a drink that looks more like crude oil than anything you would want to pour down your throat.

Today is 17th March. Today is St. Patrick's Day. And here I am living a cliché. Sitting inside a dark wooden pub in the heart of Ireland's capital as people all around me celebrate the existence of a largely unimportant man who has turned everyone's blood green for one otherwise non-descript day in late-winter. A fire roars in the corner of McCarthy's Bar, — I swear that is what it was called — trying to compete with the two fiddlers playing at the bar as to who can warm people's hearts more effectively. The two girls with violins win. Their emerald eyes and jet-black hair bring more fire to the loins of most male inhabitants of the pub than any burning wood could ever hope to achieve.

Tables are in short supply in this particular venue. Not just

because the place is packed to the rafters with people, but because tables are a little too insular for the liking of most Irish. I
mean, how are you supposed to strike up a conversation with the
stranger sitting next to you if he has his back to you and is deep in
thought in his own personal corner of the pub. Here, you either
perch on a barstool or lean on the nearest thing at hand, which,
judging from the number of people falling into me, seems quite
often to be another person.

It really could be a Guinness commercial. That most famous of Irish exports that tastes like no other beer, sits like no
other beer and takes a ludicrously long amount of time to pour.
But then again, when you are already leaning on the bar discussing the trials and tribulations of life with your new best friend,
what difference does two minutes make, waiting for your drink to
settle? — particularly when a couple of pints of the black stuff
can quite probably replace an entire meal.

I look around at the green and orange decorations hanging
around the pub, take a sip from my viscous pint, take in the rhythmic sounds emanating from the far corner and wonder if it can all
be real. Surely this is just the stereotype. Nothing is ever quite as
you expect it to be when you travel around the world to experience something that you have heard so much about. Surely all
those theme pubs cannot have got it so close to the truth. Surely
they must have exaggerated the 'Irish experience' just a little.

But apparently not. From where I am standing, everything
is just as it should be. The smiles are there, the singing and dancing is there and the copious amount of beer is most certainly
there. But maybe I am being naïve, as I am in the tourist capital
of the country on the most tourist-friendly day of the year after
all. But whether it is culturally correct or not matters little to me
at the moment. What is real is the happiness exuding from the
people in this low-ceilinged place, whether it is natural or en-

forced by expectation. I don't care and nor does anyone else by the looks of it.

Or maybe it is just the chemicals racing around my brain that are bringing this new-found sense of contentment. After all, I did spend the majority of the day getting to know my surroundings a little better via an extended visit to the Guinness Storehouse and Museum — the place that, in many people's opinion, put Dublin and Ireland firmly on the world map.

And it certainly stood up to examination, offering an ultra-modern exploration of every step of the beer-making process. From being able to get a nose for what hops smells like — not pleasant — to seeing how Guinness goes from vats to cans and bottles, the museum makes sure that you are well aware of quite how much craftsmanship and tender loving care goes into each pint. It also gives an opportunity to take a trip down memory lane and re-acquaint yourself with the classic commercials Guinness has churned out throughout the ages. White horses, funny dances and beer-drinking Toucans are all present and correct as the spirit of this most famous of drinks is emphasized throughout.

But they saved the best for last. Once the tour had been completed, I took a glass elevator up to the pinnacle of the storehouse — a transparent circular roof-bar overlooking Dublin, forming the creamy head of an enormous pint with the rest of the building making the dark body. I sat amongst the rain clouds, drinking my specially poured beer complete with shamrock etched into the head by the barman, and I could see why these people are so revered across the world. And as one pint became two, and two became three – there was supposed to be a limit but such things did not appear to matter to the cheery-eyed bar-staff – I fell in love. I loved the way this city knew how to have a good time and made no pretences about it whatsoever. If it's raining, then go inside and warm up with a beer and some festivities. That is the sort of mentality the world needs today. At least that was my thought process as I cast an eye across the gray metropolis below me.

I had planned to pay a quick visit to Trinity College, Ireland's renowned center of education, or perhaps take a wander around Dublin Castle and then drop into the Writers' Museum to pay my respects to Jonathan Swift, James Joyce and the other great wordsmiths this city has produced. But alas, it was raining, it was cold and the pub looked just that little too tempting to resist.

But then again, maybe that's what this place is all about. Doing what you feel and not getting too hung up about what else you should be doing. So here I was, tucking into a hefty portion of Paddy's Stew at seven in the evening, feeling as though it should be later, but wishing it was earlier. That guy in the Guinness commercial got it spot on. Let the good times roll. ...

Martin Ashplant is a freelance sports and travel writer currently living in England. He is presently working for a press agency in London but cannot wait to get out of the rat race to explore more of the world. Having had many wonderful times in Europe, Asia and Oceania, he has set his sights on taking his backpack to South America as soon as humanly possible.

A Week's Worth of Blisters

England

Joanna Nesbit

"You want to walk to Jerusalem?" I asked. The idea was startling, incongruous with the morning light. Gavin nodded, handing me a cup of tea.

"I'll start in Manchester," he said casually, as if everyone happened upon the idea at least once. "It'll probably take a year, give or take." Gavin had grown up in Manchester; hence, the not-so-arbitrary starting point.

"Why walk?"

"I dunno exactly. Just that Jerusalem is a holy city and deserves to be walked to, I 'spose."

I had once dreamed of cycling across the United States, inspired by the idea of crossing a continent because it is there, but I had never thought to walk anywhere. Gavin's was an adventurous plan, not unlike my yen for traveling without a time limit.

"Would you like to come?" he said. "I think you're perfect for the trip. Right now it's Roshan and me, and we need another person."

I hadn't seen Gavin since I was thirteen, though I recalled easy conversations and fits of giggles. He had spent a month with his aunt, our neighbor, during which my sisters and I had gleefully educated him about American teenagers. Now, eight years later, he offered his London home in return, allowing me to delay, if only for a few days, the real reason I was in London: to begin a solo trip around Europe.

At twenty-one, I was naïve and eager, with no itinerary other than to go where serendipity sent me. Make no mistake; this was no unplanned journey. I had dreamed of it for years with the tenacity someone might apply to acting or writing poetry. Not only did I want to see the world, I wanted to be a "traveler." Growing up on a small Pacific Northwest island, surrounded by people who'd lived there for decades, I ached to be worldly, to meet with adventure, but at the same time I dreaded the basics — negotiating buses, finding accommodation, dining alone. Gavin provided an easy segue by meeting me at Heathrow. At his house, he brewed me a cup of tea and introduced Roshan, an Indian friend visiting from Manchester for a few days. That night we went to a lively pub and talked into the wee hours about politics, work, college, and personal dreams. I went to bed intoxicated with possibility.

I was elated with Gavin's Walk: it was an adventure falling into my lap, but more than that, it was a plan that gave focus to a journey I wasn't sure how to begin.

"Yes," I said to the question that hung between us.

Gavin beamed. "I think the three of us get on well together," he said. I beamed back, flattered.

"I have several weeks of work to finish before we can start," he said. "Why don't you do some traveling in the meantime?"

I agreed, unwilling to admit I was terrified to venture out on my own, and bought a ticket to Scotland. The train took me past green fields, stone walls, and small villages, my first view of England outside London. In Edinburgh, I met my first travelers and hitchhiked to Inverness with a German woman, where I visited the Loch Ness amid barren, windblown hills and studied grainy pictures of its mythical monster in a small museum. On a split-second decision — the kind I craved — I went to Northern Ireland with someone who asked if I'd go, where we hitchhiked along the rugged coast, getting drenched by cold April rain. Negotiating transport and finding accommodation turned out to be easy, and my confidence grew volumes. The business of travel began to feel realistic. The commitment I'd made to Gavin's Walk hovered at the back of my mind; it didn't feel quite so grand as during those first nervous days in London, but several weeks later I returned to convene with Gavin and travel north to our starting point.

We started at the outskirts of Manchester on a gray day. I had not thought England could be ugly, but in the next couple of days we walked through mind-numbing industrial towns, and my spirits plummeted. I had imagined narrow, leafy lanes and wildflowers and country pubs, and, as if in agreement, my heels sprouted huge blisters in the boots acquired in Scotland for this trip.

But by the third day, our legs propelled us along the lanes I'd imagined, and the weather perked up, providing watery sun in which to bask when we were tired. We picnicked on a grassy bank and stopped at the country pub I'd envisioned to fill water bottles. But also on the third day, Roshan hitchhiked ahead, discouraged by the aching arches in his feet. He said. But I had seen his lack of commitment on the first day as he ambled ahead of us, wondering aloud where we should eat, offering nothing to our conversation about which route to take through England.

"What do you think, Roshan?" I said, irritated by his disinterest.

"About what?"

"The route!"

"Oh, I dunno. Whatever you two decide. What do you say we stop at the next pub? I'm famished."

I wondered why he had come, pondered our goals. Did he have one? He seemed childish and flighty, unwilling or unable to stick to a plan. Gavin, in contrast, walked with purpose, his steadfast demeanor providing the leadership we needed. I admired his determination and drew on it, hoping to edge out the doubts already surfacing. During Roshan's absences — often most of a day — we talked easily as we walked the country lanes. But despite the pleasant walking, we always arrived hours after Roshan, exhausted and annoyed by his cheery greeting from a pub doorway. Dropping into a chair, I fretted about the cost of pub meals, wishing I could cook in a youth hostel or eat bread and cheese from a shop.

"I don't understand," Roshan said. "You've got to eat, which means you've got to spend something." He ordered more beer as I silently fumed. Gavin observed our differing attitudes and tried to keep the peace. He desperately wanted this plan to work out, and we knew it.

Despite the discord, we had small, happy adventures: camping in a farmer's field, an invitation to someone's house, conversations with locals who raised their eyebrows at our plan. Kind people sent us on our way with sandwiches, sweets, and good wishes, but I arose each morning, feeling increasingly trapped by Gavin's doggedness. By afternoon, my blisters acting up, I cursed myself for accepting this invitation, knowing each step was one more away from my own path, whatever that was. Roshan continued hitchhiking ahead, wondering why he'd ever considered walking, as if he'd just realized the trip wasn't for him. My dislike for him grew, but I watched enviously as he flew past in a car, and only my pity for Gavin kept me from doing the same. As we walked, drifting in and out of conversation, I daydreamed about earlier travels north and places I'd rather be. Paris, maybe, or Spain. Jerusalem, perhaps? Clouded by indecision, I knew only that I resented our plodding pace.

At the end of the week, we limped into Shrewsbury, a Tudor town on the Severn River, sixty-eight miles from our starting point. In a youth hostel, our first, I cooked an inexpensive meal of rice and vegetables and looked around for other travelers. But the hostel seemed taken over by a huge group of twelve-year-old boy scouts, or some equivalent, and I felt more irritated than I had all week. My ankles were ringed with rash from sweaty socks, my feet ached, and I cared little about the picturesque town. What's the point of walking somewhere, I thought for the umpteenth time in six days, if you're too tired to enjoy it when you get there? But it wasn't fatigue getting the best of me, and I knew it. That evening, Gavin and I sat in the hostel dining room while Roshan wandered off to a pub.

"Gavin," I said, "I don't think this walk is for me."

He nodded; he had known this was coming, and I felt terrible. But by the end of the evening we'd acknowledged our threesome's lack of compatibility, differing goals, and financial concerns, and I felt better.

"I'll give it a little more thought," I said. But I knew what I would say in the morning. The next day, after gently announcing my departure, steeling myself against Gavin's sad eyes, and saying goodbye to Roshan, I shouldered my pack and walked to the main road to hitchhike south. My feet still ached and my blisters required bandages, but I felt ten pounds lighter and deliriously happy to be on my own with a plan — my plan — that I'd hatched during my daydreams. I knew, as I hadn't when I'd arrived in London, that I would go to Jerusalem myself, though I would hitchhike, train, boat — anything but walk — to get there.

Joanna Nesbit is a technical writer finally writing about her four-year solo journey around the world. Currently, she lives in Bellingham, Washington, with her husband and two children. Her work has been published in several parenting magazines.

City Reflection

London, England

BILLY ANDERSON

THERE ARE TWO REASONS TO GO TO LONDON, ENGLAND: 1) YOU win the lottery and need help spending obscene amounts of money in a very short period of time; 2) you want to experience one of the most incredible cities in the world.

With 12 million people and nearly two thousand years of history, it's no wonder that London is such an intriguing place, a sensory buffet that feeds your every interest. Night life? Got it. Shopping? Go that too. Tourist attractions? Like nowhere else.

And it certainly has its share of "old stuff." Even if you're not a history buff, you will be by the time your London visit is over. Why? Because it's everywhere you go. Forget about learning through books, just look around you.

The Tower of London, for example, has been sitting on the banks of the Thames River since its completion in 1098. That's not a typo either; the Tower is more than 900 years old. So when Christopher Columbus strolled onto unfamiliar soil, the Tower (which is more like a castle than a tower) had already been beheading prisoners for hundreds of years. Within the Tower sits the Crown Jewels, the biggest chunk of expensive rock you'll ever see in your life. If you honeymoon in London you may want to skip the Crown Jewels for fear of diamond envy. I asked the guard if I could photograph the Jewels but was told, "If you do so, I will be forced to cut off your head, mount it on a spike and parade it through the streets." I'm pretty sure he was kidding, but a few hundred years ago that kind of thing actually happened.

While waiting for a ferry ride, I noticed a few holes at the base of a bronze statue. The nearby plaque told me that the damage was sustained in a World War II bombing raid. Bombs had fallen right where I was standing. Now, seeing such a classy, architecturally gorgeous city, it was hard to believe the devastation London endured during the war.

Once on the ferry the tour guide filled us in on the multitude of sites we passed on the way to Greenwich. He pointed out docks to which criminals had been fastened at low tide and left there as the water slowly rose above their heads.

But London's history isn't all about beheading and various forms of maiming. Upon arrival at Greenwich, you can stand on the Greenwich Meridian, which represents zero degrees longitude. I figure it must be a pretty important city to warrant such a feature on every world map. It's possible to stand with one leg in the Western hemisphere and the other in the Eastern. Just one step and you're instantly a world traveler.

Perhaps the most enjoyable aspect of London is the lifestyle. Londoners work hard and play hard. The best place to witness this is at a pub, which you can find on almost every corner in London. It is totally acceptable to go straight to the pub after work and not be considered an alcoholic. The British really have life figured out: Their pubs close at 11p.m. That may sound lame to North Americans, but it actually makes perfect sense. Instead of going out to the bar at 10 p.m. and staying until closing at 2 or 3 a.m., you go to the pub after work and you leave at 11 p.m. Same amount of quality party time and you're in bed by midnight and raring to go the next morning before the day is half over — unless, of course, you opt to go clubbing after the pub, where you can boogie 'til the sun comes up.

While it is indeed a social hub, the pub is also family oriented, with children permitted to accompany their parents until 9 p.m. It is a superb place for one of traveling's greatest pasttimes:

eavesdropping. What better way to learn the goings-on inside the heads of locals? I soon realized why so many Londoners don't really care if you eavesdrop: chances are you won't understand a word they're saying. At times it's difficult to believe they're speaking English. "I had a row with me boss after work. It was a trifle dodgy-looking outside so I had to catch the Tube 'cause I'd forgotten me brolly. I'm knackered, I tell ya. Hey honey, can I bum a fag? And where are me bangers and mash?" Translation: "I had an argument with my boss today. It was looking a little like rain so I took the subway because I didn't have my umbrella. I'm exhausted. Waitress, can I have a cigarette, and where's my dinner?"

The inside of a London pub exposes you to a perplexing phenomenon — beer being served at room temperature. Back home you'd rather take out a second mortgage for a good fridge than serve beer anything but freezing cold. We even go to such lengths as frosting mugs to ensure our "loud-mouth soup" is no warmer than a penguin's behind. But there is logic in this seemingly unintelligible act: If beer is too cold, it masks the flavor. These folks are true connoisseurs of suds.

Accepting this exposes you to a world beyond ale and lager. You can have "stout" and "bitter" among other beer types. I don't see how a "bitter" beer could be tasty but hey, these folks have been brewing beer since before the Dead Sea was even sick, so I'm not going to question them. And beers have the coolest names too — some so original, you'd think whoever came up with them had already downed a keg or two: Old Speckled Hen, Oatmeal Stout (part of a well-balanced breakfast, I'm sure), Dirty Dick's Ale, Fiddler's Elbow, Old Peculiar. I can imagine a small town on the English coast as a fisherman strolls into the pub after a hard day at sea and barks at the barman: "Give me a mouthful of Dirty Dick."

In London, a beer is one of the few things that won't set you back the net worth of a small country. London is expensive in every way. Rent is astronomical. A friend of mine who lives in a small apartment in one of the wealthier neighborhoods forks out U.S. $3,000 a month. So does his roommate. The choice of restaurants in London is superb, but bring along your retirement fund if you want more than an appetizer. In the city center you can grab a movie for the nasty price of U.S. $15. Each! So a simple night out at the movies with your better half can easily cost you $40 if you throw in some munchies.

Many place names in London are pronounced strangely. Just because a word is 10 letters long doesn't mean you need to pronounce them all. In the center of London sits Leicester Square — a hub-bub of activity and entertainment. But pronounce it as it reads and you'll be met with a look of utter confusion. It is pronounced "Lester" Square. I guess Londoners are either too busy to pronounce everything or they are Scrabble-aholics and feel that longer words are worth more. Tottenham Court is "Tottnam" and Beauchamp is "Beechum" (the latter arising from an inherent dislike of all things French). But since I'm speaking a language that originated here, I guess I should be a bit more understanding.

One thing that is difficult to get used to (and not doing so could put your life in grave danger) is that people drive on the "other" side of the road. London is thoughtful enough to have painted "Look Left" and "Look Right" on the roads at intersections for us forgetful sorts. Tourists stick out like a sore thumb as they look down at the ground every time they cross a street.

If you're feeling *really* adventurous after mastering the art of crossing the road, you can treat yourself to a ride in one of London's black taxi cabs. These have more leg room than an NBA team's bus, and the seats are comfier than mommy's womb.

But then you start moving. You remind yourself that yes, it's okay that we're on the left side of the road. But soon you're darting down miniscule side streets on BOTH sides of the road and wondering if the cabbie had too many Dirty Dicks and Oatmeal Stouts at breakfast. But they always get you there alive. London cabbies, in reality, know every nook and cranny in the city and could teach Mario Andretti a thing or two about driving.

So, have I told you about all of London's highlights? Not even close, I'm afraid. To do so would take a book on its own and it is so much better to experience it firsthand anyway. So sell your car, your house and your best friend, and hop on a plane to London. The sites, the history and the overall energy of the place will ensure an authentic experience that's worth every single penny.

After two years of London living, Billy returned to his home in Canada. Cleaner cities, fewer people and the endless expanse of Mother Nature made for a pleasant return, but the history and culture of Europe is still greatly missed. Now a freelance writer and adventure guide, Billy hopes to eventually lead trips in Europe.

Lambing Season: Life and loss

Scotland

Jason Stevenson

JUST BEFORE DAWN I PULLED THREE WET AND GASPING LAMBS FROM the warmth into the cold. They were the first arrivals of the new day, beating the sun by a few minutes. I sat back and rested, wiping my hands on my pants.

These births had not been easy and my forearms burned from the constant tugging on heads and legs. The first lamb's neck twisted the wrong way, and the second one started as a breech birth. All three survived, however, and now shivered and steamed on the wet straw. The pre-dawn chill cooled the lambs rapidly, even though lambing season occurs during the warming months of the spring.

The exhausted ewe lay on the ground, my knee pressing against her neck to keep her down. I lifted her lambs, still warm and slick, and laid them next to her head. The ewe strained to lick the birth residue from their bodies, her eyes wide and liquid. The lambs' eyes remained closed as they rolled and kicked in their new found freedom.

When I learned my university in Scotland would close a month for Easter break, I sought a job to occupy the vacant time. The walls of the student employment office were thick with postings for caterers, traffic counters, and office workers. The solitary notice seeking a lambing assistant on a sheep farm stood out. It was the only phone number I copied down.

Although I was not a veterinary student, which the posting requested, my father's relatives had farmed in western Pennsylvania since colonial times. I grew up visiting my great aunt's farm north of Pittsburgh for many family gatherings. There I fed cows and plinked coffee cans with an old .22 rifle, excited to escape the confines of suburbia. I realized these vacations did not constitute a realistic farm experience, but I considered them lessons in a rural vocabulary without the tougher grammar of actual responsibility. When I called up the sheep farmer listed on the posting, I overcame his reservations with persistence and a little bluffing and convinced him to hire me as a lambing assistant for two weeks in April.

The colorless cold morning marked my final day on the farm. Crouching over the ewe and her newborn lambs, I realized I would board a bus in a few hours and return to my life as a graduate student in Edinburgh, a place that now seemed as foreign as a sheep farm once did. Before I could think of leaving, however, I had to finish the morning chores. Using a trick the farmer taught me, I lured the new mother into an empty pen by dragging her three bleating lambs along the straw. She followed anxiously, her nose tracking their scent. With the new family reunited in a cramped pen, I began to bundle hay to feed the two hundred sheep entrusted to my care.

My world for most of each day and night was a single-story barn the size of two basketball courts. Tin sheeting stretched over the roof and walls, allowing only thin cracks of sunlight to reach inside. Slat-board fences of rotting wood divided the barn's interior into the enclosures and pens that held the ewes and their offspring. I learned to step over these fences while carrying water buckets, feed bags, and even ewes, because the few metal gates were solid rust. Straw covered the ground three inches deep, forming a springy carpet over the dirt. Outside the barn, green and brown fields rolled in all directions, dotted by white clumps of grazing sheep. Despite my desire to be a shepherd wandering amid the green pastures, I spent almost all my time working alone inside the barn's translucent shell.

The isolation bothered me at first; I missed the reassurance of a large and bustling community around me. In two weeks I had seen only six other people, four of them being the farmer and his family. My life suddenly shrank from my globe-spanning circles in Edinburgh to the farmer's house, the barn, and the journey in between.

But now, on my last day, I realized how much I had come to value the solitude and routine that safeguarded this existence. Silence forced me to rely on imagination to a degree dormant since childhood. I constantly dredged up old memories and subjected them to microscopic study, weighing perspectives that busier surroundings would have drowned out. During lazier moments, I jotted journal entries for a future time when I would lack the patience of reflection.

The constancy of morning chores, however, restricted my idle time to later in the day. To feed the sheep, I walked around the barn dropping a handful of hay into each pen. The ewes rushed to eat, raising dust clouds of pulverized straw to fill the barn. The air reeked of universal decomposition, a smell dominated by wet and rotting hay and the steely odor of matted wool. Yet somehow the barn's odor felt comfortable to me, like the dankness of a familiar basement. I had spent so much time inside the barn that its environment had become a part of me. To an outside observer, however, I am sure both the barn and my own clothes produced an unbearable smell.

With the feeding completed, I refilled the dozens of water buckets emptied or spilled during the night. The freezing spray from the spigot numbed my fingers still warm from handling the newborn lambs. By now all my senses were accustomed to the sudden shocks of farm work. I shifted a dozen times each day between the mental and physical extremes of boredom, panic, comfort and pain.

Some days I waited lazily for a single birth, watching the shadows stretch themselves across the ground. The warm afternoon breeze cast a quiet spell over the barn, and for long hours I would lean back against a fence, watching the drowsy sheep and letting my mind wander over distant memories.

But other times the births came so frequently that my cracked and infected fingers swelled with purple bruises. The crisis of a suffocating lamb or burst uterus broke the calm like a nightmare shattering sound sleep. My hands throbbed as I slipped and clawed against the pressure of bone and muscle. Some times the lambs did not make it out. Other times only parts of them did. Sitting alone amid the blood, straw and mud, I struggled and pleaded between the two outcomes of birth and death. Often I gave up, drained and depressed, and waited for the calm to return again.

The dawn of my last day, however, began peacefully. No other lambs were born, and the barn fell still except for the quiet crunch of chewing sheep. I completed my chores by placing fresh straw in each pen and checking again on the newborn lambs now struggling to stand up by themselves.

Secretly, however, I knew the morning's calm to be a lie. All of my efforts, from delivering the pre-dawn triplets, to cleaning the pens, were a deception. Everything I helped to create during these two weeks would be erased completely. Watching the first sunlight slip through the gaps in the wall, I reminded myself that all these sheep would be killed today.

In fact, they had only a short while to live. Within the hour, dark green jeeps and flatbed trucks hauling bulldozers would roll up to the farm gate. The muddy lane would fill with army soldiers, veterinarians, and the loud-talking men known simply as "shooters." I would help them round up the sheep, separate the ewes from their terrified lambs, and clear space for the bulldozers and trucks to work. Then the killing would begin.

From conversations with the farmer I already knew how it would occur. Retractable bolt guns would punch a small, neat hole through the ewes' skulls, pumping their blood high in the air. The lambs would go easier, collapsing with a sharp cry after the injection of a sedative into their hearts. When it was all over, the barn would be perfectly quiet for the first time.

Just one week earlier the epidemic of foot-and-mouth disease ravaging Great Britain jumped a range of hills to infect the livestock of a neighboring farm. We had considered ourselves safe from the disease due to our isolation in a little-trafficked valley north of the Cheviot Hills. But the news arrived late on a Friday evening while the farmer's family and I watched *Who Wants To Be a Millionaire* and cradled cups of lukewarm tea. The farmer picked up the ringing phone, and after a moment, cursed loudly. The children were sent to bed and I flipped aimlessly through a magazine while watching the farmer and his wife debate in hushed voices. The TV droned on without an audience.

A few days later I learned that a thousand sheep were to die on my last morning of work. Our farm lay within the government's mandatory cull zone to contain the disease. Until that day, the farmer told me, I was to continue to deliver lambs and care for the sheep as if nothing was different. I felt like a death row warden guarding inmates who were both innocent and ignorant of their punishment.

From outward appearances, my routine changed little during that week of waiting. I delivered dozens of lambs a day and completed all the necessary chores. When a sick ewe died after giving birth, I nursed her two orphaned lambs using a plastic syringe and tube. I nicknamed one of the orphans Blackfoot and let him ride atop my shoulder as I went about my tasks.

Yet I could not ignore sense of impending violence. The

farmer told me the main roads were blocked by checkpoints and patrolled by soldiers. Cars, tractors, boots, and clothes had to be disinfected every time we came and went from the farm. A few times I thought I heard gunshots from over the hills, and finally, one afternoon I saw the pillars of smoke from burning carcasses. The most wrenching image, however, was to watch my sheep and to know it would happen here.

At first I told myself that I would not participate in the cull. These were my sheep, especially the hundreds of lambs I had pulled into the world, and I wanted no part in their slaughter. But I also knew that farm work frequently demands unpleasant tasks. I could not sit on the sidelines when difficult work needed to be done, even if that work was killing.

An hour after sunrise on that last morning I waited patiently for my imagination to resolve itself into reality. I was standing over the pen containing the newborn triplets when I heard the first growl of the army trucks from the road. The lambs, only a few thousand heartbeats into the world, wobbled on timid legs to suck their mother's milk. When I heard the truck engines quit and the doors slam shut, I turned my eyes away from the lambs to focus on the soldiers dressed all in white walking up the lane.

Although I was not a farmer by any means, I knew there was nothing sacred about loss on a farm. New life arrived every day under the watchful presence of death. The bodies of stillborn lambs and those that died soon after birth grew to a large pile outside the barn. When it rained I covered them with a shroud made from empty feedbags. With this mortality, however, there was always the continuation of life. Something always survived. The weakest triplet could die during the night, but I would find its two siblings bouncing with bright eyes and full bellies in the morning. I learned to accept nature's rule that the death of a few allowed for the many to survive.

I also killed many times before that final morning. But it was a different kind of killing. Lambs weakened by sickness or starvation curl into tiny balls of hollow stomachs and twitching muscles. They gasp for air through the cold saliva that collects in their mouths and chokes them. Other lambs are born with twisted backs and disabilities that make them unable to stand. These lambs I killed to end their suffering.

"Look away if you don't want to see this," the farmer warned me on my second day, carrying a lamb paralyzed by a joint disease. Don't look away, I told myself. You need to see how this is done.

Holding the lamb on its back, he lifted its tiny body high into the air and brought its head down hard on the top of a fence post. Once. Twice. It made the sound of wood striking wood. He held up the still-twitching body and felt for a heartbeat. The next day I killed a stricken lamb the same way. I wanted to close my eyes when its head hit the post, but I was afraid that I would miss. After a few more times it was just another part of my job I learned how to do.

Although I had killed before as an act of mercy, I had never killed the way we did on that last morning. The perfect efficiency of mass slaughter overwhelms any single act of compassionate killing in both action and theory. No lamb or ewe would survive the work of the shooters and the army to eradicate the threat of foot-and-mouth disease from the farm. Nature was not allowed to play its course.

As I describe these events, I realize I have not completely accepted my complicity in the death of the animals I struggled to keep alive. At some point I convinced myself I was just doing another job required by a lambing assistant. Although my efforts had switched from life to death, I blocked out the impact of my work and focused only on the process. I remember telling myself the faster I worked, the sooner it would be over, and I could go home and forget what had happened.

It only took an hour to kill the hundreds of sheep in the barn. After separating the ewes from the lambs, I went outside, wanting to maintain different memories of the place I spent so many hours. When it was done, soldiers worked in pairs to heave the carcasses into the bloodied buckets of the bulldozers. An open-backed gravel truck waited on the road to receive the bodies that fell like a shower of heavy stones.

As I watched them clean up, the farmer came over and told me to guide a convoy of shooters to get the sheep in the fields. Climbing into the back of a truck, I felt exhausted from a full day, though it was only nine o'clock in the morning. I sat with my back against the wheel hub, across from some of the farmer's friends from the village. As we drove away, I looked back at the wheeling bulldozers and falling bodies and was captivated by the easy mechanics of death.

In the fields we did exactly the same thing. With help from several border collies, we drove the sheep into a fenced corner of the field, and then blocked their escape with portable metal barriers. Stray sheep were chased down and captured. Then we pulled the lambs away from their mothers and placed them in a separate enclosure. When everything was ready, the shooters and the vets stepped forward. Again I tried to escape by turning to face the now empty fields. But behind me I heard the conversations of the shooters mixed with the regular snap of their bolt guns.

I stood near a makeshift pen, a small space surging with hundreds of terrified lambs. From here soldiers carried the lambs to the veterinarians standing nearby to administer the lethal injections. A pile of completely still bodies grew in the grass just behind them.

As more lambs were caught and crammed into the tiny pen,

I saw the smaller lambs at the bottom being trampled, almost drowning. One of the shooters, his clothes splattered in blood, paused from his work and waved me over.

"Don't put any more lambs in there," he said pointing to the overcrowded pen. "We don't want them to suffocate."

I nodded, a small part of my brain registering the irony of his words. He frowned, his eyes flashing contempt, so I scooped up a large lamb from the pen and walked over to the vets.

I watched how the lambs were killed while I waited behind a line of soldiers for my turn. A soldier held out a struggling lamb, and the vet probed the animal's torso with his fingers. After choosing a spot just behind the lamb's shoulder, the vet inserted a needle. A quick burst of blood shot into the syringe as the needle must have pricked the lamb's heart. The vet thumbed the plunger to force the poison into the lamb's body. In two seconds it was over. The lamb cried out as it slumped down, its final protest fading like a tape player running on dead batteries.

I reached the front of the line and stood before a vet dressed in blue coveralls and a poncho. Several glass medicine bottles swirling with red liquid bulged from her pockets.

"You're the lad in charge of the lambing, right?" She asked as I held the lamb's legs tight to keep it still.

I nodded yes, too nervous to speak and wondering how she could tell. The vet bit her lip as she searched the lamb's body and inserted the needle. In a few seconds it was done and the lamb was dead. I walked over to the pile of bodies and set it down as one would stack firewood. The pile was starting to collapse and a soldier worked patiently to rearrange the bodies.

"Are you a vet student?" the same woman asked when I carried over another lamb, this one with a brilliant white head.

"No, I'm a history student at Edinburgh," I replied.

She nodded, but her eyebrows went up. She noticed my

American accent.

"Where are you from?" She asked, her attention focused on the lamb. Her first attempt to pierce its heart failed. The lamb kicked and I pressed it against my body to keep it still.

"I'm from Ohio in the United States," I responded.

"Really." She looked at me, her mouth making a questioning frown. "What are you doing out here?" Very dark blood rushed into the syringe with the lamb's final heartbeat. She pushed down the plunger.

"A bit of adventure during my Easter Break from university," I replied, watching everything, blood and poison, disappear from the clear plastic tube.

The lamb raised its head and cried out once and then was still against my chest.

"My God" was all she said.

Jason Stevenson spent a year in Scotland studying British battleships during the Second World War, and he even earned a master's degree to prove it. Raised on Midwestern meatloaf and steaks, he recently has been introduced to fruit and vegetables. A history graduate of Harvard College, he currently writes essays and stories in the margins of his life as an economic development consultant in Boston.

I have found out that there ain't no surer way to find out whether you like people or hate them than to travel with them.

MARK TWAIN

Netherlands

Romancing Amsterdam

Amsterdam, Netherlands

VICTOR PAUL BORG

"I FEEL DEFEATED," ANGELICA LEHMANN SAID.

I sighed under my breath, and lay down on the bed next to her. "Why?"

"I think you don't like me anymore."

I rolled on my back, scrambling for words. Tucked here in the Bulldog Hostel, the claustrophobia of our attic room — gray wallpaper on the walls and ceiling, dull green paint for the bedside table and bathroom door, a dark-gray carpet, a cramped bathroom that smelled of sewage — made me feel more trapped and morose. How could I explain to Angelica that two days in Amsterdam was all it took for me to realize I didn't want to be with her? That my test had already failed? That I didn't find her attractive anymore? That now, in this wonderful city, I yearned to be alone and free, because the state of aloneness would open possibilities while being with her had emasculated me?

"Well," I said, "I am not as madly in love with you as I thought I was before meeting here."

"Thanks."

"I still like you. Maybe you expect too much from me?" I was being diplomatic, perhaps even subtly manipulative — but I didn't have the courage to walk away, completely and forever.

"Perhaps I am too romantic for you?"

Outside, the bells of the Nieuwe Kerk in Dam Square started chiming on the quarter, a lilting and melodious and tentatively desirous chime. It gave Amsterdam the provincial atmosphere of a small town. I stood up and gazed out the window. The gothic spire of the church was set against a sky the color of dirty dishwater, dusted with the orange of the streetlights. For a moment I stood transfixed at the window, peering over the back-gardens of the townhouses, the gardens as small as shafts, the jumble of houses following the twisty course of the alleys in central Amsterdam. From my vantage point, the exaggerated, tilting gables of the houses were both homely and spooky — grayish and smoky silhouettes. I watched the lights in the windows go on and followed the movements of the occupants. Amsterdam, with its high-density living, and the Dutch irreverence or oblivious-ness for privacy, is the most public of cities. The bell chimed again, and this time it sounded like a weep over lost love, and it made me restless. I said, "Let's enjoy our time and then see what happens. ... Take it day by day."

She nodded, but her eyes were hollow. Our brief honeymoon had already ended, and I wondered how much she could read into my thoughts. Did she realize that our sojourn in Amsterdam would probably be the last muted gasp of our short relationship — a relationship I should never have pursued?

It had all started in Malta eight weeks earlier, when love — or so I thought — had blazed across our vista like an unforgettable sunset. She had been studying English when we met, six days before she was due to leave for Hamburg, her home town. For her last weekend, we planned a three-day trip to Gozo, Malta's rural sister island. It was a romantic, intimate weekend on a legendary island. We lodged in a 150-year-old farmhouse and were awakened in the mornings by the crowing of the roosters and the mooing of the cows. We ate the traditional pizzas cooked in wood-fired ovens, and ravioli as large as purses bursting with sheep's cheese. We got drunk on the fortified walls of a 500-year-old castle whose limestone face is weathered to the color of sandstone. We skirted along a 200-meter-high sea cliff, the blue sky and sun-dappled sea unfolding before us forever. We chased crimson sunsets. And we had sex in the car in a remote corner of the island, and when we looked up we saw a bright and populated Milky Way. "It seems to be there for us," I murmured.

That's when we decided to meet again in Amsterdam. In Gozo, the romance had been safe because it could exist in a state of suspended reality. It may have remained so if we had made our next meetings in places where each of us would fill the other's vista, as in Gozo: another short time period in a hotel in a village or near a lake, somewhere amenable to nature walks, candle-lit dinners, long intimate nights and terrace breakfasts. But I needed to test the solidity of our relationship in a broader milieu, and for me, Amsterdam posed that challenge: If I could love Angelica in Amsterdam in January, I could love her anywhere. Now, I could see, I had been superstitious about love: I had believed that our love would triumph over the ubiquitous pickings of Amsterdam's hedonism, and I had been wrong.

Escaping from our room, I went down to the hostel's common area to wait for Angelica to shower. It was the happy hour, and the bar was full of backpackers squatting or reclining on a piece of elevated floor covered by carpets. The large room was full of smoke and beer, excited cackle and techno music. Joints and bongs were making the rounds; the air reeked of the leathery, narcotic smell of Himalayan hash. I sat on a stool at the bar counter, sipping a coffee, feeling an awkward otherness and separation. I wished I was free to associate, to make new friends, to hang out, to go partying, to cavort around Amsterdam, to join the backpackers huddled behind me — but I was trapped in an intense and melancholic holiday romance. An Australian traveler who had just arrived in Amsterdam quizzed me about the coffee shops and sex. He planned a binge of booze and drugs, and what were the women like? A Peruvian man joined us, and we discussed what nationalities of women are the best looking. Silly, superficial conversations at another time and in another mood, but now they were conversations that taunted me.

Everything taunted me — the sexy Dutch woman behind the bar, the Spanish twins with faces rounded and cute like kittens', the large group drinking whiskey straight from the bottle and puffing on a bong. Everyone here basked in Amsterdam's hedonistic allure, and I wondered why Angelica and I thought we could cultivate our love to blossom in this lust-crazed city.

That night we ate falafel in a cheap restaurant that smelled of dirty clothes in a closed room. Afterward we went on a civil touristy stroll, ambling to Leidseplein, Amsterdam's tourist-ridden area, to our favorite coffee shop. The Rokeru was a hybrid between an opium den (dimly lit by candles, a pervasive narcotic reek) and a New Age shrine (the Buddhist *mandala* etched on one wall, benches woven from rope, oriental carpets, and so on). I liked the music with its distorted, superimposed shreds of sounds and its unrhythmic, sputtering beats; and after some cannabis, it became even more wholesome, filling everything so that the music became part of everything — it became the walls, the people — instead of simply a transmitted or invasive sound.

But, as for the question about Angelica and I, there were constant reminders of the cruel difference in the change of milieu. I had to lean close to hear Angelica's faint voice. In Gozo, I remembered, her small voice had blended with the natural setting, a whisper like the hum of wind filtering through grass and trees — here, her voice sounded like a whimper. It got worse that evening: fifteen-minute silences dissected our discourse, and every spell of self-conscious silence, in a place where everyone else was talking and laughing animatedly, dealt us another blow.

The next day I had the good sense of going my own way for the day. After several days of grayness and rain, the cloudless day was promising. Amsterdam, with its narrow, winding alleys, with its compact center, with its bicycles floating past in a flurry of clinking bells, and with its disdain for motor vehicles (we had driven here from Hamburg but left the car out of town to avoid the stiff parking fees), is a city made for walking. It is a city that is quaint and sophisticated at the same time. It is liberal and unpretentious and unhurried — unlike other capitals of Europe, few people wear formal suits for work, and none of them are in a hurry, as though every day is a public holiday. And yet Amsterdam is one of the leading lights of the New Economy and all kinds of design, and it has some formidably creative artists. That day I roamed through the cobbled streets and past the canals, watching the ducks and coots and grebes and water traffic from the arched stone bridges. How I wished to be staying in one of the boat-houses — we had checked, and they were expensive, well beyond our budget. In the red-light district, I was struck by the marriage of the oldest profession and the oldest building in Amsterdam — prostitutes in bikinis in their window-booths surrounded the Oude Kerk, the oldest church. A smell of urine whiffed the air near a sign showing the half-body of a man spewing a dotted line of piss, indicating the open-air booth that enclosed a toilet.

"Coke! Ecstasy!" When I whirled my head I saw a dark man in a corner, his lips moving. "Coke! Ecstasy!" Shaking my head, I smiled at the flatness of his voice, the economic use of his words. No hard drugs for me, not as long as Angelica was around.

I visited the Marijuana Museum and the Sex Museum. Both assumed an educational and academic mission, the Marijuana Museum devoted largely to the history of hemp and its uses and environmental tributes, and the Sex Museum with the theme 'Pornography through the Ages.' But what does hemp have to do with mind-altering hash? What's the link between cannabis plants growing in a hothouse "in natural surroundings" and industrial hemp? In the Sex Museum, what's educational about centuries-old sex aids and pictures, and the clips of porno films produced through the decades? These educational sideshows seemed a pretense for a celebration of sex and cannabis. And both taunted me: I felt like a tethered and hungry dog that couldn't reach the meat in the mid-distance.

Angelica and I fell into a kind of dull routine. We spent most weeknights reading and sipping tea in the hostel's bar. Sometimes I would lift my head from the book and catch her staring at me, her eyes burning. In Gozo I had considered those gazes affectionately, as though she was peering into my heart; here her unflinching eyes seemed to be judging me. The nights were long and we devoured each other in feverish intimacy, moaning like wounded animals. She laughed breezily in the middle of the night, recklessly mumbling that the sex was good. But was she deluding herself, thinking that sudden sexual intimacy could patch up our discomfort and incompatibility? Because the sex was good only while it lasted, furious in its romantic finality, the way a pricked balloon swishes through the air before it falls flat on the ground.

Yet the days became easier and unhurried as some of our soreness eased. We did enjoyable and uneventful sight-seeing. We visited the Van Gogh Museum and the Stedelijk Museum of Modern Art, where Rembrandt's celebrated *The Nightwatch* is housed. We strolled in the Vondelpark, Amsterdam's largest park. We rambled through the city center, soaking up the atmosphere. We sat in cafes with their sweet coffee flavor and took in the city's face: its buildings, like stacks of books propped on a shelf, some teetering forward, others slightly tilted, their confident facades pockmarked by hollow-eyed windows, and higher up, their gables pompous and eloquent. The lines of buildings, and indeed the whole vista of streetscapes and elm trees and canals, looked elegant in their lopsidedness, as if it was a conscious effect (technically, the buildings were ever shifting and sinking on unstable foundations). We pointed out the sights, we wallowed in our flights of fanciful imagination, we discussed the Dutch way of doing politics and business in growing admiration. There were moments when instead of emasculation I felt freely associated, the same way I would feel with someone I had met in the hostel and paired up for a day or two for company.

Some nights we went clubbing, and the soreness returned. Angelica hadn't been to many dance clubs in her life, and now she struggled to blend into clubs and enjoy the music. She acted like someone who didn't belong, following me as though she was my shadow, and such an intense and awkward presence by my side deflated me. Her boredom and cluelessness dragged us to the corners and edges of clubs. I thought, *You can be with a lover one-to-one and grow into each other's presence, but the make-or-break test for a couple comes when you mix with people socially, and Angelica and I were failing.* In Gozo, I had taken her timidity as signs of dedication and propriety, while in Amsterdam her lack of assertiveness and her weariness made me feel socially incompetent, guilty by association. In Amsterdam, while everyone was partying, we were watching from the shadows.

If I couldn't party, at least I had to check out the clubs Amsterdam had to offer, information that might serve me well if I decided to revisit. Mazzo, on our last night, struck me as an unpretentious club, with red umbrella-shaped paper lamps dangling from the ceiling as décor. The DJ spun dance-floor acid jazz, with lilting basslines and rhythmic beats, and the dance floor soon filled up. After a while I felt pity for Angelica, and said, "Do you feel like going home now?"

She shook her head. Her gestures, however, suggested boredom. Her face was down-turned, her arms and legs crossed, and not a twitch escaped her limply reticent posture. At least we never argued or made a scene, I thought when we left Amsterdam, back to our separate homes. We never met or spoke again, and some years have passed now, and my one wish remains unfulfilled: to go back to Amsterdam, this time by myself, the only way I could be open to whims and opportunities and associations — an openness, coupled with the Dutch way, a marriage between pragmatism and idealism, that is crucial for the enjoyment of Amsterdam.

Angelica Lehmann is a fictitious name, to protect the privacy of the real person.

Victor Paul Borg, who grew up in Malta, is a freelance travel writer and photographer. He has had over 500 articles published worldwide. His pictures - travel and photojournalism - have been published widely, and he has recently shot 250 subjects for a new pictorial guide to London. He is also the author of The Rough Guide to Malta & Gozo, *and is currently in Asia writing a travel book. His website can be found at www.victorborg.com.*

Boy, those French. They have a different word for everything.

France

Parisian Angel

Paris, France

JANNA GRABER

MY FRIEND LISA IS PLANNING A TRIP TO PARIS. WE ARE SITTING IN my kitchen, where she has spread out several maps and dumped a towering stack of French guidebooks on the table. Using her forefinger with its perfectly polished red nail, she points out all the places that she and her husband will visit, commenting on each exotic destination.

"Can you imagine?" she asks. "All that great food, the quaint cafés, walking along the river banks. ..." Her voice drops off as she envisions herself in such locations. Lisa, it's obvious, has already fallen under the city's spell and can't wait to return.

"Don't you just love Paris," she asks dreamily.

Frankly, I don't know how to answer. For others, Paris is the most romantic of all locales. For me, it's the city of unfinished business, where a story that was once started hasn't yet found its end.

It stems from my first impression of Paris. Lasting memories are formed by virgin encounters with the places we see, the food we eat, the bed we sleep in, and most of all, the people we meet.

I was studying in Vienna, and as any college student abroad will tell you, exploring the continent during school breaks is half the fun. There is no other feeling like grabbing your rail ticket and backpack, opening a new, crisp map of Europe on a bright and shiny Saturday morning, and picking, either on a whim or some rumor you have heard, the place that you want to visit next.

That's how I ended up on the overnight train to Paris.

I slept most of the way and awoke as I felt the wheels slow for our arrival in the French capital. Drowsily, I grabbed my backpack and searched for my small shoulder bag, the one with money and a credit card inside. It was nowhere to be found.

My shoulders slumped as I realized that I had been robbed. I couldn't figure out how. Several others and I shared the closed train compartment. I didn't remember anyone else coming in.

I left the train and decided to go to the police — if I could only find them. Stopping here and there, I asked vendors for directions. Most stared at me dumbly, amused at my English words. Finally, a woman pointed out a small police office.

A policeman in a stiff uniform and proper hat motioned for me to sit down in front of him. He pulled up a small black typewriter, stuck in a triplicate form, and began firing away questions in French. I couldn't understand a word he said. I told him so in English, but he asked another question — in French. I just stared at him dumbly. Finally, he shrugged his shoulders and rolled his eyes with exasperation.

"Sprechen Sie Deutsch?" I asked. No response.

"Hablas Espanol?" I asked again. No response again.

Tired and fed up, I blurted out my story in English, pausing briefly between sentences for breath. When I stopped, the policeman stared at me a minute and then began typing in a two-fingered fashion. He did understand what I was saying! Or else he was typing, "This stupid American girl doesn't speak even one word of French. Who knows what she is gesturing wildly about?"

When he was done, the policeman spoke again in French and pointed me to the door. So that was the end of that.

Later I heard that there had been a rash of train robberies that month. Now, I was in Paris with less than $20 worth of currency in my pocket and no credit card. A fine state!

One bright spot — before setting out for Paris, my uncle

had given me the name of a place to stay. "The Palais de la Femme," he suggested. "They were very nice. And don't worry. It's cheap."

I looked at the slip of paper now, fingering the little money I had in my pockets. I hoped the hotel was cheap; otherwise, I'd be sleeping on the street. For now, I had the whole day ahead of me, so I tossed my backpack over my shoulder and set off to at least see SOME of Paris. I grabbed a map of the subway system and went exploring.

The cozy cafes that I passed looked warm and inviting — young couples were staring at each other over tumblers of red wine. I saw children eating cakes and bread while their mothers talked happily together. I had no money to enjoy these tempting places, so I just walked on, watching these happy scenes through the windows.

Determined not to let that get to me, I hauled my backpack across the city to see the outside of Notre Dame, free to view, and I walked along the Seine River, also free.

It was getting dark as I walked into the park under the Eiffel Tower. As a recently robbed student, I couldn't afford the ticket to the top of the Tower. So, I sat down on a park bench and stared at its twinkling lights. It was strange to look at a monument that I had seen so many times in pictures.

Couples walked by arm in arm, others sat on a nearby bench kissing. I was overcome with a feeling of loneliness. Suddenly, all I wanted to do was leave this city of lights and these people I couldn't understand far behind. But first, I had to find somewhere to spend the night.

I walked over to stand in the light of a pub, and pulled out my map. While I searched for the street I needed, a group of three young men noticed me. They were sitting around a tiny table, drinking wine and smoking. Their pointing fingers and rapid

French made me wonder, but when they stood and wobbled toward me, I felt uneasy.

Quickly, I stuffed the map back into my pack, pulled it over my shoulders and walked away. One of the drunks began to follow me, speaking and joking in French. I ignored him because I had no idea what he was telling me.

A block later, I turned to see him still coming behind me. The glass of wine was gone; an intent look now covered his face.

It's nothing! I told myself. I crossed the street, noticing with sinking dread that the sun was now gone. The drunk was still following.

I was really scared. There were fewer people on the street, and the area was looking more suburban. Who could help me when I can't even speak French?

Then I saw it — Palais de la Femme — in bright lights ahead. I felt like jumping for joy. It was a nondescript building, but right then it looked like the Hilton. With one more quick glance at the man, I slipped in the door.

The place was simple and clean. At the front desk, two women were working. One, who was a young woman about my age, smiled at me.

I hesitated and took a deep breath before asking in English for a room. She smiled, but it seemed that she didn't understand very well. "Hablas Espanol?" I asked tentatively.

"Si!" she replied. Relieved, I asked for a room. She took out a key and then told me the price. It was about ten euros more than I had with me. My shoulders fell and I turned to leave, stuffing my money back into my pack.

"Wait," she called, motioning me back. Then she pulled out her purse from a drawer, opened a tiny pouch and drew out several notes.

"Here, now you have enough," she said, handing me a form

and pen to register.

I looked at her with shock. Did she just GIVE me money? With her simple gesture, this young woman, who told me her name was Pacquita, had turned around an entire city for me.

I thanked her profusely while she gave me the keys to the room. I have never been so relieved at the sight of clean, white sheets in a small, ugly room. For the first time that night, I took a deep breath and felt safe.

Later that evening, I went down to talk with her. She was a university student who had a French father and a Spanish mother. We talked of America and Spain and France. She told me of her studies, and I talked of my school life in Vienna.

Pacquita wasn't working that next morning, and I never saw her again. But when I left for the train station, I noticed that Paris had taken on a fresh hue. Sparkling sunlight reflected in the windows as the sleeping city woke up. I could smell baking bread and rich coffee from the cafés as I walked back to the station.

A few weeks later, back in Vienna, I got a postcard from Pacquita. "I hope you had a nice trip home, and a great year at university," she wrote in Spanish. I pinned her card up on my bulletin board, and later packed it home to America.

"That card is probably still in a box in my basement some-where," I now tell my friend Lisa, who has been listening to my story. "I haven't thought about Pacquita for a long time. ..."

Is it possible? Have I let the fright I felt in Paris overcome my memory of the kindness I found there? I breathe slowly, re-membering how that one small gesture of compassion changed everything.

"Let me see those brochures," I say, grabbing a stack of them. I open up a map of France to see the page dotted with tiny vil-lages, blue lakes, and then Paris, big and shiny on the page.

Maybe places, like people, deserve second chances.

"Paris really *did* look beautiful in the moonlight," I tell Lisa, a smile on my face. This French city, I have decided, is worth seeing with fresh eyes.

Janna Graber is a freelance journalist who has covered stories from Haiti to New Zealand for publications including the Chicago Tribune, Denver Post, Reader's Digest, Parade, Redbook *and* Alaska Airlines. *Having studied international relations in Vienna, she has a special passion for bringing the world home to readers. Besides freelance writing, she is an editor at* Go World Travel Magazine *(www.goworldtravel.com), an international publication covering the world's most fascinating people and places.*

Living with an Aristocrat

Paris, France

COURTNEY LOCHNER

"GOODBYE!"

I hear the final echoes of my friends' and family's farewells as I move from the airport lounge to the plane that would carry me to Paris, France. I'd been studying French for seven years, and for the past few months, working at a miserable job, I'd been motivating myself with the word "Paris" written on my palm. As a little girl, I had begged my parents for French lessons, given my Barbie dolls French names, and played "restaurant" with a French menu. I was great friends with my high-school French teacher, studied the French dictionary during my spare time, and befriended the French high-school exchange student on his first step into class. France had always been a part of me, yet I'd never been there.

I didn't sleep the whole way to Amsterdam, my layover point, and I picked up a copy of *Le Monde*, in order to prove to myself that France really existed. This was not another French class reading exercise — it was the paper of French people, and I was almost there!

Through my jet-lag haze at Charles deGaulle Airport, I made it onto my Paris-bound bus, and then I saw it, that most magnificent of wonders, the Eiffel Tower. I sat up, immediately energized, and looked around me, a full 360, and that's when it really hit me: *I'm alone.* I had no one but strangers to tell. When I finally stood outside my new university, luggage and all, I could barely even get myself to go in. *I'm in France!* I thought, mesmerized by the street, the French signs, the corner *patisserie* oozing the rich

112

scents of sugar and butter, the stylish people carrying fresh baguettes home, the dogwalkers, the woman sweeping the sidewalk outside her boutique.

When I finally shook myself out of the trance and walked in, I entered a room full of people mid-conversation. A tall brunette in an elaborate scarf turned to me, "Ah! Vous etes qui!?" This was the moment that my ear would begin accepting French language as its norm. I introduced myself and learned that my new French "mother" would arrive any minute, as would many others for the 41 other students as big-eyed as myself. Minutes later I discovered what a puppy at the shelter must feel like: dozens of French ladies appeared, announcing American names with their best effort. With each one I thought, *She looks nice, could this be the one that takes me home?*

The one who did was a small woman in her sixties, immaculately dressed. The brunette pronounced my name for her, she whisked us into her oh-so-small but chic car, and she took on the crazy drivers of Paris. As we sped by monuments I had only dreamed of, Madame told me about "la perspectif de Paris," spilling out impressive historical dates and architectural facts that make Paris what she is today. It felt like an out-of-body experience, yet I had never felt more alive.

Nothing could have prepared me for the sight of my new residence. After punching a code into a large stone wall by the street, we passed through a courtyard to a residence building, then punched another code for entrance through a thick wooden door. A ride up a tiny elevator brought us to Madame's floor, where she entered an old-fashioned key into an even thicker door. In the foyer my jaw dropped: the ceilings were so high I feared my voice would echo. It was furnished with what I guessed were antique Greek busts, Oriental rugs that probably cost more than a year's tuition at the university, and a chandelier that made me gasp.

Showing me quickly to my bedroom, Madame informed me that dinner was about to be served. I dropped my things in another high-ceilinged room, with another chandelier, a large bed covered in thick toile blankets, and French doors that opened on that peaceful courtyard and a view of miles of Parisian rooftops beyond. Still in a daze, I made my debut in the dining room, where an incredibly long table was set to perfection. French doors opened to a small balcony with a bird's eye view of Paris and the Eiffel Tower in the hazy distance. Just when I thought it couldn't get any more unreal, Maria, the server, arrived with our first course on her wheeled cart. I sat down and took my *serviette* (napkin), anxiously eyeing the quantity of shiny silverware as Maria put an herb-stuffed tomato in front of me. Aromas of French tarragon and anise filled the room as my glass was filled with the fullest-bodied Bordeaux wine this 20-year-old American had ever encountered. Was it a kind of wine so rich and tannic that it needed to be taken with food, or was I just that unaccustomed to it? After each tiny sip, Maria immediately poured more into my glass. My cheeks were turning very rosy, my insides ignited, as I listened to Madame proudly tell me about Paris. I told her that I was mesmerized and immediately in love with the city. *My little American,* she replied in French, *you have such a good accent.* Emotions flooded me and I smiled so big I had to look down.

Dinner finally came to an end after three hours of the best food I'd ever eaten, and I was advised to turn in. But first, Madame gave me directions to my school: Metro stop this, metro stop that. … After forty-eight hours without sleep and three glasses of wine, making sense of directions given in a different language was a challenge. I slept very well in my big French bed.

Day one opened with me putting to the test those directions I'd heard last night: metro Monceau … Metro? Ah! There was the sign, and the stairs leading down into Paris' mysterious underworld of transportation. I ran to the underground ticket window to purchase my *carte orange* — my new metro identity — from the ticket seller. In test number two, speaking with a fast-talking native, my years of devotion to French paid off. She handed me my little booklet and map; all I needed to complete it now was my photo.

I felt so empowered, so independent getting on the metro — I now had access to every corner of Paris. Trying to hide my enormous smile and not blow my cover, I sat down and noted my fellow riders' attitudes and apparel: *don't carry a backpack, get a chic bag; act like you know where you're going; get some new shoes; and hey, stop smiling.*

At Rue Daguerre — these words stuck with me from Madame's instructions last night — I hopped off the metro and ran back down that first enchanting street to my new university. We students received an incredible welcome: an orientation, great quiche, class schedules, and a lecture by a *gendarme* (policeman) about the laws in our new country.

I made friends with two American students, and, after class, we got on the metro with no direction, using our new *cartes oranges* as keys to the city. This would become one of my favorite things to do. After our day of exploring, we found a small restaurant in the middle of a narrow cobblestone street, where we feasted on authentic paninis and a bottle of wine. The air carried French voices, the bright crescent moon hung between two old buildings and illuminated the smiling faces of my new friends. We had no idea where exactly we were, but Paris was answer enough for me.

Every day was spectacular, beginning with the cart outside my bedroom every morning holding a carafe of fresh orange juice, a croissant, and a rotation of almond tart, pain au chocolat, or an éclair. After breakfast, I parted for the metro, hiding my pride that I knew my path so well underground, even at the overwhelmingly large interchange of Charles de Gaulle Etoile. I started a new ritual of getting a *café au lait* right before class. Class was where I found my second home in Paris: the more people who know your name in a foreign country, the less of a foreigner you become.

I often ate lunch in one of the university cafeterias available to students throughout the city. I loved that a delicious piece of French bread accompanied every dish, that the French loved eggs cracked over their pizzas, and that I met someone new each time.

Every other night I ate dinner with Madame, usually alone, but once in a while joined by a niece, nephew, or sister. All the dinners lasted three hours, and every minute was enjoyable. Madame was incredibly formal, and she didn't speak a word of English, but we were able to cover all topics in great depth, aided slightly by the wine. As the sun set through the open French doors, we'd dine on the fine food, discussing politics, history, and culture until our bellies were nice and full and it was time to retreat to our respective rooms.

In a foreign country, small things seem so big. I found it exciting to visit the post office, amusing to see the insane amount of yogurt at the grocery store, and an awakening to see a wine and beer machine at the school cafeteria, like any pop machine in America. Every little event seemed magnified: getting a note from my French mother that I'd received a phone call from my French friend was a marvelous novelty; sitting in a park with a journal and a head about to explode with inspiration was a thrill; seeing almost as many types of cheese in the French grocery as there are total items in an American grocery was surprisingly unusual.

I enjoyed my school, and that my teachers didn't pretend — they were just themselves, real people that we got to know during the course of the year. My grammar professor wasn't worth talking to until she'd had her 8 a.m. *café*; asking my sociology professor about film noir was a sure way to get him in a good mood, and he took our class to a movie that would have prompted a Dateline special back in the States. But we were different people here; we were Parisians. I now carried a sleek bag onto the metro, and I hid my smile within to fit in with my surroundings.

I was beginning to feel really comfortable in Paris. I knew my metro route, I was a regular in my block's café and the city's busiest Internet café, and I knew where everything was, from les Champs Elysees to *le quartier latin* (the Latin Quarter). I even fooled the locals. As I sat on a bench on the Champs Elysees waiting to meet some friends, a Parisian tried to pick me up by asking if I knew how to find the Champs Elysees. He was probably hoping to have found a foreigner that would go weak at his French. "You're standing in the Champs Elysees," I laughed. "*Merde,*" he replied, "a little embarrassing asking a French person that." Days later, a French woman asked if I could tell her how to get to the Monceau metro stop. I gave her the directions (I live across the street from it), and she said, "How lucky I am to have asked a Parisian with all of the tourists around here today." You couldn't dream of a prouder moment in my world.

But I had my difficult times as well. One night I partied and didn't come home, which set me up for a shock the next morning when Madame screamed at me, "*Where have you been? I couldn't breathe, I was so scared! You didn't call!*" I felt absolutely horrible and I cried for hours. How could I have forgotten to call her, for she was my mother here, and she took care of me. I couldn't think at school that day, I was without appetite watching my sugar cubes spin around my café au lait, I didn't know what to say, how to apologize, how many I'm sorry's could make a wrong right.

That evening, I came home just past dark, after a solitary sketching on a bench at the *l'arc de triomphe*. In front of my bedroom was a cart, holding three exquisite desserts and a small card that said, "*Pour ma petite americaine.*" There were no more words to be said. This was Madame's truce. I was still her daughter.

My last day of school, the tall brunette woman with the scarf pulled me aside. "You know who your mother is, don't you?" I did not. "She is the former President's sister. Mitterand's sister." There it was. I lived with a legend. Some things about Madame suddenly made more sense. I nodded back at the brunette, sophisticatedly holding in my smile as I'd learned so well to do *a la mode Parisienne.*

That night was Fete de la Musique in Paris. The city was alive with music: In the streets, every five feet or so, was a band, a musician, someone singing. Surely the whole world could hear! I sat with my new best friend near the Pantheon, drinking a *kir* and humming as my contribution to the classic French songs sung live just in front of us.

"Things will be different when we go back, huh?" she said.

"Yeah, they said we'd be pretty depressed, at my pre-departure orientation."

"Do you think you will be?"

I thought about it. "Yes, I do, I will be. But I'm here now."

Yes, I was depressed leaving France, and for some time after I got back to the States. I didn't find life as exciting when everyone spoke English, when all I wanted to talk about was France and people were getting sick of hearing it, and when I knew life went on at home without me — and worse yet, I knew it was going on in France without me. But if I close my eyes and think of it, there I am, back in Paris. I can smell the croissants in the pastry shop, I can feel the brick roads twisting through the Latin Quarter, I can hear Madame's voice, I can see the Eiffel Tower against the black Parisian sky. I was reborn with passion in Paris — knowledge that more is out there, that, oceans apart from us, there are people, cultures and places that are completely foreign, but where you can still find a home.

Courtney Lochner holds degrees in French and Communication Studies from the University of Minnesota. She lives in Prague, where she writes, teaches English, and listens to house music with a glass of wine. Watch for her novel, Night and Dia.

Dancing Like a Chicken in Paris

Paris, France

LEE ANNE HASSELBACHER

As I LAY IN THE DARK HOSTEL ROOM, THE SILENCE INTERRUPTED OCCA-
sionally by the softly snoring German girl in the next bed, I felt for the
first time that I might really be dangerously alone and adrift in the world.
The twenty-four hours leading up to this moment were an adrenaline-
soaked blur of crowded airports, soggy train-station sandwiches and
fleeting images of European landscapes as they slipped by my windows
on the plane, train and subway.

I was going to be studying abroad in England, and, before classes
began, I set out with two traveling companions, Jenny and Kelly, to
embark on a whirlwind tour of Western Europe. Our first day of travel
was, some might say, a tad on the ambitious side: from Green Bay,
Wisconsin, to Chicago to London to Winchester (to dispose of several
suitcases at our university) back to London and on to Paris. Nonstop.
Well, we did stop once when my suitcase strap broke, my bag fell, I lost
my balance and caused a minor traffic jam on Platform B of the train
station; but otherwise nonstop.

Exhausted from the travel and, after apologizing our way down
many a narrow aisle with overstuffed backpacks, we finally arrived at the
Aloha Hostel in downtown Paris around midnight. Sunny yellow walls,
the disco beat of ABBA and a friendly English-speaking clerk greeted
us as we wearily stumbled into our temporary home. Relieved, though
a bit overwhelmed, we gratefully took our key and wound our way carefully up more narrow passageways to our attic room. Ready to unwind,
we opened the door to find a large room with nine beds, six of them
already filled with sleeping hostelers. Not sure of proper hostel eti-
quette regarding the lights and not wanting to wake anyone, we quietly

119

put our things down and claimed beds in the dark. It was then that I found myself lying in my sewn-together sheet with my heart racing and my mind highly alert to the fact that I was thousands of miles away from anything familiar.

In the months before leaving, I felt an almost electric excitement whenever I imagined myself exploring foreign cities and cultures. Yet, there in the hostel that first night, I was not feeling excited or enlightened; I felt absolutely panicked. I lay there unblinking, sweaty, consciously forcing my breathing to slow; pathetically, one lone tear escaped to my makeshift pillow. I remembered the Internet station downstairs and silently slipped out of the room. In the lobby I paid my 10 francs to use the computer and typed a few short sentences to my parents. Somehow, writing the words "Getting here was an adventure, but all right" and "It's awesome to finally be in Paris" helped me believe they were true. Though I still contemplated all the ways I could get lost, confused or laughed at, I did sleep a little easier knowing my world was still in existence and a mouse click away.

My spirit of adventure slowly returned the next morning as we stepped out of the blue hostel door and into the sunlit new world before us. Feeling fairly self-satisfied after finding a way to communicate our desire for some honey-drenched croissants at a local shop (through the universally acknowledged "pointing" method), I was more hopeful about our situation. The idea of actually *being* in Europe was still so surreal that we decided to visit the most prominent verification: the Eiffel Tower.

Khaki-clad in a sea of sleek black pants, we made our way on this Parisian pilgrimage, and I found myself in awe of the city unfolding before me. With delight, I felt the knobby cobblestones of the sidewalk through the soles of my shoes and drank in an air heavy with history. I cannot describe how or why, but I *felt* the old age of the city; the atmosphere was like nothing I had experienced in my relatively teenage Wisconsin. We arrived at the Eiffel Tower and took turns taking the obligatory pictures of ourselves in front of the famous landmark. Throughout our travels we took many of these sorts of pictures; they are now displayed in my album like evidence to prove my memories.

I spent the rest of the day trying to hold onto every sight, sound and smell as we explored some of the well-known places. I was overwhelmed with cultural stimulation; I went from solemnly contemplating the religious devotion that inspired the gothic beauty of Notre Dame to pondering a life spent writing revolutionary literature from a wrought-iron café chair in the Latin Quarter. We also visited the Pantheon, a museum that toured like the index of a history textbook. Legends became human as I wandered among the tombs of such French notables as Victor Hugo, Marie Curie and Jean-Jaques Rosseau.

After a day of walking around like porous sponges absorbing every sensation, we were thoroughly exhausted. We picked up some groceries for a simple dinner and made our way back to the Aloha. That evening, "Son of a Preacher Man" and the happy chatter of excited travelers spilled out of the blue door, and I found myself aching to be a part of the fun. My fellow travelers were ready to retire to our room, write in their journals and get some sleep. After a moment's hesitation, I too pulled out my journal, but instead headed back down to the buzzing lobby.

The hostel had a small bar and several high café-style tables spread around the cozy first floor and, a legal drinker there at 19, I ordered a cold Heineken and sat down at an empty table. I had my journal open in front of me and began to write, but secretly I was hoping to connect with some of the energy that filled the room as fellow travelers were conversing around me. However, considering that before this trip I was nervous about calling a stranger to order a pizza, I wasn't exactly outgoing in this situation. Yet, just as I was documenting the previous night's flirt with fear, a smiling dark-haired young man came over and introduced himself in such a warm and unassuming manner that I immediately felt at ease. His name was Sameh and he was originally from Cairo,

Egypt, where he was studying to be a doctor. In endearingly labored English, he told me of his travels thus far.

He had just gotten to a fascinating part about the Parque Guell, in Barcelona, when we attracted the attention of three more hostelers who joined our conversation, urging us to see Gaudi's bizarrely orchestrated park. Stefan, Biola and Daisuke were from Austria (Daisuke was originally from Japan) and talk quickly turned to all of our native countries, with questions flying back and forth. The highlights included Daisuke's ability to pinpoint my Midwestern accent (he had studied in Minnesota) and Sameh's patient effort to describe the Arabic alphabet, complete with illustrations in my journal. Amusing in his sincere regret, Sameh added, "I am quite sorry, but my alphabet does not have any letters of 'p' or 'v'. But there are ways to work around it, do not worry."

That night I fell asleep enveloped in feeling of genuine contentment and looked forward not only to seeing my guidebook's recommended sights, but also to the evening plans I had made with new friends.

Our second full day in Paris was a very warm one and, quite honestly, the Metro does not smell pleasant on very warm days. And, since our exploring had been going so smoothly, it was inevitable that we would get lost on the Metro. Once underground, in the cavernous cement tunnels, it becomes easy to lose your bearings. Mostly, we just guessed at routes and, as a result, we got turned around ... a few times. Finally, Rick Steves' phrasebook in hand, we decided to ask for help. After losing at paper-rock-scissors, I was the one pushed forward on an unsuspecting Frenchwoman. I was terrified, like I was being asked to represent the earth in an alien encounter. I tried to be brief and apologetic; five stressful minutes later I grasped some of her advice. We finally made the cross-town transit to Sacré Coeur, a breathtakingly white cathedral resting atop what appears to be an altar of vibrant flowers. What it really rested on was a fairly steep hill, and we gladly took refuge in the darker, cooler interior and gazed once again at faith's manifestations, this time in the form of gold-plated ceilings and walls.

When we got back to the hostel later that day, a small group was gathering for a night out. Jenny and Kelly decided to delay sleep this evening and join us as we came up with a plan. It was a beautiful night, so we thought we'd see the lights of the Eiffel Tower. We began walking and, along the way, Daisuke and Sameh darted into a shop and emerged with a few bottles of cheap red wine and, of all things, potato chips. Picnic provisions in hand, we continued walking and mingling, the same spirited energy of the previous night creating an aura of possibility and adventure. Upon reaching the park surrounding the Eiffel Tower, we found a spot on the grass and, with that, one of the best nights I have ever spent traveling was underway.

Along with our original crew, we had added Mark (Costa Rican), Kylie (Australian) and George (Canadian) to make an even ten, with six countries represented. For hours we sat on that lawn, the lights of Paris in the backdrop, discussing everything from government structure to standards of living to favorite desserts. A long conversation was dedicated to the differences in our respective education systems, including approaches to learning about the history and language of foreign nations. I was humbled when it hit me that this exchange would not be possible if half our group was not bilingual. Daisuke alone spoke five languages proficiently.

We traded traveling tales, drank wine and teased each other like old friends. Any fear of being somewhere "unfamiliar" and "strange" melted away as I recognized so many reflections of myself in these other travelers. That night I understood the possibilities that could await a global community, the opportunities we have to learn from each other and experience life from a different perspective. That night I also discovered one of the great universal truths: Everybody loves a good chicken dance.

During the course of a discussion on varying traditions, I jokingly remarked that no Wisconsin wedding would really be complete without the "chicken dance." I got a laugh from Jenny, Kelly and George, who knew what I was referring to. The rest of the crowd gave me blank looks, so, with the wine's help, I placed my dignity on pause and volunteered to demonstrate. I leapt to my feet, pinched my hands like a chicken beak, flapped my arms like wings, twisted like Chubby Checker and clapped four times to finish. By the time I was through, all of the blank stares had become smiles of recognition and I realized the world was a little sillier than I had imagined. Apparently, representing a chicken through interpretive dance is enjoyed in at least six of our world's nations (and I later learned of at least three more). I still have no explanation for this phenomenon.

That third night in Paris greatly shaped my backpacking experience because it made me consider where I should look for meaning while traveling. Seeing famous sights and exploring landscapes was wonderful, but the *people* I encountered brought out the rich colors of the places I visited, be it fellow travelers or foreign citizens. I recall the Italian-speaking family on the train who communicated not through words, but their generosity in sharing dinner; I think of the British friends I found amidst cider and karaoke at the pub across from the university. Like the laughing faces of nine fellow hostelers doing the chicken dance in the light of the Eiffel Tower, my trip was illuminated by the people I met along the way.

Lee Anne Hasselbacher studied literature and environmental issues at the University of Wisconsin-Madison and has served as a researcher and writer for several nonprofit organizations. She has traveled around the United States, in Europe and in South America, with plans to work with a social-justice organization in Belize.

Will Work for Food

Paris, France

LISA CORDEIRO

IF YOU'RE LIKE ME, YOU REVIEW YOUR ITINERARY DOZENS OF TIMES before you travel, imagining, fine-tuning and re-imagining the adventures that lie ahead. For me, it's partly because I always hear my father's voice echoing in my ear: "You need a plan, Lisa. Did you make reservations? Where are you going to be each night?" But when I start traveling, things don't always go as I plan. What should you do when that happens? Follow your itinerary so as not to miss anything you want to see? Or go with the flow and see what you'll discover?

As I grew up, I didn't know what I wanted to be. I just knew I wanted it to be in Paris. I had savored its details, dreamed about Europe, filled my room with postcards of France and a door-sized poster of the Eiffel Tower. I watched any movie that had anything to do with Paris. I listened with eager fascination and delirious envy to my friend Zepure, discussing the details of a trip to Paris. *When would I make it to Paris?* I thought.

So, as I finished my service in the Marine Corps, I decided that I'd leave Okinawa, take the plunge and go on a three-month European tour, even if I had to do it alone. I planned the trip for months beforehand, detailing where I'd be, when, and what activities I'd do (thanks, Dad), savoring the details as I read about each destination, and hungrily anticipating the moment I would arrive in Paris.

My landing point on European soil was London. I spent a few days wandering through Picadilly Square, Westminster Abbey, and the usual tourist haunts. None too soon, I boarded the overnight ferry from Dover, England, to Calais, France. I could barely contain myself, knowing that I'd soon be on French soil. I stopped immediately at a cafe in Calais, and spoke French in France for my very first time. "Un café, s'il vous plait," I ordered, and almost swooned.

When I finally arrived in Paris, my head was swimming in the clouds and I wandered the streets in awe. After a couple of hours, my backpack grew heavy as the night settled over Paris. I needed a place to stay quickly. I was trying to be spontaneous, evading my father's "plan-ahead" voice, but like a bad B-movie, everything started to go wrong.

I tried to use the phone to call a hostel, but a phone card was required. I found a pay-phone that took coins, but the youth hostel I called was booked. There were hostels on the other side of Paris, and perhaps cheap hotels somewhere nearer, but I had used my only francs on the phone call. Then, it started to rain. My high from hours ago settled into a desperate low as I wandered the streets cold, tired, hungry, and wet. Maybe I should have listened to my dad after all, I thought.

Then, I stumbled onto a police station and used a combination of Franglais and body language to get directions to the booked youth hostel. Surely, they'd have a patch of land where they'd let me pitch my tent? But when I arrived, the gaudy green building hadn't enough spare land to pitch a shovel. Regardless, I walked in, not knowing what I'd say.

That's when the miracle occurred. I saw a help-wanted sign for an au pair waiter/waitress: two weeks' work at the hostel in exchange for room and board. I can do that! I thought. I'll do anything at this point. Of course, there were obstacles: (1) I'd never waitressed before; (2) I wasn't fluent in French; and (3) I didn't have working papers. I humbly walked up to the desk and asked about the job anyway.

"There's no pay, just room and board, and some tips. You'd work every night in the restaurant. Are you interested?"

Without hesitation, I said, "Yes!" This was incredible. Moments later I was in my room overlooking a shady section of Paris. I was *living* in Paris!

When Jean-Marc, the English waiter who was training me to take his place, asked me if I'd ever waitressed before, I lied and said I had. I didn't want to blow this chance. How hard could waitressing be?

It turned out I wasn't the greatest, but I survived. Most of the travelers were Australian, so I usually spoke English at the tables and practiced my French with the cooks. By day I explored the city as a tourist; by night I worked in the restaurant. The worst part about my shift was having to announce over the loudspeaker each evening, first in French and then in English, that the restaurant was now open, its hours, and so forth. I felt quite self-conscious about speaking French over a loudspeaker with not only an American accent, but a Bostonian one, but it was a small price to pay to live in Paris for free.

I was the only American who worked at the youth hostel. It was great to be fully immersed amid an international staff. The cooks were French, the receptionists Spanish, Brazilian and French; the other waiter, Edgar, was Columbian. He had lived for a year in London and spoke English perfectly, and now he was planning on a year in France. His plan was to spend four years abroad — one year in England to learn English, one year in Paris to learn French, one year in Italy to learn Italian, and he didn't know which the fourth country would be yet.

If there were few customers, I could chat with them while sipping red wine and smoking cigarettes. Could you imagine a job in America where it was OK to drink while you worked? I didn't smoke before coming to Paris, but there was so much smoke in the air everywhere I walked that I figured I might as well join them.

Most nights I worked hard from 1800h to 00h (6 p.m. to 12 a.m.), the sole waitress for the bar and 20 or so tables. Americans were the toughest customers, demanded the most of me, and were usually the only ones who tipped. Europeans imagined that the tip was included in the bill, as it typically was in France. So I made very little tip money, but it was enough to finance my daily sightseeing through Paris.

The customers came from around the world. The Australians were the ones who showed me a new way to look at travel. "We're going to be working hard for the rest of our lives," one traveler told me, "so after we finish school, we save up to travel for a year."

"How can you possibly save enough money to travel for a year?" I asked, thinking about how I tried to save $5,000 to last me a few *months* in Europe, but only managed to save $2,000 or $3,000.

"If we need to make more money, we go work in England for a few months," he replied. *Fascinating,* I thought, *working your way around Europe for as long as you want to stay. What a great idea.*

I'd end my midnight shift in the bar downstairs, where Serge the bartender added a few drops of grenadine to the French beer to give it a twist. Here, I partied with the travelers or the workers, each night different from the night before, depending on who was in the hostel that night. When the South Americans came, the dance floor was filled with wild bodies moving, gyrating, and making me wish I had some Spanish blood. The bartender/DJ played Elvis, and Edgar grabbed me, saying, "Shall we dance?" Edgar always asked his questions using "shall," which I found quite endearing. Next thing I knew, he was spinning me in a mix of '50s dance moves that I'd seen only on comedies such as Happy

Days.

I got over my fear of working as an illegal immigrant without papers, because technically, I was a volunteer, not an employee. I was so deliriously happy, living out my dream. Who cared about the rest of Europe, and keeping to that itinerary I had created so many months before?

I guess I did. The two weeks quickly passed, and I left Paris with a heavy heart for other adventures in Europe. But I knew I'd return to Paris, and that time, I vowed, I would stay.

Lisa Cordeiro served in Okinawa, Japan, while enlisted in the Marine Corps. Living in another country ignited her wanderlust, and she went on several other solo adventures across Europe and the United States. Currently, she is a writer outside of Boston who travels with her new companions, her husband, Eric, and son, Nicholas.

April 29, 2003

Paris, France

EUNICE CHUNG

YESTERDAY I HAPPENED TO BE PAINTING THE EIFFEL TOWER. IT WAS A magnificent spring day in the last week of April. My friend Shirley had said that there was a 40% chance of rain forecast for every day of this week. I laughed. The monstrous clouds were being lit by such a brilliant sun, whipped along so quickly by the wind, in such a deep blue sky, that you couldn't take such threats seriously.

Monsieur Denny, our painting teacher, and Shirley and I had settled down with our paints and papers in a green park, hidden from the touristy base of the tower by large trees. We sat under a tree where blossoms were falling, little bunches of ragged white petals laced with red.

I loved being there at that moment, in that place, on that flowery-damp shady patch of grass, with the Eiffel Tower rising before us, almost tipping over us. I squeezed out my colors, red and brown for the beams; blue, white, and gold for sky; and yellows, greens, and browns for the trees. "Voila! Tu es courageuse aujourd-hui!" said Monsieur Denny as he watched me throw down the first lines. I started midway up the tower, with the structure of beams that formed a window framing the sky. Then, I painted the scintillating bright piece of sky in that window. As I filled in the rest, each stroke seemed to lift, filled with air and speed, so that even the trees were apparitions of the sun and the wind. I made the blues bluer and the reds redder so that the tower gleamed against the sky. After a few hours, I was almost done, but the wind blew the clouds so hard that the sky kept changing its light. Each time I had almost captured the moment, the moment changed.

Suddenly, Monsieur Denny, who had disappeared for a few moments, came back to tell us that while he had been standing by one of its legs, a man had begun climbing up the Eiffel Tower. I thought it was probably a daredevil mountain climber, or maybe a record breaker sponsored by an athletic sneaker company. However, Monsieur Denny said that the police had come and were trying to talk the man down. I still didn't pay attention, because after all, nothing ever happened while I was around. No one ever died or fell in love or had a heart attack. Of course the man would be rescued. I continued painting. A little while later, I heard the scream of a crowd. Before I had time to think, the crowd screamed again and I heard a thud. I looked down to the base of the tower and saw some of the tourists who had been standing there, watching, running away.

I cannot say exactly how it felt to be there. I saw nothing but a few people running and heard nothing but two screams and thud, and then a little later, sirens. Where we were, nothing seemed to change. We were hidden by our trees in the park. People continued to pass by, the children around us continued to play, and we continued to paint.

However, something had happened. On a magnificent spring day in Paris, someone had decided to jump off the Eiffel Tower. I had heard him fall and it had been a strange sound. It was as strange as if a star that had been furiously exploding its whole life decided to fizzle out like a match.

What had that man been thinking? When he had reached his destination did he cling onto his life for a moment, wondering if he should really leave the dazzling blue and red world? Maybe he was tired of being ignored. Maybe he was tired of passing people every day who didn't see him. Maybe he had decided that he wanted his death to be a tourist attraction. That is, until he saw that the eyes and cameras and camcorders looking up at him were curious, not compassionate. Maybe he thought, out of that crowd of hundreds

of people, someone's life would change because he jumped off the
Eiffel Tower. Or maybe he was like me, who always said that if I
knew I had to die, I'd jump off of a cliff, or something very tall, so I
could know what it felt like to fly. Maybe he discovered, like I did
when I jumped out of a plane, that flying is not the same as falling.
But then again, I was scared of death. Maybe he wasn't.

Today, the day after the beginning of my story, it's raining. Already the reality of yesterday is fading. Today, I recall mostly the
wind and how it blew those dark clouds edged with light across the
sky.

Yesterday, I put down my blue and red painting of the Eiffel
Tower to do another. The first painting was finished because I ended
it, but it was not completed because the sky had kept changing.

Today, maybe someone who hears about his death will feel some
kind of thud, like the one I heard, and it will make them sick and sad.
But maybe yesterday, at that moment, there was no one except but
me to be sad for him. Not disgusted, not shocked, not judgmental,
nor disappointed, but just sad because he should have been feeling
as I was feeling in that place, at that moment, at that time.

Yesterday I did another painting of the Eiffel Tower. It started
out in black and white but at the last minute I added a little bit of
pale yellow sun and little bit of pale blue sky.

I hoped he decided to jump off the Eiffel Tower because he
wanted to know what it feels like to fly before he died. I want to
believe that, at least for a moment, while clinging to the red beam I
was painting, the man who jumped off the Eiffel Tower felt the beauty
around him. I hope when he jumped, he didn't go head first but
instead looking up at the sun and the sky.

*Eunice Chung is a graduate of Stanford University, where she ma-
jored in symbolic systems. She has lived abroad in Paris for five months,
studying French, painting and photography.*

Fiasco By Train

en route to Nice, France

SARAH HAINLEY

BACKPACKING AROUND EUROPE FOR TWO MONTHS IN THE SUMMER after graduating high school, my friend Bryan and I decided on the spur of the moment that we *had* to see Italy. The Vatican, the beaches off Naples, the artwork of Florence, and all the other sights make it one of the most beautiful countries in the world. Since we were in Paris at the time, we decided to use our Eurail passes to head into southern France, spend a few days in Nice, and then make our way over to Rome. Every backpacker knows that trains are the optimal way to travel. Train rides can pass in a wink of the eye, or they can be long and drawn out experiences.

As the trip south would take us at least six hours, we figured it would be best to take an overnight train and sleep the journey away. We packed our bags, headed to the Paris train station around 10 p.m., and jumped on the first overnight train to Nice we found. <u>Note to travelers</u>: Always, always, always check to see what kind of train you board. If only we had checked.

Once on the train, Bryan and I headed through the second-class cars looking for seats, as outlined on our rail passes. Of course, there are never seats available when you really need them, so after finding absolutely nothing open, Bryan and I decided that, hey, if nothing in second class is open, then it was our *right* to sit in the first-class cars. So, we hurried on to first class and deviously tried to open the compartment doors, only to discover that all of them were locked. This was starting to get frustrating. I mean, we had bought and paid for our tickets; shouldn't *something* be available? Finally we saw one open cabin, a heavenly light waiting just for us. We climbed in and put our bags in the overhead compartment just in time for the conductor to come in asking for our tickets. "Bon soir. Les billets s'il vous plait," he said to us. We handed over the tickets and waited ... and waited ... and waited. Finally in broken English he let us know that our Eurail passes were invalid.

Bryan gave me a questioning look, assuming that since I knew a bit of French I could figure out what was wrong. I simply told the man "Oui, Oui" and moved like I was getting up to leave. The ticket man left and Bryan whispered, "What are you doing? We can't leave!" "I know, I know," I said. "I just wanted him to leave so he wouldn't kick us off the train." "Why should we leave? We paid for the pass, and that includes overnight trains!" Bryan muttered.

We moved into the hallway. The ticket man walked by us again and, without warning, deftly reached behind me and locked up the car we had just been in. "What the...?" we both said in disbelief as he walked off. It was clear the man was making the point that we were not staying in a compartment on *his* car tonight. Up to that point, Bryan and I figured we would have to leave. We knew we held second-class tickets and shouldn't be anywhere near the holy realm of first class. But being *locked out* of the first-class car annoyed us beyond belief. We were *going* to get our sleeper car back, no matter what. Bryan unleashed his Swiss Army knife, and while I kept watch, he began to pick the pathetic excuse for a lock. Moments later we were back in the car, giggling like schoolgirls at a slumber party. We slammed the door shut, turned off the light, jumped in our sleeping bags, and sat in silence, our hearts pumping madly as we lay waiting for the inevitable battle to come.

It was only a few minutes before we heard the click of the ticket collector's heels stop outside our car. Muttering to himself in French, it was clear that he could see the lock had been tampered with. He fumbled with his keys, and, after what seemed like hours, threw open the door. "Out, Out, OUT!!" he screamed. As the train began to slow down, it became apparent that he expected us to get off at this stop. Bryan and I both looked at each other and a silent agreement passed between us that we would do whatever it took to stay on this train tonight. We took out our Eurail rules packet and began fumbling through it, saying to the conductor: "No, we paid for this ticket! We paid for the overnight car! Ummmm, yeah, it's right here. ... Give me one second. ..." We were obviously taking too long to get to the section on overnight trains, and he grabbed it out of our hands, frantically looking through the packet. The train had now stopped. After realizing our attempts to stall him, he threw down the packet. "No, no, no, you must LEAVE!" he said. "It says nothing." And he began physically pushing us toward the door. But it was too late. The train was already moving.

We all stopped in our path. The ticket collector slowly turned to us and through clenched teeth whispered, "Move." We gathered our stuff and followed him to the passageway between the two cars. "If you are to stay on my train, you must sit out here," he said, glaring at us, then turned and left. We had three hours before the next stop. Looking around, we wondered if maybe we should have gotten off. The hallway reeked with the stench from the nearby toilet, and every turn the train made flung us into the exit doors. This should be fun, I thought. But apparently Bryan was not done tormenting our little friend.

"Check this out," he said, pulling our pop-top bottle of the cheapest wine in France out of his bag. "He may think he has won, but what better blasphemy than to party out in the hallway? He'll be even more disgusted with us when he sees our taste in wine!" And with that, he popped off the top. We passed the bottle back and forth, cracking up at the situation and trying not to shudder from the vinegar smell coming from the bottle. The ticket man went back and forth every ten minutes or so, and every time he passed, we raised our bottle, toasting him and our stinking hallway. I suppose there was no real reason to spite the man; it was simply one of those "well, there's nothing else to do" type situations.

When we finally arrived at the next station, we peacefully got off, waved a friendly goodbye to the ticket man, and planted ourselves on the floor once again to wait for the next train. After two hours of slapping ourselves to stay awake, another train pulled into the station on the way to Nice. We gathered our belongings and climbed aboard. Of course the people on this train had taken up all of the seats and had been sleeping serenely all night. With nothing available, not even the smelly passageway in between the cars, Bryan and I were banished by this train conductor to the storage car, which was filled to the brim with bicycles. We wedged ourselves in between a few bikes in the back and, with my face nestled snugly against a pedal, I finally collapsed into sleep. After what seemed like minutes, I awoke to the sound of screeching brakes, the sun pouring in the window, and tire marks on my face. As we climbed out of the train and into the beautiful world of southern France, I couldn't help thinking to myself, "Oh, what a night. …"

Sarah Hainley grew up in Portland, Oregon and will soon graduate with a degree in english literature from Seattle University. She has spent quite a lot of time abroad, traveling through most of western Europe as well as studying abroad in Galway Ireland during her junior year of college. Although she loves exploring what the world has to offer, she will always return to the northwest and could never imagine living away from the ocean or her family. After college, Sarah plans on moving away from the literature realm a bit to pursue a career as a midwife. As for traveling and trains, she hopes to encounter more of both in the future, since the traveling bug that bit her years ago is just too strong to resist.

Freedom From the Future

Guise, France

BRADLEY CHARBONNEAU

"HAVE YOU BEEN HERE BEFORE?" I ASKED IN FRENCH.

"Non. C'est la première fois," he responded with my favorite answer: no, first time.

"Bon. On y va?" and we were off. Out of their view, I smiled to myself in triumph, for only I knew I was living a dream.

"Le Château fort de Guise a connu, au cours de la première moitié du vingtième siècle ..." I rambled on about the history of the castle. The castle I was living in. The castle in France where I gave tours to French tourists about the history of their own country, their own castle.

A few months prior, I had met an old French man on a train who told me I was doing the right thing. Always eager to hear more about *that* topic, I listened intently. At my age, he said, I should be living and seeing all that I could see while I still had my youth, my health, my energy. He said that he was old and he could see things more clearly now that it was all behind him. He said that I should live in foreign countries and learn foreign languages. That I'd learn more about my own country now that I'd left it, that I could see things more clearly if I wasn't so close to them. I tried to scribble in my memory. He regretted not having lived the life he dreamt of and it was too late for him to be young. He didn't blame himself, he didn't blame anyone; it was just the choices he had made. In some way, I was learning about the life he had lived — and the life he didn't. Later, he said, I'd have time to earn lots of money and have a family, a car and a house. "Two houses maybe!" he exclaimed. But later. Now, I needed to have freedom, he said, freedom from the future.

I didn't completely understand everything he said, as it was in French and he was very old and spoke with a thick accent, but I was riveted by his every idea. He was a philosopher and I was his pupil. He wore polished shoes and an old plaid jacket, he looked distinguished. I wanted the man to adopt me. He smoked terrible cigarettes that smelled like burnt earth, but it just added to his authenticity. I wanted my own father to believe in what I was doing and not push me so hard to get the job, move up the career ladder, buy a house. I would do all that, I knew I would. I was twenty-one. I had time. I had my youth. I had to get off at the next stop, but I wanted the train trip to last forever.

"Les souterrains?" I repeated. The tourists at the castle always asked about the underground tunnels, especially the kids. I told them how the castle had hundreds of kilometers of secret passageways leading out to nearby villages. They were used when the castle was attacked by invading armies, I told them. The kids always wanted to go into them, but I pretended that it was too dangerous and dark and spooky, which just made them all the more excited. So I brought the family down into the opening of one of the tunnels with my flashlight lighting the way, walked in just enough to where it was darker than night, then turned off my flashlight. The kids sometimes screamed, sometimes just went silent, but it was all they talked about after the tour was over.

They were the tourists, I was the local.

I'd been living in the castle for just over a month as a volunteer for the Club du Vieux Manoir, a group that engaged foreign students to restore old monuments. I had found their address in a book on volunteerism. I wrote, they replied, I arrived. I was studying its history, giving tours of the underground tunnels, chopping back the rose bushes with a machete when we didn't have any visitors. I chopped a *lot* of rose bushes.

The first question I asked the tourists was if they had been to the castle before. It was an important question because I got some real historians in there once in a while and they'd catch me on the little stuff. The old men liked to test my knowledge of the castle, but I managed. I studied like a madman — then I learned from the old men. This time, the mother broke up the interrogation by asking where I was from, because she noticed my accent, and that got us off the topic of the castle and onto the topic of me — which was far easier to talk about, vocabulary-wise.

"Ooh, cheri," she said to her husband, "Our little Pierre could go and live in the United States and do a volunteer program like this young man is doing, non?"

Other people talked about living in another country. People talk about doing lots of things they'd like to do. I was doing them.

I was reading Don Quixote at night by dim candlelight. I learned how to make a stained-glass window. I ate warm baguettes with fresh jam in the mornings and each day I felt like a prince. The prince of the castle. I wasn't the king; he had too many responsibilities; I was the prince.

The old man on the train said that usually youth is wasted on the young. He shook his head. Then he put his hand on my shoulder and looked into my eyes with a seriousness that scared me, but that I admired. He said that I wasn't wasting my youth. He was old, he was history, he knew things. I was young, I knew nothing in comparison. I was all alone talking to an old man on a train in France, rolling through the countryside like a '50s black and white film. I couldn't think of a place I'd rather have been. I shivered with pride as if a pretty girl said she liked me, but that seemed so trivial compared to these discussions. I wanted to video tape the whole thing so that I would have a record of someone, a respectable someone, telling the world that I was doing the right thing. I thought hard about what he said; I turned it over in my mind. I tried to plan the rest of my life according to how I would feel about it when I was the old man in the train talking to the young boy.

"Mais cherie," the tourist's husband answered, "it is very expensive to do such a thing." He thought a moment. Aand the visa, the paperwork … bah!" He huffed and raised his eyebrows and curved his lips, as the French do so well, and that was the end of the discussion.

"Mais non, ce n'est pas vrai— " I started, but the husband wasn't really listening any longer. I looked to the mother, she looked to her husband, then back at me and she smiled politely. I wanted to tell him that it didn't have to be so expensive, *where there's a will there's a way* and all that.

It was a simple matter of priorities, what you wanted. I chose not to have a car, I didn't have a job waiting for me, I left my friends back home, but none of it mattered. Maybe he didn't want to hear the reasons because he didn't really want his little Pierre to do it. That was fine, he didn't need to do it, not everyone needs to live in a foreign country, not everyone needs to go after their dreams — or do they?

"Le château … " I continued my stories of the castle. The boy wanted to see the dungeon, and there we all talked about the prisoners who were trapped inside the thick walls for years and years. Trapped alone with their thoughts of their past, their present and their future — but with little choice about the present.

Bradley Charbonneau can hardly remember the high-paying corporate job he got a few years later, but the old man on the train and a few months living in a French castle were worth any rungs of the corporate ladder he may have missed. He later managed to find a balance between living for the moment and paying the rent, and is currently shopping a narrative non-fiction book about a yearlong love story through Africa and Asia. He also works as a branding consultant in San Francisco. His website is www.bradleycharbonneau.com.

Guest Lessons

Montpellier, France

Sarah Steegar

I SOON FORGOT THE FOREBODING LAST COUNSEL MY FATHER GAVE me and my best friend Heather before we departed for our semester abroad in Montpellier, France.

"Be realistic about what to expect from your French families. I am sure you will get along fine, but don't expect to feel like part of the family. They will welcome you, but always remember that you are a guest."

We were matched to a dream family, the Dominiques: enthusiastic parents Rosalyne and GéGé and their daughter Delphine, who was our age. They welcomed two American girls into their home with open arms. Our stay evolved happily. The Dominiques included us smoothly into their daily routine, made us feel part of their close, comfortable family, and initiated us into their quintessential French, almost sacredly elaborate family dining routine.

Each night on her way home from work, Rosalyne would buy two fresh baguettes for the family dinner, a meal she often began preparing during her lunch-hour visit to the house.

On these occasions, Rosalyne would efficiently breeze in the door around noon and get straight to work. I was so awestruck watching her effortlessly flick herbs into a heavy pot like some good witch charming her magic spices, I didn't hear a word of her cheery, busy French chatter. From my observation post at the door frame between the kitchen and dining room, I'd expect every moment to see a quick flame or hear a sizzle from the pot where she dramatically tossed her rapidly chopped fresh vegetables. She'd tidy up and disappear back to work without pause, leaving the concoction to slowly simmer all day for *Ratatouille*, *blanket de veau* or whatever that night's magic dinner would be.

No earlier than 8 p.m. each evening, the family would gather for an aperitif: kirs and appetizers for all, around the family room coffee table. After bonding with polite conversation, we'd move to the dining-room table for a multi-course meal complete with cheese course, wine and dessert.

Heather's and my one difficulty with this ritual was our hunger. Accustomed to a 6 p.m. southern U.S. dinnertime, we were ravenous by the time the Dominiques were ready to sit down at their table. They never announced ahead of time when the evening's dinner could be expected. Rosalyne, in fact, sometimes busied herself gardening after work, as if she didn't intend to serve at all the food I'd seen her prepare that noon. Not wanting to seem greedy, Heather and I would often wait for what must have been hours, looking desperately for hints that the family still planned to eat an evening meal.

Even when Rosalyne made a considerate effort to eat early, we never seemed to sit down any sooner. "Girls," she would occasionally announce, "in honor of you, we are going to eat early tomorrow. Raclette, your favorite. At ... what is your dinnertime? Six? Six o'clock. So save your appetite!" Sometimes she would even attempt the announcement in her slow, forced English to show she really meant it this time.

At 10 p.m., Heather and I would be rolling on the stone floor together, clutching our stomachs in hunger, without a nod from Rosalyne toward the kitchen. Suddenly, she would stop waxing her skis, shining the outdoor grill, or whatever the evening's pressing *cours* (chore) was, then walk in casually, with the air of discovering a sudden bright idea.

"Girls, did you want to have some dinner tonight? We'll just throw together something light. How about some salad and yo-gurt?"

"Sure," we'd manage with confused smiles, actually pining for the promised Raceltte and wondering who had abducted our French mother and replaced her with a dizzy clone.

Heather and I learned to cope with our cultural dinner shock and well-intentioned mother. Mostly we compensated by nibbling on the daily baguettes. Normally only one baguette total was consumed at dinner, and the remaining one (minus a few nibbles) was had for breakfast the next morning. It was all part of the ritual.

One afternoon, some especially gossip-worthy events had occurred at school, and Heather and I excitedly exchanged stories sitting around the kitchen table, pulling off our pinches of bread. Our French sister Delphine joined us, eager to be included in her new sisters' stories.

Our conversation was interrupted only by our awareness that we were out of fuel. An entire baguette was gone. Heather and I mourned our lack of snack, playfully chastised each other for our piggery, and colluded on how to cover. We figured that if we abstained from eating any more bread with dinner, only one-half would be needed and there would still be some for breakfast. Our gaff would go unnoticed.

Of course, this one night, everything took a rare turn. The father was out of town, so on this one-time occasion, we four ladies of the house allowed ourselves to relax in front of the television as we ate. Rosalyne and Delphine — who hardly ever ate *anything* — consumed the entire second baguette.

Halfway through the meal Rosalyne mumbled for Delphine to get the rest of the bread from the kitchen. In slow motion we waited for Delphine's confession, but instead of fessing up she sauntered into the kitchen as if to fetch it.

She's covering, we thought. *It must be bad.*

From the other room Delphine yelled, "Maman! What's wrong with you? There's no more bread!"

We froze. *She's really going through with it,* we thought.

Rosalyne yelled back, "Of course there is. We only ate one. Open your eyes, *ma fille.*"

Rustling came from the kitchen as Delphine searched various corners. Heather and I exchanged glances, unsure of what to do. A full-fledged argument between mother and daughter ensued about the missing food. We kept our mouths shut and our heads low. We caught snatches of their bickering. This was all taken quite seriously.

"Mom, I'm telling you there's no more bread here."

"There must be!"

Worse, Rosalyne continued the conversation to herself, staring down into her plate. "Am I crazy? I always buy two. ... Why would I have not bought two? It can't be ... maybe I've been distracted. ... This can't be. ... What's wrong with me?"

Instead of blowing over, the search intensified. A ransacking of not only the kitchen, but the dining room, master bedroom, purse, garage and car ensued. Bags were dumped upside-down, cabinet doors banged. Finally the question came our way.

"Girls, did you see the second baguette?"

I looked up, ready to confess, but Heather was always faster at everything. She piped up, my own mouth still only half open. "Non. Pas du tout." An earnest shake of the head.

Laughter scraped out the back of my throat, the way it bursts free against one's will, like it was popped out by the Heimlich maneuver.

Rosalyne looked at me suspiciously. "Ma fille? Is something funny?"

I swallowed the food that survived in my mouth and pointed to the TV with my fork. "The TV. 'Sister Act II.' That Whoopi Goldberg ... funny lady."

I hoped my inability to look her in the eye would appear as distracted nonchalance, or, at worst, rude deference to the TV. Somehow she believed us and dinner continued, but not without random mutterings from Rosalyne to herself under her breath about her sanity.

The event was never mentioned by Delphine, so we let it lie, assuming her silence was all in sisterhood.

Fast forward a month or so. I was given an assignment in class to write an essay about an anecdote of something that had happened to us during our time in France. Having completed the essay telling my story of bread gluttony and embarrassing guest manners, I accepted Delpine's offer to proofread for "Frenchness" — that intangible, frustrating quality of writing being the downfall of my grades rather than grammar.

("Of course it 'just doesn't sound French'; that's because I am *not* French" never worked to dissuade my professor from issuing a low grade.)

Delphine burst into my room as I crawl into bed. "You bitch!" she spouted, her English well advanced by the months spent with Heather and I.

I looked at her, stunned.

"How could you not tell us you ate the baguette? My mother thinks she's crazy now! We tore up the house looking."

I stuttered, confused. "We thought you were covering for us, meaning we shouldn't admit it."

"Of course not," she snapped. "Why would I do that?"

I pulled back quizzically. "But you sat right there and watched us eat it!"

"I remember no such thing."

"But you sat right on the kitchen table—"

"Then I wasn't paying attention."

"But you ate some with us, didn't you?"

"I don't remember that. ... Anyway, here's your paper." She tossed it on the bed.

Regardless of her tone, I couldn't tell whether or not she was actually mad. "Please don't tell Rosalyne. We're embarrassed enough as it is. Now we lied on top of it."

She pursed her lips. "I won't. But I hope you're ashamed."

"We are," I agreed quickly.

She shifted her weight. "Well, other than that, your essay is good. Be careful, or you two will become the fat Americans we had expected."

Again, I was not sure whether she was serious. I scrambled to Heather's room for a laugh as soon as Delphine left.

At the end of our stay, my sisters came for a visit. Enjoying lunch in the garden, recounting memories of a semester well-spent, my sister made a comment about our gluttony, expecting a laugh. Heather and I tried to silence her with a stern widening of our eyes.

"Shut up," I mouthed with terse lips.

Rosalyne cut the awkward pause with a laugh. "Oh, my dears. You can't keep secrets from mothers."

Heather and I looked at her warily.

"Have you not noticed the appearance of a third nightly baguette? One for breakfast, one for family dinner, and one for you two starving girls."

I couldn't believe that Delphine had betrayed us. And even though Heather and I were red-faced (especially now that we each carried an extra 15 pounds on our small frames), I wish I could say that was the most embarrassing part of the story.

But no. That moment belongs solely to me, at the moment

in class when I was chosen to read my essay out loud. I was a few paragraphs into the tale of confession. My classmates were looking at me with odd puzzled expressions. The professor stood up as I read and wrote something on the blackboard. Everyone began laughing. For a moment I thought I was a hit. My story was funny!

That was not the case. The professor had written the title of the assignment on the board, "Un Souvenir d'Enfance" (A Memory from Childhood"). Mine was titled "Un Souvenir d'en France" (A Memory from France).

It was offered that if I had studied as much as I had eaten, perhaps I would have written the correct paper and saved myself from simultaneously confessing to both my bad manners and my weakness in French comprehension.

Rest assured, both quickly improved.

Sarah is a North Carolina native who currently works as an international flight attendant and French translator. You can find her working from New York to Paris for her weekly baguette fix, where she now buys her own.

Wine and the Blues in St. Emilion

St. Emilion, France

ADELE MCDONALD

WHAT DRAWS ME TO ST. EMILION IS NOT ANY PARTICULAR INTEREST
in the art of making wine. Rather, it is the wanderer's pot of gold
— a free place to stay. I am a backpacking vagabond on an open-
ended journey, meandering across Europe to destinations unknown. For this trip I have brought along a tall, charismatic
husband, a talent for playing the piano, and some rusty French.

From the start, we have followed the budget travel adage
"Plan your itinerary around visits to anyone who is kind or foolish enough to give you their phone number." Thanks to Madame
Annie we have the names and phone number of her friends in the
wine country. When I call them, despite my halting French, I
manage to extract an invitation to come visit. We know very
little about Alain and Brigitte, only that he is in the wine business, they speak no English, and they will put us up for a few
nights at their home.

We are on the train to Libourne where Alain will meet us at
the station. There's only one problem: We have no idea what he
looks like. Stepping off the train, we scan the sea of faces for our
host. No one looks in our direction. We stand on the quay,
clearly visible as tourists with our enormous backpacks. Nobody
approaches. We move inside to nonchalantly inspect each trinket
in the little gift shop. Looks like we've been stood up. The station is nearly empty when a man in a maroon sweater and gray
flannel slacks looks up from the post card rack and says, "Les
Americains?" We pile into his Audi for a wild ride through the
vineyard countryside.

149

During the drive, Alain delivers a running stream of tourist facts and local history. When filtered through the language barrier, this translates to "wine, family, wine, caves, wine, and mushrooms." He is genteel and a little reserved as he gives us an auto tour of St. Emilion, a red-tile-roof-and-stone town with narrow cobblestone streets. Most of the town was built in the 1100s, and where they quarried rock to build the town, they now have enormous caves five stories deep. "They use the caves to grow mushrooms," Alain says. "People often get lost down there and the police have to rescue them." We pass an ancient church; the only thing visible above ground is the bell tower. This little village seems to be burying itself. Already the visit has taken on a surreal character.

We are in the heart of the French wine country, so our first stop is at the family bottling plant, a stone "shed" built in the 1300s, with enormous vats that each hold 20,000 liters of wine. Work proceeds with a timeless grace; nothing can be hurried when making wine. The shed is dark and steeped with age — aged wine, aged casks, ancient appellation, and pride of ancestry. We have stepped into a scene from the Middle Ages.

His day's work done, Alain is ready to take us home to meet Brigitte and their two children. We climb back into the Audi for the 10-kilometer drive to the house. It's February and the vines are dormant. The view out the window is a lithograph in brown tone, endless rows of grapes etching the contours of the landscape. At last, the car turns onto a small lane. We follow a circular drive and stop in front of a majestic stone building on a square of lawn surrounded by water. Dumbfounded, we realize that their house is a thirteenth-century chateau, complete with tower and moat.

Brigitte is light and fair; Alain is short, dark, and handsome; the children are well behaved. They all seem to float on a cushion of air with a graceful, collected demeanor. They are the current genteel generation of vineyard aristocracy. As we enter the stone foyer, following the kindness of these strangers who are welcoming us into their home and their world, we are about to see how the old wine families live.

Our hostess leads the way up the ancient stone stairs, past a glowing stained-glass window gracing a medieval water font, to our room on the third floor. I quickly change into my finest clothes; a long, dark velvet dress would seem appropriate, but my cleanest jeans will have to do. Before reappearing downstairs for dinner, we furtively explore the rooms nearby, finding magnificence and grandeur everywhere.

In the dining room, the family is gathered around an enormous table as wine is poured from a five gallon Gerry can filled from the casks in the cellar. This is not your average house wine; this is the pride of Alain's winemaking heritage. During dinner, as each Gerry can of "the red" is emptied down our thirsty gullets, champagne is offered to cut the "heaviness." Dinner conversation provides a lesson in wine-tasting technique. "Swirl the wine and watch the tears run down the glass. They should weep evenly in fine rivulets." The evening consists of wine and food and champagne and wine and champagne and wine with several trips down to the cellar for a Gerry can refill. After dinner, we retire to the salon and an old Pleyel grand piano. While I play, we drink and party through the night.

Alain is the product of five generations of winemakers who have carried on the pride of the family business and the St. Emilion appellation. Here, everything centers around the wine. Today we are honored to visit the family patriarch at home where we are treated to a gourmet lunch, surrounded by white doves. These are kind people, generous with their apparent affluence, but conversation between father and son hints of serious financial straits.

All is not as jolly as it seems.

By the second evening the word is out: "Two young Americans are visiting Alain. The woman plays the piano." Sitting twenty at dinner, wine and champagne flowing, there is a babble of conversation between table neighbors. We speak in French and a sign language of exaggerated pantomimes. Our inebriated voices bombard the language barrier with sheer volume. Amidst the cacophony, a middle-aged man sits quietly, not engaged in conversation. Watching the American guests, he is riveted on our every gesture, mulling something over in his mind, cataloguing each nugget of information about us. At last the light bulb goes on in his brain and he bellows, "Ils sont heeepeeees (They're hippies)!" Conversation stops. Silence reigns. All eyes are on us. Is this an accusation? Time to retreat to safer ground? Where? The man is seated calmly now, at peace with himself, dilemma solved. We finally break the deathly silence with our only defense — a self-deprecating smile, a nervous chuckle. Thankfully, we are answered with a rippling of laughter around the table. Amity prevails and cultural barriers crumble.

Time now for some music. Guests, champagne, and Gerry can retreat to the music room where the grand piano awaits my eager fingers, my throne upon the bench. Alain has cued up the reel-to-reel; he is ready to document the "St. Emilion Sessions." The guests are my audience; Alain is my proud patron. The performance begins as I play polished old chestnuts with fluid ease. These tunes are invaluable as icebreakers, like knowing how to say hello in any language. More wine, some requests, more wine, and a couple dances. Alain beams as host and promoter of this visiting American artiste. Glasses are refilled. Euphoria settles in. The French reserve is gone now as we sit three on the bench, guests draping the piano. Alcohol runs through our veins, mainlining the music. My playing loses its technical accuracy and I am way beyond rifling off familiar ditties as ambassador tunes. No, now there's only one soundtrack for this movie: The Blues.

It starts with a wailing cry from my right hand, which slides down the keyboard to jump-start my left hand into its rhythmic bass line. Eyes closed, head rolled back, body wrapping itself around the keyboard, my fingers are linked directly with musical soul totally bypassing anesthetized mind. Feeling is the universe now. The walking bass line dissolves into a solid thrumming. The intensity grows. I'm in the trance state of the blues. A voice rises above the piano and belts out "Oh Fifi, veux-tu coucher avec moi". This French aristocrat is wailing a bawdy impromptu verse. On and on he goes, telling the universal story of hard times and lost dreams, the heart and soul of the Blues. I look up to discover that the vocalist is the "heepees" man. We're all in the same condition now, eyes half-lidded with drink, each of us connected to our interior space of blue memories. We are numb to the world, free falling on the music. The reel-to-reel records this bacchanalia, this cross-cultural exchange, this musical communion of the heart. We are speaking the international language of the blues.

On this European journey we are masquerading as shoe-string-budget gypsies, carrying the appearance that everything we own is on our backs. In truth, we are privileged young Americans, beneficiaries of family largesse. And what of our hosts and their flamboyant lifestyle of wine and music in this massive chateau? They, too, are living a masquerade concealing the decay and poverty afflicting the gentility that has been their birthright. The truth is they have plenty of wine and little else. Here in the chateau, the wine and the music have unveiled our various deceptions and left us on common ground. The following morning another deception is stripped away.

It's time to continue on to new adventures. Parting hugs for

Brigitte and the little ones, into the car, out the circular driveway, across the moat, and a turn onto the road. The chateau looms on our right. Here is our first view of the back of this massive structure. What's *that?* A laundry line, several strange children playing in the yard, another grand entrance, another family. With a jolt, we realize that our noble hosts of the grand chateau live in a duplex.

The train leaves Libourne following a river flanked by vineyards and rolling hills. As it rounds a bend we spy another chateau. The view reveals the hidden side, the back entrance to this home from an historic era of graceful gentility. A time when French wines were unmatched in the world and the wine aristocracy lived a life of ease and gaiety. We ride on, laden with memories and several bottles of St. Emilion's finest.

Adele currently flies for a living as a charter pilot. Prior to that, she had a successful career as a performing pianist. She makes her home on a wilderness farm in the Smoky Mountains. For Adele, life continues to be a colorful adventure.

I love to travel, but hate to arrive.

ALBERT EINSTEIN

Germany

German Follies

Munich, Germany

Jennelle Menendez

From somewhere in the train comes a loud metallic clang, and it echoes down through the empty cars. "That sounds ominous," my friend says, laughing. "I'll wait for you out on the platform."

I am about halfway through my three-week backpacking trip and have just arrived in Munich on an overnight train. After narrowly averting a train strike in Italy (and after a bottle of wine at dinner), we have declared ourselves to be "European Traveling Superheroes." We toast to our excellent ability to deal with maps, hostels, and most of all, trains. What we don't realize is that due to our blatant lack of humility, it will only be a matter of time before a disaster proves us wrong.

This isn't my first overnight train, and being the travel pro I am, I expect a wake-up announcement in the morning. I hadn't even bothered to set my alarm clock. I discovered early on in the trip that sleeping cars on trains are great ways to catch up on some much-needed sleep. Dorm-style hostels, although cheap, are not really the best place to rest up for the next day (especially when randomly sharing a room with six snoring Englishmen). I am actually looking forward to the train, because the only thing anyone is concerned about on these overnight trips is getting some sleep.

When the train finally does stop in Munich, my wakeup call doesn't come from the conductor or the cabin speaker, but from the two Mexican guys sleeping below us. Apparently the cabin speaker is broken, so the guys inform me that the train has been

158

stopped in Munich for a while already. While my friend and I scramble to get our stuff together, we realize we are the only people left on the train. Still, we aren't too worried. I mean, this *is* the last stop, it isn't like the train is going anywhere. Plus, they check the train to make sure everyone is off ... right?

That is what I'm thinking as my friend hops off the train, because my half-asleep brain is more concerned with tugging on my other sneaker. I finally wander into the hallway, and it takes me a few seconds to understand what is going on. The train is moving. It is chugging backwards, and I am still on it. Alone.

I stare at my friend through a window; she is running after the train just like in a scene from a movie. Then train starts really picking up speed. She reaches the end of the platform with a look of defeat and disbelief, and we wave goodbye to each other. "This should be interesting," I say out loud to myself.

Because I am relatively calm up until this point, I am even laughing at my unique ability to get into ridiculous situations. But once I realize I am truly alone, the panic sets in. I start running up and down the train car screaming, hoping that there is someone left on the train who can help me get off. Even in this state I know how ridiculous I must look. I'm still wearing my pajamas and a pair of sneakers, carrying a backpack that is taller than I am, complete with a yoga mat and my spare pair of sneakers bobbing up and down on the back. The yoga mat is just slightly too wide to fit through all the car doors, so it gets caught in every door I run through, and then snaps back to hit me in the butt, adding to my overall feeling of stupidity.

It starts to feel like I'm in an episode of The Twilight Zone. I run alone in an abandoned, moving train. I see *evidence* of people everywhere — in every compartment, the seats and beds are strewn with pillows and blankets from their sleeping. Even the conductor's compartment is empty. I see function buttons on his control panel, but their labels are all written in German. I want to hit one to help myself, but with the luck I'm having now, I hesitate to touch any of them.

My next thought is to pull the emergency brake. Every time I go to do it, though, I chicken out. All I can think of is what I've seen in movies, where people pull the emergency brake and the train sparks and screeches, then inevitably derails. This is not something I want to explain to the German police.

Meanwhile, the train is passing stations, apparently in a big hurry to get somewhere. I assume it's going to a train yard to be cleaned, but it doesn't really matter. I have already been on the train for fifteen minutes, and I have no idea where I am, where I'm going, or how I'm going to get back. I tell myself I just need to calm down and think about this rationally.

Pretty quickly I determine that my current courses of action (screaming, crying and panicking) are not getting me anywhere. I lean against the wall and just try to think clearly. I go to a side door and see a latch at the bottom with a picture of a person and a fire, so I think it's safe to assume this is the emergency exit. I lift up the latch and kick the door open. It isn't very difficult; but then again with all the adrenaline in my system at the moment I can probably lift a large car off a small child. I decide my best bet is to just get off the train any way I can, so I resolve to jump off the train as soon as it starts slowing down.

Now, I like a little adventure as much as the next person, but I'm not what you would call daring. And I'm *definitely* not one to leap from large, fast moving things just for kicks. Being a college girl from New York, staying in a hostel that doesn't have a shower in the room is what I consider an adventure. Yet here I am, seriously contemplating passing myself off as the female Harrison Ford from *The Fugitive*.

Finally, I feel the train begin to slow down. It seems to be slowing for some kind of signal up ahead, and I see my chance. Standing in the doorframe of the emergency exit, I look down. There is about a six-foot drop to the rocky track below, and I try not to think about all the things that can potentially happen to someone who jumps from a moving train wearing a 40-pound bag. I wait until the train is barely creeping along and then jump out onto the tracks.

I'm lucky enough to land without breaking anything, and I can't believe I'm just a little dirty and banged up. I just sit there for a few minutes, watching as the train passes through the signal, picks up speed once again, and continues on its way. Then I start walking back toward Munich. I know that if I follow the tracks I'll eventually find people, and a way back. Somehow, after what I just went through, it doesn't seem that intimidating. I begin the long walk back, laughing at myself again and promising to always set my alarm clock, just in case.

Jennelle Menendez is currently studying broadcast journalism and dramatic literature at New York University. Spending a semester in Spain allowed her to travel around Europe for the first time. Jennelle has interned for the law firm Shearman & Sterling, where she was a contributing writer to the firm's ProBono Newsletter.

Dachau: A place to remember

Dachau, Germany

HOLLISTER MARIE MARX

IT WAS DURING A SUMMER EUROPEAN BACKPACKING TRIP THAT I felt compelled by curiosity to get an up-close glimpse of a Nazi concentration camp. I was in Munich, Germany, not far from the little town of Dachau, once a beautiful, 1200-year-old Bavarian town. There, on March 22, 1933, the Nazis initiated the "Final Solution" to rid Europe of Jews by opening the first of their concentration camps within the walls of an old Dachau powder factory. Over the next 12 years, until it closed on April 29, 1945, the camp's guards and managers processed about 200,000 prisoners and killed more than 32,000 by execution, burning and torture. Today, Dachau is known only for the terror of the Nazi regime.

My first impression when I reached the town was, "This is not so bad." It was when I headed out of town, toward the camp, that I got a sick feeling I couldn't shake. The first stop within the concentration camp was the museum, where the walls were covered with collages of pictures: faces of Jews and some Nazi staff, images of fear, sadness, terror; black and white documents of the horrifying things that took place in that camp.

I wanted to know everything, because I wanted answers to the questions we all ask: "How could something like this have ever happened? How could people do this to one another?"

Our tour guide, a German-American, showed our group through those faces, each with a more unthinkable story than the last. I stationed myself at the front of the tour group, sponging up every morsel of information that our guide shared with us. I paused in front of one picture that haunts me still — of a man not much older than I, wearing an aviator's harness. The tour guide noticed my interest and explained that the man was part of an experiment to learn why German pilots, whose planes were shot down between England and the Continent, were dying. The pilots would parachute safely into the cold sea waters and get rescued, but would die shortly afterward. To learn the answer, Dachau doctors dressed Jewish prisoners in parachute harnesses and lowered them into freezing water, to see how long it would take them to die, and what processes they would go through on their way there. I looked at that man's face for a very long time. If I had been alive then, that could have been me or someone I knew.

We were then shuttled into a theater to see black-and-white film of daily life at the camp, shot by Nazi film crews. It was the most astonishing thing I had ever seen in my life. The footage matter-of-factly showed Jews digging their own graves, piles and piles of dead, skeletal bodies stacked on top of one other, stripped of any dignity. The Nazi camp staff appeared, sometimes smiling, even proud to serve as guides. I wanted to scream, "What monsters! How could anyone allow such maliciousness against another human being?"

Outside, we were shown the line of grass that Jews were forbidden to touch, with even a toe, or they were shot. Our tour guide explained that the Nazis would compel prisoners to carry rocks up a hill and, when they reached the top, to carry them back down again. In this and other ways, Jews would be worked until a minute after the dinner bell, then would be sent to bed in their barracks without supper, never knowing when their captors would serve them their next meal. The Nazi rationale was that in the concentration camps, it was easier to work inmates to death than to expend cost and effort on killing them outright with bullets or gas. Using this form of mental torture, those who ran Dachau were able to break the spirits of large numbers of prisoners.

It was hard to believe I could see anything worse after that. But I was not prepared for the crematorium. Through their tall, cylindrical brick chimneys and into the sky rose the smoke and ashes from bodies of those, dead and alive, burned in the huge gray ovens on the ground. Our tour guide gathered us around a single, small oven, that stood by a memorial to "The Unknown Prisoner." Around it were ashes from those thousands of people burned in the full-size ovens. Just for a moment, I perceived the sense of chaos and horror that must have reigned here some 55 years before.

Then, I noticed an old man standing about 15 feet from me, watching the tourists, not moving a muscle, as if he were a monument himself. He was a survivor of Dachau, a Jewish veteran of the Polish Army, captured by the Germans as a prisoner of war. The Nazis never found out that he was a Jew, so he was put with the POWs. It was the only thing that saved him. He comes to the camp to be a living testimonial to the horrors of Dachau. He answers questions for anyone who asks, because he wants the world to know what happened here.

From the ovens, we proceeded to the gas chamber, which was built late in the war. It was never used at Dachau; the war ended before it could kill a single person. But many gas chambers like this prototype were used at the other camps to kill hundreds of thousands of people with Zyklon B gas.

Our next stop was the barracks. The originals are no longer standing, but a replica showed the small sleeping spaces allowed for the hungry, the helpless, those who hoped for and dreaded one more day of life for themselves, their families and friends.

When there was nothing left to see, we were shuttled out and left standing on the ground were we had started. I felt gloomy and defeated. Why Dachau? There was no answer for me. And Dachau was not the worst of the concentration camps.

The people who live in the charming little village of Dachau express deep regrets for the innumerable crimes that were committed in the camp. Many even assert that Dachau was not consulted about the opening of the camp, and that the citizens of the town had voted against the rise of national socialism. Several townspeople smuggled food to prisoners or occasionally passed a letter on for some of them. And near the end of the war, before American troops liberated the camp, a few citizens helped escaped prisoners, and worked to help drive the Nazis out of Dachau.

Today, Dachau stands as a memorial to those who died here during World War II, and as a reminder to all of us that tolerance and understanding are crucial to the survival of the human race. It is within the walls of this memorial that the visitor can almost feel the souls of departed calling out to us: "REMEMBER!"

Hollister Marie Marx holds a master's degree from Northern Arizona University. Hollister spends her time traveling, writing, and counseling at-risk youth. She is currently writing a children's book series called Meg's Friends. *The series deals with real issues surrounding children in the new millennium.*

The Hofbräuhaus: A shared space

Munich, Germany

SPENCER STONER

AFTER MY FIRST AND LAST EXPERIENCE WITH A TOUR GROUP —
those packaged, processed glances at "local culture" that say as
much about the nature of foreign life as Disneyland says about
our own — I chose a new type of travel: nothing but local reality.
It was becoming my obsession. I didn't want to be a list
checker, a snapshot grabber, a tropical-flowered-shirt-wearing loud
American, a visiting-all-the-landmarks-I-could-easily-see-on-a-
postcard-just-so-I-could-say-I'd-been-there type of person. I didn't
want to be a tourist. I wanted to be a traveler, one who viewed a
place and culture not with foreign eyes, but with a resident's eyes,
with understanding and familiarity, as if I had helped round the
cobblestones of the town's streets with my own two feet.

Thus, I was surprised to discover that the Hofbräuhaus, or
Bavarian beer hall, belongs as much to *Münchners* as it does to the
throngs of international tourists who flock to Munich every year.
In my naievete, I overlooked that, in order for it to become the
world-famous magnet it is, the world must eat and drink there.

The day I chose to visit the Hofbräuhaus, a chilling March
mist fell, its dampness seeping under my jacket. My walk through
plaza after plaza of nondescript shops was broken by the occasional warmth of chestnuts roasting on glowing orange fires in
metal carts. I passed the Glockenspiel, Munich's world-famous
giant cuckoo clock, layered with years of black industrial and
fireplace soot, and felt the city was alive but lifeless under the
Prussian gray sky.

At last, I stood before the large, wooden doors, brass-laden and crowned by two regal lions. When I pulled them open, I entered another world. It shook with the energy of hearty laughter and the oompah of a polka-playing quartet in the corner. I was struck by the physical and psychological warmth of the place, the contrast between the coldness of the streets and this inviting interior. It was like being a little kid and plopping myself down in front of the fire with my comforter and jammy-jams — only, with more beer.

I was seated at a weathered old family-sized wooden table and handed a menu. The Hofbräuhaus is a fully staffed restaurant, but there are really only two things you get there: sausage, and the restaurant's lifeblood, beer. Beer is the *raison d'etre* of the whole institution. Were it not for King Wilhelm V's desire to shorten the distances of his late-night beer runs in the 16th century, the Hofbräuhaus brewery never would have come into existence, and the world surely would have been the poorer for it.

Though I had never seen this place before, sitting down there was like finally coming home. The warmth of the building and the joviality of the regulars' tables was familiarity bottled; the essence and ease of walking into a party where you've been expected, and you let the creamy house brew melt the weight of the world off your shoulders. My presence there felt both natural and at odds. I was pop culture, they were a world apart, where the corseted lass off the Swiss Miss package really serves pretzels, and guys named Franz walk from table to table, carrying 17 beers in both hands at once. In the distance, a yodeler wearing lederhosen shot off into a ballistic rendition of a traditional Bavarian shepherding song, and I felt the barrier between this culture and mine melting away. I began to merge with my surroundings. I drank beer, I ate sausages. I ate sauerkraut. I don't even like sauerkraut. The idea of slippery, flavorless cabbage is often enough in itself to squelch any emerging hunger I may have. However, that afternoon I ate and enjoyed every bite. In the Hofbräuhaus, it felt as natural to me as taking communion in church. It was just what was done.

"*Haben Sie eine Spiesekarte?*" Several 30-somethings from Minneapolis tried asking me for menus in heavily accented German. I assured them very casually that I was American as well.

"We're in town for a convention, ya know? So we thought we'd let the wives go shopping and come on in here. Can we sit with you? That all right? Yah?"

No, no it is not all right. I disliked their intrusion into this place, this gem that I had found and felt was mine alone. Their presence exposed me as a tourist when I desperately wanted to blend in. "Sure, why not?" I replied. The Minnesotans took places to my right.

To my left was a table filled with aged German men adorned with feathered alpine caps. I had been in the Dachau concentration camp earlier that day, and it occurred to me that the men sitting to my left were surely my age when Hitler rose to power in this town. They had seen and experienced things I could never fathom. Then and now, this place was part of their routine. As the beers kept coming and the yodeling grew more intense, it became increasingly difficult to discern between what was authentic and what was presented for my benefit as the tourist. It all seemed too contrived, too "It's a small world after all" to qualify as reality. And yet, it also felt as genuine and tasteful as if I was eating a meal at my Bavarian grandmother's.

Somewhere between the Minnesotans and the Germans, there was I. I had never seen a place I could appreciate on so many levels before, an experience which led me to question what it really means to be representative of a city and its people. What happens to the soul of a place when it becomes overrun by mobs of people who, as much as I hate to admit it, were hardly different from me? Yet the Hofbräuhaus somehow managed to keep its soul, despite its globalized clientele. In my home town of San Antonio, everyone knows which places are overrun by tourists and avoids them and their inflated prices like the plague, but in the Hofbräuhaus, the place is embraced despite the vacationing families and the loud Americans and the flower-shirt-wearing, snapshot-taking tourists. For many of the regulars there, a beer at the Hofbräuhaus is not an exercise in the esoteric, but rather a continuation of what they've always done and will continue to do.

Spencer Stoner is a junior at Georgetown University, where he studies international politics, Spanish, and Portuguese. Stoner enjoys photography and comedies, though he is neither talented nor funny. He will be spending a year abroad, studying at the University of Auckland in New Zealand.

The Berlin Love Parade

Berlin, Germany

TINA GREGORY

AS I MARCHED AROUND MY TINY SQUARE OF AN APARTMENT IN A Bonn *Studentenwohnheim*, tossing clothes into a daypack from piles strewn on the floor, I got it again: the half-smile, the quizzical stare, the you-have-no-idea. No matter. I was going to Berlin.

"Du weisst was da am Wochenende passiert, oder?"

Of course I knew what was happening there this weekend, or I thought I did. Not from television (I didn't have one), not from the foreboding-looking *Frankfurter-Allgemeine Zeitung* (which I never read), not from my now dog-eared guidebook (it wasn't mentioned). Even the source of bemused looks, the uni student cross-legged on my bed, who was both my best friend of recent months and my impromptu German grammar coach, could only offer up a shrug. I'd had to piece it together myself, from fliers in the lobby, from a pair of overenthusiastic British techo-head tourists I'd met in a railcar, from eavesdropped conversations in that institution of German student life, the omnipresent dormitory basement bar. What I'd pieced together was this: it was a techno party, it was massive, and that I shouldn't bother looking for a room, because I'd never find one.

Undeterred, I hunted in the clutter for my railpass. Bonn, a city with few virtues (and no vices) did have the advantage of being a mere eight hours from Berlin. When I got tired, I reasoned, I would just come home. When the alternative was another weekend in this small, sleepy city, restoring my studio to the orderly standards of our strict *Hausmeister* or sorting trash according to Byzantine recycling laws, such reasoning seemed sound.

It earned me another shrug from my bemused mentor, which I returned. We'd broached the cultural divide in many ways, but found ourselves now in split camps: he was an aficionado of that *other* nineties musical movement, grunge.

Then again, if you were to ask any average raving polyglot lucid enough to have a conversation (as I later did) you would learn that it's not about camps at all, but something universal, something inclusive. Emerging bleary-eyed from the Berlin Zoo station, I nearly walked into a clutch of wholesome blonde youths, chained together by manacles attached to their black leather. I spun around to find the source of a distant throbbing noise, and was faced with one of many banners proclaiming that year's theme: WE ARE ONE FAMILY.

A bold statement from a city so historically divided, I thought as I dodged my way through the ever-denser crowds of leather- and fur-clad, fuchsia- and lime-bedecked "family" on my way to the Tiergarten, which seemed to be the center of the action and the destination of the bright, vibrating floats, the source of the pulsing beat. I passed the high gates of the zoo, its ornate iron-work hinting at the exotic inside, and smiled. If this were a family of tropical birds, then I was a peahen; my enterprising solution to the backpacker's quandary of having clothes for all occasions (always wear black) had finally fallen flat. Even my hair, which I'd tinted a deep indigo in the cramped railcar toilets, seemed so subdued as to be barely noticeable.

Although the crowds grew tighter on the way to the main avenue, I could still observe the flocks with some detachment. Like the heavy, pulsing beat that was everywhere, that penetrated your consciousness until you forgot the sound of silence, people's garb was something ... tribal. Naturally, it was Europe's answer to tribal: two tall boys, holding hands, sported matching crew cuts dyed an unmistakably Swedish yellow and blue, while an extraordinarily tall, bewigged figure on teetering platforms show-cased a Union Jack mini, redone in a decidedly Teutonic red, yellow, and black. In this vast carnival, a sort of Mardi Gras with vague pretexts at the political rather than the devout, costumes propped up prevarications of gender and nationalism, only to knock them down — or, as I observed later on a float packed with nude, writhing figures — to strip them off.

As if to bring me back down to the spirit of blithe revelry, a gaggle of girls in matching pink furry bikinis pushed past, armed with huge water guns. One spun on her heel, aimed, and caught me in a sticky-sweet spray. Pushing after them, I broke through the crowd to the Tiergarten itself, a vast concrete expanse alive with movement; an indiscernible riot of jumping, writhing, seething color. The huge obelisk at the Tiergarten's center, strewn with streamers and obscured by balloons, might have been a pagan maypole, if not for the ethereal winged statue at its top.

If the crowd had reached an even more fevered pitch, I hadn't noticed; but before long stark blocks of black and white began to appear amid the color, and the din of shouts, whistles, and the ever-present beat was interspersed with sirens. *Die Polizei!* came the yell, as the crowd formed ever wider circles around the cars, and then began to disperse entirely. I shrank back, expecting an ensuing riot, and searched for higher ground so as not to be trampled. But this was Berlin and not my native New York, and this was, after all, a march rooted not in rage, but in love.

Love was a word bandied about often: *love* on banners, *love* on backpacks, *love* out of the mouths of schoolgirls bedecked in red and pink and orange. *We love our new neighbors in the East!* proclaimed a scrawl of graffiti on the last standing bit of the Berlin Wall that I decided to visit after the police caused the Tiergarten party to peter out. Taking the empty train from the brightly animated Zoo station in West Berlin to the desolate and ramshackle

Hauptbahnhof in the East, I emerged in what seemed like a different time, a different day; one cold, gray, and abandoned. It was but several years after the Fall (*Too late to dance on the wall!* smirked my guidebook), and alone in the stillness, I wondered if this summer's festival of *love* was any match for the jubilation of that November. Maybe they were equal in scope, if not in meaning — maybe the driving force of the Love Parade draws from the same source, as if the energy spawned from this political hotbed had not yet run out.

Traveling on the empty train back to the Zoo, from East to West, I felt again the vibration of the beat — so simple and staccato that it might be mistaken for the click of the rails. I looked over the stark, boxlike Bauhaus skyline, and thought of the art and culture of German modernity; of the Expressionists and Objectivists, who eschewed representation in their painting and sought to find a universal visual language of basic elements of color and line. Techno, a global trend with its most rabid followers in this historically split part of the world, aspires to something much the same. Drop the instruments, strip down the lyrics, and what's left is the beat — and an attempt at something like a shared revelry, a universal understanding, in a city where cultural barricades are all too visible.

Back in this temporary utopia of Love (never *Liebe*, never *amour*, no such linguistic pretensions) it was now nightfall, and the scattered party had begun to reorganize. Crowds gathered around makeshift platforms of stairs and crates; boomboxes hitched to amps spewed out track after track of songs that were becoming differentiable, recognizable; and back to the Zoo station flocked the largest crowd of all, which had started to include ordinary, workaday Berliners in spectacles and suits. It was easy, effortless, to fall into the crowd and dance until I was exhausted, to climb on the shoulders of strangers, to join in a cacophony of *more, more!* until I awoke to another morning, my head pillowed by the curb, one of hundreds sprawled on the surface of a suddenly quiet street. I walked back to the station for the last time and began the long ride home, soothed by the rhythmic clicking of the rails.

Tina Gregory has settled in New York's Lower East Side after extended stays in Bonn and Prague. She is working on a Ph.D. at the City University of New York, where she also teaches undergraduate writing. She misses the heyday of house music.

Reinventing Berlin

Berlin, Germany

VICTOR PAUL BORG

THE ONLY ODD THING ABOUT VOLKSPARK PRENZLAUER PARK IS that it is on a hill, a geographical anomaly in a city built on swampland. Otherwise it looks like any city park should, with poplars and pines and chestnuts, with meadows of wild buttercups, with benches and playing field, with a pond fringed by reeds and inhabited by moorhens — and a couple sunbathing naked, taking full advantage of the hot day in this July afternoon. Only that couple was present in the park, and they didn't cringe or cover themselves when I stepped in full view, a reminder of Berlin's irreverent openness. I walked toward the summit, cutting straight up the hill. The ground appeared stony and rough and hard to me, but perhaps I wouldn't have noticed this if I didn't know what lay under the grass: the detritus of World War II Berlin. All the rubble from bombed-out Berlin after the war was heaped in this artificial hill in Hohenschonhausen, and a park created on top. It's this fact that had lured me to the park, but history was buried and forgotten here — not even a memorial had been put up to explain how the hill came to be.

It had been the same in other places I visited. Historical notoriety had slipped away, or just didn't match up. In Glienicker Brucke, the metal bridge that links Berlin and Potsdam — renowned as the point where, from the 1950s to the 1990s, Soviet and American Cold War warriors exchanged captured high-profile spies — it was impossible to feel the old tension in this lovely setting of lakes and parks. There were schoolchildren on picnics, couples on bicycles, gulls making a fuss, and a genial pollen-scented air. I lay down by the water's edge, reading and napping. The world of Cold War Berlin couldn't be further away. Across the city, Karlshorst was also deserted; the only person present was a guard languidly sitting by the gate, sweating profusely. Karlshorst had been, until 1994, the KGB's international operations base, the vast complex that the CIA never managed, despite ingenious and daring attempts, to penetrate. Behind the guard, beyond the gate, grass had grown through the cracks in the cement, doors and windows were sagging or missing, and the interior seemed dim and blank and dusty. Across the street, the formerly lovely KGB top-guard bungalows were starting to crumble.

On another day I went to see what remains of The Berlin Wall, perhaps the most potent feature of my generation, symbol of the greatest human tragedy of all: the walls of division we create, past and present. The Wall once stretched for about 25 kilometers, but only scattered pieces survive; most of it was hacked away in the euphoria during the German reunification, and chunks of it sold as mementoes. (Something you put on the mantelpiece, with a note: *This is part of the Berlin Wall.*) The largest stretch that survives intact, perhaps a mile long, stands between the river Spree and an arterial traffic road, Muhlen Strasse. It is covered with graffiti, another Berlin specialty. A message says: "East Side Gallery — the largest open-air gallery in the world."

I strolled along the wall as traffic roared past. There were no other visitors. Even the travelers who had camped in old trucks and buses behind The Wall had left, and the area behind the wall was like a scrapyard, with heaps of rubble and corpses of cars. The Wall is covered with murals expressing political freedom, environmental doom, and the shades of human obsessions. The best mural shows Soviet Premier Brezhnev and East German leader Honecker locked in a mouth-to-mouth kiss, and the inscription "God, help me survive this deadly love."

But The Wall, for all its symbolism, failed to stir any emotions in me other than boredom. It seemed like another historical leftover, like last-election posters no one had bothered to remove. Berlin, I was finding out, buries its history well. It is a city on fast forward, and the past is only as good as its usefulness in the future. This is not deliberate amnesia; it is just that the city is restless, ever metamorphosing. The city is now busy morphing into its new incarnation, finding another pivotal point in history, as always. This is how Berlin remains relevant: It reinvents itself. In the past 100 years Berlin reinvented itself five times, and it was almost destroyed completely twice in the world wars. Now the cliches about the city's emerging role are bandied about recklessly — "from the city at the frontline to the bridge of Europe"; "the meeting place between east and west," and so on — but you know the city is serious about its new role when you see the forest of construction cranes cluttering the cityscape. In the beginning of the 1990s, when the largest urban renewal project was unveiled in Berlin, costing $116 billion, there were about 2,000 construction sites; ten years later, there were still 2,000 construction sites.

The heart of the reconstruction could be found at Potsdamer Platz. In the 1920s and 1930s this was Europe's busiest square, and the first place where traffic lights were installed. Then it was razed in the war, and during the Cold War it degenerated into poisoned open scrubland in the shadow of The Wall, a no man's land. Now it is a gleaming futuristic square, and once again one of Europe's busiest, and it is amazing seeing it today when you remember that ten years ago there was nothing here, just a piece of dead land. During its construction in the 1990s, Potsdamer Platz was billed as "Europe's largest construction site." Now it feels like you're entering the promised city. It is framed by two glass skyscrapers, which cost $2.3 billion, and behind them there is a straight run of office blocks, cinemas, the Grand Hyatt Hotel, cafes, restaurants, and shops, all linked by a new underground train station. There is even an artificial lake, where office workers lounge during lunchtime.

Potsdamer Platz is a statement that Berlin is reclaiming its former glory. It is not gaudy or showy — the Germans are beyond that — but I found it sterile, and too confident in its capitalist smirk, because the skyscrapers are owned by Daimler-Benz and Sony, the two largest international companies in Germany. I was seeking, instead, the rough edge of frontline Berlin, because this is how Berlin has always commanded fear and admiration. In essence, I was seeking continuity, not a buried history. Given the reconstruction, the beginning of a new era Berliners called *The Wende* (The Change), would Berlin loose its soul? There were some good signs: the city still had an air of buzz and energy so fiery it felt like defiance. And the reconstruction, however radical and sweeping, hadn't hidden the city's grimy damaged look (and in East Berlin, some shrapnel-ridden facades). Besides, the contrasting architecture set-pieces that are so bullyish in Berlin were still here. A drive through Berlin took me past these architectural monuments of ideological expression, etched in stone — faithful imprints or representations of ideology: uniform Communism, brash Capitalism, callous Nazism, fairytale Royalty — all of them embodying some triumph in living beyond the utilitarian into current immortality.

The artists and political activists who became the very image of Berlin during the Cold War, when it was an island of the West surrounded by East Germany, have moved from the Turkish district across the old dividing line, into the former East Berlin districts of Mitte and Prenzlauer Berg, new territory for them, more amenable to their living arrangements and inspiration. They are occupying the worn old buildings that survived World War II, and had lain derelict since, and transforming them into chapels of post-modern art. During the Cold War; West Berlin had been an easy city, propped up by lavish, nearly unlimited subsidies from the West German government. Now the subsidies have dried up, but the artists still pour in, creatures with an affinity for the fringes and the frontlines and the gray areas, lured by the city's artistic fame and excellence, and by duty: they have to have a hand in the great reshaping of Berlin.

The art here has the rough conceptual edge of post-modernism; it is no-bluff, undignified, crude, unpretentious, and angry art, and it seeks to express, by its presence and context and countenance, the tribulations and ugly truths of modern life. These are natural themes for Berlin artists; after all, these are the kind of people for whom hedonism and decadence isn't just about indulging, but a lifestyle informed by philosophical and political convictions. Nothing is apolitical, nothing is flippant, which is why these artists are dead serious about their art, as devoted to their work as religious fanatics. Even the graffiti artists dedicate their life to their peculiar brand of outside art, and in the late 1990s, when the authorities decided that the ubiquitous graffiti was incongruous with the new image of a modern capitalist city, the graffiti artists had a fight on their hands. They will not lay down the spray can without a fight, and at night, organized gangs of them fan out throughout the city to continue doing what they have always done, armed with pistols to confront the police who are looking for them.

Berlin artists have an uncanny ability to keep one step ahead, and while the mainstream in Berlin is the alternative and radical elsewhere, the radical in Berlin gives the word a harder and more extraordinary meaning — perhaps another example of how Berlin constantly reinvents itself. Berlin, for example, is known for the Love Parade — a celebration of drugs and music and hedonism and openness — but when it became too famous, and started attracting young airy ravers from all over the world, it was time to move on: the Hate Parade came into being. It is held simultaneously with the Love Parade, and it winds down Oranienburger Strasse in Mitte, finishing with a clamour of hard beats and hooting horns and savage screams in front of the city hall, just for the political effect. The Hate Parade now embodies the politicized arm of dance music, the new underground. Here, in Mitte (perhaps it's shut by the time you read this; this is Berlin, where things change fast), you can visit the Eimer, an illegal club located in a house that doesn't exist officially (it's shown as derelict land on official maps), and try dancing to Gabba or Gabber, the music that rattles your teeth and numbs you with its 250-plus beats per minute. It's the Berlin version of the new underground, a furious music, because mainstream dance music has become too soft and meaningless.

No, Berlin remains at the frontline, and that is the city's allure. No longer a military frontline, of course; Berliners are fierce pacifists, and a current point of discourse among the intelligentsia is the trepidation that a reunified and reinvigorated Germany might once again build a powerful military and start meddling with other countries. If you're an observer of German politics, you might think that this fear is unfounded and exaggerated. And a visit to the Reichstag will confirm this. It's the most inclusive parliament in the world, its history (the history of Berlin) preserved in layers, serving as an illustration of the torturous road of German politics in the last one hundred years. In the renovation, Norman Foster, the celebrated British architect, wanted the Reichstag to perform two roles: to be the transparent and open heart of Germany's democracy, and to be a testimony and reminder of 100 years of historical twists. Parts of the building gutted during the war were left deliberately gutted, and the missing dome was only replaced by a spherical glass dome — as an expression of transparent politics — and everything else was left as testimony; even the graffiti and messages engraved with coins or penknives were left untouched, as though in an archeological dig where artifacts are left in situ. It is, in a sense, like visiting a museum, and a potent living organ that illustrates how Berlin reinvents itself — not to banish its past as I had initially thought, but to remain at the frontline.

Victor Paul Borg, who grew up in Malta, is a freelance travel writer and photographer. He has had over 500 articles published worldwide. His pictures - travel and photojournalism - have been published widely, and he has recently shot 250 subjects for a new pictorial guide to London. He is also the author of The Rough Guide to Malta & Gozo, *and is currently in Asia writing a travel book. His website can be found at www.victorborg.com.*

To travel is to discover that everyone is wrong about other countries.

ALDOUS HUXLEY

Czech Republic

"Do You Like Beer?"

Prague, Czech Republic

MELANIE CURTIN

PRAGUE'S MOST FAMOUS LANDMARK, THE BEAUTIFUL, GOTHIC
Charles Bridge, makes an unlikely background for my traveling
companion Dana's strapless bikini top, French braids and sunglasses as she puts her back into pulling us upstream on the Vltava
river.

"Do you like beer?"

The question comes unexpectedly from behind. The two
Czech boys who have been (unbeknownst to us) checking us out
for the past five minutes have apparently gotten up the nerve to
approach. Their "Do you like beer?" makes us laugh not only
because of the adorably heavy Czech accent it's uttered in (not to
mention the frankness of the question itself), but because it so
perfectly matches the unconscious humor of their overzealous
stick legs powering the paddleboat they arrive in.

We are all drifting around on the Vltava; in rowboats,
paddleboats, and kayaks, we are enjoying the warmth of a summer day on the water, not to mention distance from the crowds.
After a few days of gray fog, locals and tourists alike are out on
the river in force, in general falling into two categories: There are
the busily active explorer types, enthusiastically discovering points
of interest along the shore, bridges, and islands; and the idle drift-
ers, peacefully letting the river push them where it will, occasionally making a half-hearted attempt at a lazy paddle. Lucky for me,
today Dana belongs in the first category, so I get all the benefits
of an energetic rower while I trail my finger in the water.

The Czech boys, meanwhile, look at us expectantly. We shrug, grin at each other and reply that we don't, in fact, mind the occasional malted beverage, provided it's of quality caliber ("Yes, we like beer!"). To our surprise, they barely indicate that they have heard us as they promptly paddle away, chattering excitedly in Czech and disappearing around a bend in as endearing and mysterious a fashion as they appeared. We shrug again, laugh, and pass it off as one of those random experiences one so often entertains while traveling. ("Maybe it's a cultural difference," I suggest).

We have nearly made it to the next bridge; Dana lets out an involuntary "oomph!" as she makes the final push toward the underpass. She stops rowing and we drift slowly under the bridge, basking in the cool, dripping shade.

This relaxed river trip is a welcome change from the rest of our stay in Prague. The second stop on our tour of Eastern Europe, my two friends and I arrived here two days ago from Budapest. Unlike Budapest, where we skipped most of the sites to just hang out at outdoor cafes on the Buda side of the river, our first two days in Prague have been a whirlwind of destination-hopping and mandatory exploration of local sites. Actually, our arrival itself was one of our grandest (as in, most nerve-wracking) adventures. The guidebook listed the wrong tram number to our hostel, so immediately after stepping off the train we took a not-so-picturesque tour of Prague's not-so-picturesque districts before realizing that we were heading not only away from the river where we were fairly certain our hostel was located (it was called The Boathouse, after all) but away from Prague itself. We were thus divested, in rapid succession, of a few myths of traveling. Myth #1: All the information in the guidebook is accurate. Myth # 2 (as we hopped out and asked the first person we saw how to get back to Prague): Everyone in foreign countries speaks English. And Myth #3 (more a product of the ego-centrism of youth and the desperation which comes from the desire to escape a Prague ghetto): Everyone who lives in [fill in the city] will know exactly how to get to your hostel on public transportation.

Eventually, of course, we made it to The Boathouse — aptly named for its picturesque location right on the Vltava and the fact that kayaks are indeed stored in its basement and can be rented to hostel-goers — and were immediately invited to accompany a group of Americans on the mandatory day-trip out of Prague: the Bone Church. Four train rides, a significant amount of walking, another encounter with Myth #2, and 10,000 fascinating yet vaguely disturbing bones later (the Bone Church is a bizarre and rather grisly phenomenon of several thousand human bones set up in various religious formations within a church on the outskirts of Prague), we were back at our hostel. But we only had a chance to change quickly before we were convinced to go get dinner with some fellow travelers, with shopping, dancing, and partying to follow. We returned to The Boathouse at 7 a.m. and got up the next day only to repeat the entire process (minus the bones and the ghetto).

After two straight days of this, we were, to say the least, ready for a break, though none of us would admit as much. Today, on our way to Prague's Historic District, we stumbled across the rowboats, and it took little to convince us to forgo more tourism for a simpler jaunt on the river.

We are thus quietly reclining in our boat and reflecting on our journey when the Czech boys return as unexpectedly as they had arrived — with four generous cups of Czech lager. We have drifted back into the sun, and the cold beer seems especially appealing in the heat of the day. We watch as they come toward us, paddling less furiously than before due to the concentration required to avoid spilling the cherished liquid.

"Beer?" they suggest hopefully as they near our rowboat.

We laugh and raft the two boats together, passing the beer between us. I am concerned that now that the beer is a reality, they will realize I don't actually like it, but my fears are quickly allayed as we begin talking — we are so distracted by the mere act of communication that we barely have time to drink. This is because by "talking" I really mean us (the Americans) repeating ourselves in various ways in English in an attempt to speak more simply so they will understand, accompanied by both their and our enthusiastic and creative yet ultimately only semi-effective hand gestures. But between their almost-legitimate English-language skills (think the equivalent of our high-school Spanish), our genuine interest in who they are, and a lot of patience, we manage to gather some information. Despite their appearances (we placed them in their mid-20's), we find that one is our age and one is younger. They come from a rural town outside Prague, and they are in the city because that's where they have to come to work. It strikes me suddenly that not everyone has the capacity and capabilities to just travel for the summer.

We wind up having a truly lovely afternoon and evening with our new friends. Returning the boats and meeting up with our third friend, our primary motivation is food. I get to know the younger Czech, Andre, while we spend an hour walking around the city, searching out a restaurant listed in the guidebook as "authentic and delicious" (Myth #4: Restaurants listed in the guidebook are always good). And although not exactly what we were expecting, the restaurant is indeed very local, so it is extraordinarily refreshing to have native speakers to navigate the menu and act as a go-between for the vegetarians. Czech people, and many Europeans in general, find it hard to wrap their minds around the fact that some people actually *choose* not to eat meat. It is just confusing for them. After dinner our new Czech friends invite us to a rock concert they are having in their town (Andre plays drums), but it is far outside the city and if we miss the last train back at 9 p.m., we will have to spend the night. After a brief group consultation, we decide we are not comfortable doing this, so it is time to say goodbye. The two conduct their own group consultation away from us (as if we could understand them) and then, mysteriously, only Chako, the older one, returns. Andre, the younger one, stays back on the side.

"Yes," says Chako, pointing to me, "he want knowing you do something."

My friends giggle.

"Do something?" I inquire politely. "What kind of something?"

"Yes," he says again, and pauses, searching for a word. "Kiss," he says finally. "Is OK?"

"Kiss!" I exclaim, thinking he means that I make out with a boy I've known for barely an evening — and in front of everyone? I shake my head emphatically so he understands me, "No!"

"No, no!" he says. "is OK. Here, like this," and he pats his cheek, makes a kissy face, and pantomimes kissing on the cheek. Now my friends are laughing in earnest; they think it's hilarious. They also think it's a little awkward, so they wander away down the street.

"Oh," I say, feeling silly and self-conscious, "well. ..." I look around, deciding. I don't really know what to do and would ask the girls to stop twittering and give me advice, but they are now distracted by, and decide they *must* take a picture of, the sign for a Czech 24-hour pizza take-out place ("Non-stop Pizza-Go-Home"). I sigh.

Ultimately, I do wind up giving Andre a kiss on the cheek — I find it endearing the way he wanted his friend to ask, and it almost seems appropriate as an innocent token for the boy who (according to him) had never spoken to an American girl before.

They are very reluctant to leave, but they have a train to catch if they're going to make the concert, so they give us all quick hugs goodbye (again), and quickly excuse themselves. And as I watch them walk away, I realize that one of the most memorable experiences I will have in Europe will not be visiting the Louvre in Paris, taking pictures of the Sistine Chapel at the Vatican, or even riding in a gondola in Venice. It will be the memory of the day when two sweet Czech boys took the time to befriend us from a paddleboat on a river in a beautiful city. It will be the value of making a connection with someone completely unlike me, someone I am unlikely ever to meet again, but someone I am unlikely to ever forget.

So my advice to even the most seasoned of travelers is this: Take the time to float on the river. You won't regret it. Oh — and be sure to answer the following question with a resounding yes:

"Do you like beer?"

Melanie received her bachelor's degree from Stanford University in 2003 in Japanese, and is currently working on a master's in communication while she contemplates whether to move to Spain or Brazil after graduation. She is a surfer, dancer, linguist, and writer, but above all, a traveler from now until her legs will carry her no further.

Prague: The time is now

Prague, Czech Republic

KARA ALAIMO

WITH ANTI-AMERICAN SENTIMENT RUNNING AT A FEVEROUS HIGH in the days before the start of the war in Iraq, Prague seemed like my safest bet for spring break 2003. The Czechs weren't staging huge protests or spitting on Americans in the street. The country had survived Nazi invasion, peacefully revolted against the Communist party, and successfully split with Slovakia. I doubted they'd feel too threatened by the presence of a 20-year-old American.

Though I left Manhattan hoping to escape the protests, terror alerts and political bickering that enveloped the city, what I found in Prague was a city full of relatively quiet people who know as much about war and peace, government and policy, and history and people, as your average ancient Greek philosopher.

I discovered my first bit of cultural information the moment I stepped foot in Ruzyne Airport. At 7:45 a.m., the airport stores were closed and the restaurants gated, but completely overflowing with people was the airport pub. Czechs are, in fact, the largest consumers of beer in the world, with every man, woman and child drinking an average of about half a liter of beer every day.

As amusing as this was to my friends and me, I would later come to understand the pub's place at the very root of Czech identity. It was there that a young group of bohemian men, under threat of death from the Communists, would meet to discuss their ideas on government and human rights. They would go on to lead the country. It is there that, today, an American college student can still sit down and talk to people who were there at pivotal moments in world history.

All of my experiences with the Czech people were permeated by a sense of the importance of this particular moment in the Czech Republic. I took a short bus trip outside the city into Bohemia, to Terezin, the infamous town where Nazis held Jews before shipping them to concentration camps. I was taken through Terezin by a 74-year-old survivor of the ghetto whose mother perished there. This man was shipped to Auschwitz at age 15, where he managed to slip into an older age group, escaping the Nazi-mandated murder of all those in his group under age 16. With this younger group of Holocaust victims gone, time is running out to hear these accounts firsthand.

Many Czech people can recall when Soviet tanks rolled into their city in August 1968, and the subsequent Communist rule until the peaceful Velvet Revolution of 1989. They have experienced something that few people of any country or time have known: a non-violent takeover by a radically different government.

So, as you can imagine, it wasn't easy to find a Czech who was convinced that violence was the answer in Iraq. These people found an answer by choosing as their president a playwright whose genre was theater of the absurd, a guy who wore jeans, rode a scooter through the Castle, and held official meetings at the pub.

That's not to say the Czechs are particularly vocal about their political beliefs. In fact, most are quite quiet and reserved, a carry-over, I'm told, from the Communist days of spies and social monitoring. In part because of this, the Czech experience as a whole is unfamiliar to many and totally unique among European countries. The same holds true for the city.

Prague to me is the up-and-coming Paris of Central Europe: a beautiful city, the people a bit more reserved than in, say, Athens or Rome (though for different reasons than the French), and even equipped with a mini Eiffel tower that serves as a viewing station outside the city. But Prague is special because, while it will be a tourist trap in ten years, its not quite there yet. From the nightly performances in Prague's black-light theaters, where artists learned to communicate with action when words were too perilous, to the jester puppets sold on the streets, I found authentic remnants of Czech history around every corner.

A trip to Prague is still a trip to a wholly unfamiliar and extraordinary place, a city where you walk charming European streets on your way to visit the former prison cells of the current leaders of the country, or the museums of torture and communism. It is still a place where the president of the country resigns so that he can have more time to write plays, and where the people remember the days when performing his work was illegal. For now at least, there's still a pint to be had with the locals, and a thing or two to be learned.

Kara Alaimo studies journalism and gender and sexuality at New York University. She has studied in London and Sydney and traveled extensively throughout Europe. Kara has written for more than a dozen newspapers and magazines in the United States and Europe and interned for Sex and the City, Reuters, Live with Regis and Kelly, *and* Jane Magazine.

If you actually look like your passport photo, you aren't well enough to travel.

SIR VIVIAN FUCHS

Hungary

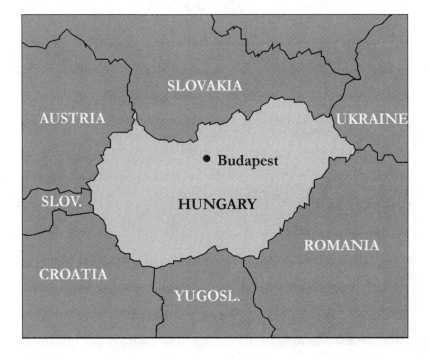

Budapest by Accident

Budapest, Hungary

LYNDA TWARDOWSKI

"TRAVEL IS ALL ABOUT THE DETAILS. JUST LIKE A RELATIONSHIP, IT'S the little things that count — the puny, minute details that you think don't matter but can make or break you."

The chilly March morning I spat this at my boyfriend, we were standing before a deserted ticket window at a train station in Caen, France. It was the morning after my brother's wedding there, and thanks to the bounty of wine provided by his French bride's family and my American family's thirst for it, the previous night's celebration had lasted until 4 a.m.

Nevertheless, my boyfriend, heady with the prospects of his first trip overseas, had hustled me up and out of bed three hours after we had collapsed into it, so we could make it to the station shortly after 7 a.m. Sunday morning, which would get us there, according to him, "right on time."

The ticket window was, of course, still closed.

"Sorry," he said, peering anxiously through the fogged Plexiglas. "I could have sworn it was supposed to be open now."

I closed my eyes and slid with my back against the wall to the cold, dusty floor, then let out a long, tired, pointed sigh. *Novice.*

This was my second trek through Europe. And like all who had already stuffed their lives into a series of Ziploc baggies, jammed those swollen baggies in an unforgiving canvas backpack and hoisted the whole lot on their backs for a two-month journey through 11-plus European countries, I saw myself as the expert, the matron saint of efficient and exemplary cross-country travel.

Clearly, I would have to show him the ropes.

196

I launched into an instructive lecture on the finer points of research and planning and was just wrapping up with a sermon on the inherent dangers of flying by the seat of one's pants when the clerk finally arrived and sold us two overnights to Frankfort, Germany — the last junction on Germany's eastern border, which would get us en route to our final destination, Poland, by nightfall. I had mapped out this journey with exacting care months before.

We soon boarded, cruised down to Paris — an intended stopover on our itinerary for which I had scheduled lunch beneath the Eiffel Tower, a tour of the Louvre and a walk to the Arc de Triumph — then jumped on the night train that would have us in Frankfurt by 8 a.m. the following day.

As we rumbled out of Paris that evening, I congratulated myself on the results of my exceptional tutelage. The seamless quality of my well-scripted Paris afternoon had clearly inspired my boyfriend. He lay curled in his berth, dutifully scouring the pages of our Germany guidebook, taking careful notes and flipping back and forth from index to map to index to map.

The methodical snaps of his page flipping lulling me to sleep, I snuggled deep into my bedroll, dreams of the cross-referencing prodigy I had created dancing in my head. Minutes later, his whisper shattered the vision.

"I have a question," he said.

I opened one eye; there was no need for both. I knew that map backward and forward.

"Which Frankfurt are we going to?" he asked.

I opened the other eye.

"There's two," he said, handing me the book.

I sat up. Surely there was some mistake. I had spent days — no, weeks — planning this trip. We were going to Frankfurt — the *only* Frankfurt — because Frankfurt was the place we needed to go to catch the train we needed to catch to get into Poland tomorrow afternoon. I peered down at the open page, each eye wide as the mouth of a stein.

He slid his finger to a dot on the map's eastern border. *Frankfurt an der Oder*. "This is one," he said, then slid his finger to another dot in the center. *Frankfurt-am-Main*. "This is two." He looked at me expectantly. "Which one are we going to?"

I stared at the map. Blinked. Looked up at him. Blinked again.

When we arrived the next morning in Frankfurt-am-Main, hundreds and hundreds and hundreds of miles from Frankfurt an der Oder, the city we were supposed to have gone to, I was still blinking.

In my defense, that's about the most a person can be expected to do when she has spent the prior eight hours listening to her boyfriend invent an endless succession of limericks, each one stupider than the last, all of which ended with a rhyming reference to the word "details" and inspired him to wiggle and dance like a child both in crowded train compartments and on empty train platforms.

No matter. Eventually he tired of scraping the bottom of the "details" verse barrel, and when he did, my catatonic state stirred him to action. He propped me up against a pole, swung up to the station's tourist information desk and began a deep, prolonged conversation with the burly man behind it. Together they decided that waiting to catch a train to the other Frankfurt was out of the question.

With a grand flourish, my boyfriend tore my lengthy Poland pages from our equally lengthy itinerary, winked at me, and turned back to the burly man. They huddled closer, and then joyfully made arrangements for us to fly by the seat of our pants.

Our new destination? Budapest, Hungary. "We're going to the baths," he told me.

I blinked. *Baths?*

He yanked me onto another train that afternoon, and off we

went. I didn't like it. I didn't like it one bit. The plan was to go to Poland, to see the land from whence my ancestors came. I had studied maps, consulted family trees, interviewed aging relatives — I had *a plan*.

We were supposed to have been eating boiled cabbage and drinking chilled vodka, exploring endless forests and towns ravaged by Nazis and rebuilt by Polish sweat. I had plotted directions to the farm where my great-grandmother was raised, and I had intended to get to its stone house, the hand-hewn floor of which she said she was on her hands and knees scrubbing at age 16, her sudsy, wet skirt piled tightly between her knees, the day my great-grandfather showed up.

A month later they had married and he had hauled her away to Detroit. She hadn't been back home since, she always cried; she was too old to go now. But I could go. I could see Poland, the place my grandpa called "the old country," the only name he saw fit to call it, and the place he rarely mentioned without waving a dismissive hand at his forever-tearful mother-in-law.

Or, at least, I could have seen it — if I hadn't overlooked that one … uh, make that *two* critical details.

And so these were the thoughts twisting my face into a pained grimace as we rolled and swayed along the long stretch of tracks toward Budapest, a city for which we had no room reservations, no map, and little more than a clue about what we were doing there.

When we finally stepped off the train and into a chaotic morning cluster of Hungarians, my first thought was that the people seemed to be divided into two groups — those who had somewhere vitally important to go; and those who didn't but hoped to give us a ride. While the members of the two groups either blew past or tugged on us, I slowly worked myself into a frenzy.

Tiny droplets of sweat pooled at the base of my neck. I turned my head left and right in search of an information booth, and as I did, an icy wind raced across the platform, sending torn tickets and cellophane wrappers spiraling around us and a chill down my ill-prepared spine. *This is way colder than Poland would have been. But then, how would I know that? I had no idea what the median temperature was in Budapest at this time of year. Why? Because I'm supposed to be in Poland.*

I stomped my feet. "I'm freezing," I called to my boyfriend, who was already racing through the crowd toward the busy intersection.

"Then run," he yelled over his shoulder.

I stared after him. "Where are you going?" I shouted.

He turned around at the curb and shrugged.

I stood planted where I was. "We have to find an information desk first," I yelled. "We need a room, a place to eat —"

He shifted his pack to his other shoulder — he refused to hang it over both, despite my advice — and walked over to me. He bent his face very close to mine. "Don't worry so much about the details," he said, his face breaking into a grin. "We're in Budapest. Fucking Budapest!"

I looked around. Austere, sculptured masses of concrete and iron office buildings stretched up from the cobbled streets before me. Miniature versions of cars zipped past, horns bleeping, engines buzzing. An old woman, her head tied under a fuchsia scarf, strolled past, cooing into a stroller. She nodded in our direction and said something I didn't understand. I blinked. She smiled anyway. I smiled back. My boyfriend was right. *Fucking Budapest!*

That morning we didn't immediately go in search of a room. We hauled out our cameras instead and walked the length of the Danube River bank, shooting the industrial scene to the east (Pest), its seemingly endless gray sky jagged with shoots of bright electric billboards and blinking letters. It was a fierce contrast to the soft, sloping hills of Buda to the west. Each hill there lay muted in a fog, dense with trees and rolling beneath tall stacks of cozy apartment flats, each layer of windows burning shades of warm yellows and fiery oranges against the charcoal sky.

When the cold bit too deeply through our fleece coats, we dove into a standup counter in the city's interior for goulash soup, and after we tottered half-drunk on paprika and heat, back into the street, we chanced upon coffee house after coffee house as we strolled the wide boulevards. Whether they were papered with fabric walls and filled with rattan chairs or gilded in gold trim and dripping with chandeliers, each served us heaping slices of pastries and steaming mugs of coffee as if we were royalty itself coming in from the cold.

As the morning faded into afternoon, we found ourselves ambling through a quiet park on the edge of town, snapping random shots of kids at a pond blowing into the sails of their homemade boats, running our fingers along icy fences and staring into the blank eyes of bronzed Hungarian heroes.

Then we spotted it. In the distance, a towering — what? Castle? Hotel? Museum? In any case, a great, glimmering building, walls the color of iced lemon and dripping with gleaming white trim, it looked like a giant, hot birthday cake sparking and steaming there in the cold.

"The baths," my boyfriend shouted, grabbing my hand and charging across the grass.

We raced for what seemed like miles and stumbled through the first opening we could find in the massive walls. Nobody stopped us so we didn't slow down. We tore up a gleaming hallway toward a glow at the building's center. Huffing and puffing, we rounded the final corner. Then we skidded to breathless halt. Before us, drowning in sun that came from God only knows where, pools of Hungarians — old ones, young ones, fat ones, skinny ones — stood schools deep in the clearest, sparkliest, most inviting waters I had ever seen.

I stood there watching them for a moment, as they swam, gossiped, floated and played chess amidst the depths. My heart was elated at the sight. "We have to go in," I said to my boyfriend.

"We can't," he moaned. "We have no suits." He looked down at me, genuinely sorry to break the news.

My heart sank like a stone. I looked up him, blinked, stared back out at the pools, then turned and walked away. As I trudged down the dark hallway, I passed a janitor's closet door, hanging open. On its floor lay a wet, mildewy lump. I walked past, blinked, then backed up.

One panicked minute later I tiptoed from the janitor's closet, my clothes in my hand and two wet, mildewy bathing suits dripping from my body. Their previous owners, both woefully oversized it seemed, likely had abandoned these suits because of the many holes gaping in the most inopportune places. But as I emerged back into the sunlight and sashayed to where my boyfriend sat at the water's edge, I didn't care. I loved these suits.

He glanced up at me when I dropped my clothes and pack into his lap, shocked no doubt, by my resourcefulness — or maybe the large chunk of Lycra hanging from my butt to my knee. "Oh my God, what did you do? What are you doing? Where did you — ?" he stuttered.

I crouched down at the water's edge and gingerly slid my toes, then my knees, then my hips into the crystalline warmth, feeling my muscles liquefy as I melted into the deep. I tilted my head up to where his face was framed by the sun and before I submerged, I grinned. "Don't worry about the details," I said. "It's fucking Budapest."

Lynda Twardowski is a freelance lifestyle and travel writer living in Northern Michigan. She recently was awarded a three-month writer-in-residency grant, which enabled her to live and write in the historic former home of Jack Kerouac in College Park, Florida. She has written nine books and more than 100 articles for various publications, including Cabin Life, Traverse Magazine *and* Playboy.com.

I'll Always Have Paris

Budapest, Hungary

Lisa Cordeiro

MY SOLO BACKPACKING TREK THROUGH EUROPE REACHED A major crossroads in Budapest. Several weeks before, I'd landed at Calais from England, spoken French for the first time on French soil to order my first cup of French roast coffee, then headed for Paris, where I landed a waitressing job in a youth hostel my first day there. I worked two weeks, then said farewell, and followed my plan to backpack around Europe. It wasn't until after I left that I realized how much I missed Paris, the city of lights, in France, the land of my dreams.

I traveled on a precariously tight budget. I thought twice before buying anything, including food. One night in expensive Zurich, in fact, I chose to buy a Swiss army knife instead of something to eat. So, initially, I was thrilled when I reached Budapest: I could live like a queen instead of a starving traveler, and enjoy the culture, too. For a few days, I gave up the Nutella diet for meals in fancy restaurants, which helped make up for those lean eating days. But something was happening to me. I had trekked across Western Europe, and couldn't care less if I stepped into another historic church or world-class museum.

Everywhere I went, there were references to Paris, and I started to become homesick — not for Boston, my hometown, but for the Paris I'd experienced for just two weeks. How strange to lament over the city I had embraced for such a short time. Still, my eyes glazed over when I heard the sound of Edith Piaf's voice. I savored menu references to French cuisine. Then, I sealed my fate in a Budapest movie theatre, watching the remake of *Sabrina*, where Julia Ormond travels to Paris and blossoms into her full potential. Why wasn't *I* in Paris? I thought. Well, I had scheduled myself for the next several weeks to explore the Czech Republic, Northern Germany, and the Netherlands. It took the blink of an eye to blow it all off. *I'm going to Paris right now*, I decided.

Instant decisions reached around midnight usually don't make for well-thought out plans, and this was no exception. I simply ran down to the subway, jumped a train, and willed it to carry me fast back to my campground. Plan A was: (1) grab my belongings, and (2) fly back to Paris.

I ran upstairs from the subway to the street, and was instantly lost. The campground's around here somewhere, I thought as I wandered off the main road and onto residential streets, where a startled dog started barking at me.

Dogs are my phobia. No matter how small or harmless they seem, I am terrified of them, because all I can see is vicious teeth, and all I can imagine is what those teeth can do to me.

"Shhh," I hissed.

Apparently, that wasn't how to calm the dog. He barked more, and excited others in the neighborhood, too. It was as if they were preying on my terror — like feeding time in a dog kennel. I was surrounded by barking dogs. I was fresh meat and they all wanted to tear me apart. My heart was racing. I ran blindly through the dark neighborhoods, my breath short, kicking myself for coming up with such a stupid plan. Who just pops over to the Budapest airport after midnight and jumps on a plane to Paris? If it was that easy, we'd all be doing it.

Then, I saw street lights. I was out on the main road again. There was the campground! I ran to the gates. They were locked. The campground was closed for the night. Foiled! Now what? Blocked from Paris, and even shut out of my bed for the night.

Unless. …

… I could infiltrate this campground. I was enlisted in the U.S. Marine Corps. I peeked to my left and right, made sure nobody was around, then scaled the fence. At the top, I swung my leg over, and —

RRRRRIIIIIIPPPPPPPPP! There went my last pair of jeans! I dropped inside to the ground.

I still had the knack. Swiftly and smugly, I ran to my camp spot, grabbed my bag, returned to scale the fence again — more carefully this time — and rushed to catch the last bus out of town. Of course, by now, they had all stopped running. So I hailed a cab. I hadn't survived a "covert op," getting lost at midnight and nearly ambushed by rabid dogs to turn back now.

"Get me to the airport," I signaled the driver.

He drove me straight there. With a keen sense of satisfaction, I paid him, slammed the cab door, and walked to the departure building's entrance. The doors were locked. I took a step back, realizing that the airport was closed until morning. As this dawned on me, I turned around to the street. The cab was long gone. A security guard approached me.

"What are you doing here?" he asked.

"I'm trying to catch a plane to Paris," I said desperately.

He looked a little astonished. "You are at the wrong airport," he said. "This is the *cargo* airport."

Now I started feeling stupid. Was that cab driver just messing with me? I mean, what did he think a girl was going to do at the *cargo* airport at one in the morning? As the failure of my irrational plan set in, the security guard said, "I'll call another cab for you."

This one took me to the right airport. I used the last of my Hungarian currency to pay the driver. Of course, this airport was closed, too. Unlike in the U.S., where I could just sleep in an departure lounge chair overnight while waiting for a flight, in Budapest, I had to I settle on the sidewalk out in front of the departure building. Now, alone, I was looking forward to freezing all night out on a curb. *Think before you act, Lisa,* I could hear my parents reminding me there in the dark.

I gave myself a mental wake-up slap. Okay, my situation seemed pretty bad right now, but tomorrow night at this time, I should be in Paris, and it would all be worth it. That's when two men walked up to the airport entrance. Who else would come to the closed airport in the middle of the night? I wondered nervously.

"Damn communism," the dark one muttered in English as he waved his hand towards the closed door. Then he turned to me. "Are you waiting for it to open, too?" he asked.

"Yes, I just got here."

"Oh, don't stay out here and freeze," he said. "You can wait in our car until it opens."

Let's see: Freeze on the sidewalk alone, or climb into a car with two strange men in the middle of the night? It was really cold; I was an former Marine. I decided to take my chances.

The men turned out to be Dutch and were returning home. They only turned on the car once every half hour to run its heater, so it was almost as cold inside with them as it was outside on the curb. Shivering in the back seat, I caught only a few fitful minutes of sleep here and there, so I felt ecstatic when the airport finally opened. I thanked the two Dutchmen for their hospitality, wished them well, and rushed off to the AirFrance counter. "I need one ticket to Paris. Now. Please," I told the agent.

She booked me on a flight to Paris then and there. All the money I had budgeted for hostels over the next few weeks went to pay for my ticket. I waited in the lounge like a restless, caged animal. When they called my flight, I could barely restrain myself from running down the jetway to my plane, elbowing passengers out of the aisle to my seat. By mid-afternoon, we were landing at Charles de Gaulle airport, clearing customs, and then I was speeding through the RER into Paris. I took in the city with all my senses. I was home again. Mission accomplished.

Now, what about Plan B?

I had told the hostel people that I wouldn't be back for another month, so there was no guarantee I'd get my waitressing job back. I felt stupid just showing up unannounced on their doorstep that night. So, I went to stay the night a nearby motel, and they offered me a job — handing out fliers to tourists at the train station. I didn't last one day at that. I had to approach the youth hostel again, find my old boss Stephan, and throw myself on his mercy.

My heart was beating out of my chest as I approached him. But before I even got the words out, Stephan said, "Yes." I could barely believe my ears.

As I went to sleep in the hostel that night, I realized that barely 36 hours ago, I had been walking out of a movie theatre in Budapest. I was a little surprised at what I'd put myself through to get what I wanted. No obstacle was big enough to stop me when my dream was the objective. Now that I had it, I wouldn't be giving it up again any time soon.

Lisa Cordeiro served in Okinawa, Japan, while enlisted in the Marine Corps. Living in another country ignited her wanderlust and she went on several other solo adventures across Europe and the United States. Currently, she is a writer outside of Boston who travels with her new companions, her husband, Eric, and son, Nicholas.

Fancy a Shag?

Hungarian border

Billy Anderson

No matter how experienced one might be in the art of traveling on a budget with one's life on one's back, surprises will happen. Sometimes they're good, sometimes bad; often they're comical. That said, I'm still surprised by my experience on the Budapest to Vienna train.

Long ago I'd learned a valuable trick for long train trips. On the way to the station, stop by a restaurant or grocery store, buy an empty wine bottle, and hide it in your pack. Arrive early for the train and find an empty compartment. Old-style European train compartments have six separate seats, a door and curtains, making it feel like your own little apartment. Spread your stuff all over the place, sprawl across the seats, hold the empty wine bottle in your hand and snore like a tractor. As people board the train they'll stick their heads in, think you're a passed-out drunk, and leave you alone. Then as the train starts moving you can sit up and enjoy your very own compartment for the duration of the trip.

This time, I followed the usual plan. The ticket collector came by about ten minutes after we left the station. I expected him to ask blandly for my ticket, then carry on to the next passengers without saying much. But this fellow was a "Guy Smiley" type. He bounced into my compartment like a rabbit, grinning like he'd just won the lottery. Instantly my backpacker defense went on alert. Money belt secure? Check. Backpack locked to rack above? Check. Chest out, scowl on face, looking mean and unapproachable? Check.

Happy boy just kept grinning. He looked me up and down (as you can imagine, this is rarely a good sign) then asked, "Sport?" I had no idea what he meant. I figured he wanted to see my passport, but as I went for it he shook his head, leaned over and squeezed my knee. As far as I know, squeezing other guys' knees isn't in a ticket collector's job description. I know I'm not from around here, but come on, is that really necessary?

He left. Thank God. But a few minutes later he came back, much to my chagrin. He made me stand up in front of him, which I happily did, in hopes that my height would deter him from groping me again. He cupped his hands in front of his chest, imitating a woman's breasts and said, "Lady, you like lady?" Again, I call your attention to the fact that this is not something you expect train employees to do. I was starting to feel more than a bit uncomfortable with this little chap. I wondered if he was coming on to me so I replied, "Yes, yes, I like lady. Very much so." From the look on his face, I could tell I wasn't getting the point. It was then that he did it. Something I never expected. He started tapping me between the legs — RIGHT between the legs.

What would *you* do at this point? Push him away? Wind up and send him into next week? Well, that's what you'd *think* you'd do, but I was in a state of shock. I knew damn well what had just happened, but I wondered, "No-o-o... he didn't just do what I think he did, did he? That's not possible — he's the ticket guy and my train ticket would never be down *there* so why would he do that?" But all doubts were erased when he did it again. This time I gave him a little push which upset him to no end and he began waving his hands in front of his face and shaking his head like I was overreacting. Call me crazy, but I think I was handling the whole thing quite well.

He left. I stood there, mouth agape, trying to figure out just exactly what was going on. Earlier that morning, when I'd planned my day I definitely hadn't included "get groped on train" in between breakfast in Budapest and lunch in Vienna. It was supposed to be a nice, peaceful train ride. After all, I was going to Vienna, a cosmopolitan city known for such distinguished citizens as Mozart and Freud, not train-riding crotch-grabbers.

Eventually I sat down. But I couldn't relax. Was this guy going to come back? What would I do then? Hurting him would only land me in more trouble, seeing as he worked for the train and I didn't speak a word of Hungarian or German. It was all so strange that I began wondering if it had really happened. Maybe that empty wine bottle wasn't empty when I got on the train. Maybe I actually drank that whole thing, passed out, and had this nasty dream. Yeah, that's what it must be.

I was wrong. I got three new visitors next — two big guys and a good-looking young lady. Like the ticket guy, they were all in official train uniforms. The two men stood outside the cabin as the lady entered, closing the door and curtains behind her. I was so utterly confused at this point that I just waited for whatever was next, like someone facing a firing squad. Bring it on, I thought, how can this possibly get any weirder?

She looked at me and asked, "Forints? You have Forints?" Forints is Hungarian currency. This lady wanted to know if I had any money on me. With the two gorillas standing outside my door, I wasn't about to admit that I had any money, so I told her "no" and shook my head. She left.

And then it hit me. Like a two-by-four. Guy Smiley was the train pimp asking me if I wanted a little excitement to help me pass the time! The two behemoths outside my door were the bouncers, and the lady, to put it politely, was "of other talents," who would have happily taken my Hungarian money in exchange for a little cross-border hokey-pokey.

I was stunned. Sure I'd expect something like this in dirty

areas of various big cities worldwide, but my poor, sheltered, Canadian mind never would have thought there could be a train tramp business. What if I'd have told her I had money? She may have started peeling off her uniform right there.

This trip, I would have been much happier *not* to be alone in my spacious compartment. When the train eventually rolled into Vienna, and I made a hasty exit. I felt violated, a little more educated, and equipped with another fantastic story to share with the boys when I got home.

Billy recovered from his train encounter and enjoyed the sights in Vienna. The experience taught him to always keep his guard up and expect the unexpected. He continued to enjoy the many delights of Europe, studying in France and then working in England. He now lives in Canada, where he is a freelance writer and an adventure guide. His Canadian train exploits have remained "grope free," much to his delight.

There is a bond among backpackers that people with suitcases and taxis and reservations will never understand.

LINDA SANDS

Austria

A First Encounter

Salzburg, Austria

Robin Gandhi

The mountainous landscape running by my window, I watched tentatively as the short Austrian lady walked into the car and stopped at each seat along the aisle to verify tickets. With my friend's yet-to-be-expired Eurailpass, I had managed to make it from Berlin to Munich with no hitches. Now, on the last leg of my journey to Salzburg, complacency had set in, but there was still the tension of things not going right.

"Ticket."

I handed her the pass. She looked it over carefully.

"Passport." I looked to her to hand back the Eurailpass, but she held onto it firmly even as I tugged on it. It wasn't something that I had expected. In fact, over the last month and half, nobody had ever bothered to crosscheck the pass with the passport. Panic mode set in and I foolishly decided that if she couldn't check the pass against a passport, I could never be identified as not being the person on the pass. While the passport sat securely against my thigh in my front pant pocket, I frantically pretended to look through my backpack, rummaging through the contents.

After five minutes of "searching," I looked up at her with a frazzled look on my face. "I'm sorry, but I can't seem to find my passport. Maybe I can just pay you for the ticket."

She stared me down with no sign of leniency. I cringed in fear. "Passport." It was obvious that she wasn't going to just let it slide, and her English was not good enough to clearly explain what she was thinking as the possible next steps.

An ex-pat behind me who spoke a bit of German tried to translate my faked situation to the lady … but to no avail. The lady held onto the pass and quickly walked it to the front of the train. Now my head was doing somersaults. Obviously, I was not the person on the pass, and I would soon be discovered. I needed to lose my identity, and quickly. While I awaited her return, I took the passport, along with my license, credit cards and any other identifiable documents and shoved them deep into my backpack. Thoughts about possible scenarios bounced chaotically about my head, as I sweated out a decision from the train. My crumbled train schedule showed no stops between the two-hour ride from Munich to Salzburg, so the possibility of jumping out at an obscure town along the way was quickly put to rest. Listening to my Discman was impossible as the impending doom weighing heavily on my mind drowned out the tunes.

Half an hour before we reached the station, the lady came back into our car with the pass and talked to the ex-pat about the situation at hand. The translation was that the company issuing the Eurailpass would be contacted and the pass would be checked to see if it had been reported stolen. A matter of five minutes, if everything checked out. Perfect, I thought. Obviously, there was no reason for concern, as I had been given the pass from my friend who had left Europe a couple days earlier. As we pulled into the station, I stood with the lady and whistled merrily to myself for having gotten away relatively cleanly.

When the train came to a complete stop, I moved to step out onto the platform. To my horror, the lady held me back with one arm and called out. "Guards!" The approach of four armed men with semi-automatics and full military gear sent the bottom of my stomach sinking straight into my legs. The situation was explained to the men in German, and pretty soon a guard who could have easily been Schwarzenegger's brother, complete with the accent and the muscles, had begun the interrogation.

"So you have the passport, yes?"

With the lady still standing over me, I decided that I might as well keep the farce of the lost passport going. "No, I can't seem to find it. I can go to the U.S. Embassy and get it in Salzburg, right?"

"You should try to find it."

"What if I can't?"

"Well, then ... that would be very baad for you."

"Bad, why?"

"Then we take you to the police station."

"Can you just send me back to Berlin?"

"No. Now it is done."

What do you mean it's done? "Okay, let me check again." I put my backpack down on the platform floor and started to unlock it while trying to figure out what the hell I would do next. Now the realm of scenarios had taken an entirely new turn. How long should I keep playing along with this lost passport story? As I crouched on the ground in contemplation, one of the guards noticed the tag on my backpack. He read off the name silently, but I could clearly see the light bulbs going off one-by-one in his head. He walked over to the guard with the pass and read the name off of the pass aloud. Suddenly there was a barrage of German that I couldn't understand with the exception of the word "arrest" intermixed into every other sentence.

Shit. This was the end. Now, I had either stolen the Eurail pass or an entire backpack. I looked up innocently from the ground to the congregation of guards. "Okay, can I tell you the truth?"

"Yes. That wud be gud."

The time had arrived to come clean. I explained that I hadn't realized that I couldn't use someone else's pass, and that I had gotten flustered when the lady on the train had wanted to compare the pass-port to Eurailpass. With their guns slung over their shoulders, the guards were eating it all up and loving every second of my anxiety. Another set of German commenced and after five minutes, all but one of the guards dispersed. He explained that he would have to take the pass and charge me the cost of the ticket from Munich to Salzburg. I couldn't have been happier. I walked over to the ATM, paid the man and headed towards the city.

When I got my bearings straight, it dawned on me that the private house that my friends were staying in was far on the outskirts of Salzburg in Kasern Berg. Back on a train to the little town, I was paranoid of everyone around me, but at the same time, I had the energy of someone who had just escaped a night at the Austrian police station. After legitimately paying my way to the Salzburg-Maria Plain stop, I walked the fifteen minutes up the hill to the Haus Moser, happy to be off the train. At the house, my friends were anticipating my arrival with evening tickets to the opera. With the cool crisp cleanliness of the mountains floating through the air along with the three hours worth of adrenaline coursing through my body, the last thing I wanted to do was sit in a concert hall and listen to music. I was looking for excitement. The woman who owned the house informed us that there was to be a huge bonfire in a neighboring village, complete with Austrian food, booze and music. That was more of what I needed, and I convinced the group that we could easily pass up a night at the opera for a night of authentic Austrian fun.

We were already in the middle of nowhere, but the dirt path to the bonfire lead straight through multiple fields of rolling green grass past old-fashioned brick red farmhouses. There was no mistaking that this was the land of *The Sound of Music*. As we walked, a couple honking cars filled to the brim with Austrian college kids passed us by. Looking back, we could see a steady stream of people walking along the path though the grass as if on some sort of pilgrimage. And we were a part of it.

A forty-foot-high pyramid of firewood stood in the middle of a circular area of dirt unfettered by guard wires or overcautious yellow police tape. Obviously, the words "risk-management nightmare" had no meaning out here. It had been lit along the base, but the fire was still in its infancy. Very quickly, it became obvious that there were not going to be any tourists at this event. Some people looked at us wondering who had let the secret out, but still they welcomed us with open arms. Lines and lines of picnic tables had been set up in front of a stage, and we could see the band practicing on the side. A couple makeshift bars had been set up amongst the various barbeque grills, and there was no question that we needed to get the party started.

As the bartenders quickly discovered that we were from the States, it became their unofficial goal to get us as drunk as humanly possible. Beers were followed by more beers. Rotisserie chicken, Austrian ribs and pretzels helped to prolong the inevitable inebriation. And then the band began to play. Soon we were dancing like fools under the starry night and the fiery glow of the bonfire. In between sets, the band would turn on the CD player and spin some American tunes, and the locals would dance even harder. It was like being in some bizarre 80's time shift. And then out of nowhere, the band began to sing John Denver's *Country Road*, and we were standing in the middle of a grassy field on the edge of Salzburg as some three hundred Austrians and five Americans belted out a rendition in unison. There would be no going home. We stayed out until the sun came up and the bonfire went down. It was a good day.

Living in New York City, Robin has been traveling the world for the last four years. He looks to continue his efforts by exploring Latin America on his next adventure. In his spare time, he works as a business consultant and continues to refine the stories of his travels.

Plenty of Salt, Not Enough Food

Salzburg, Austria

DAVIS BAWTINHEIMER

HUNGER IS AN INTERESTING TRAVEL COMPANION. IT CAN TRANS-form dry, crunchy buns into a wondrous feast and make the most amazing experiences seem tedious and exhausting. Essentially, as my three friends and I toured Europe on an attempted budget of fifty dollars a day, we invited hunger along.

On a more human level, people say that traveling with a friend, partner or family member results in a thorough exploration of the relationship. This is apparent and trite, but it is too broad a statement to be one hundred percent truthful. It's the little things that occur while you travel that truly delve into how much of each other you are willing to bear, appreciate, forgive, explore, accept, and love.

A certain experience on a certain day comes to mind. A small annoyance, on one of the best days I've had in my short twenty-two years.

When you are accustomed to eating "Dijon sandwiches" and "wet dog sandwiches" (not quite as bad as it sounds, but still bad enough to be shameful), chocolate bars are as heavenly as any-thing else that the mind can fathom. Subsequently, the purchase of a chocolate bar does not entail the consumption of a treat. It is considered, under those circumstances, to be an investment in the harmony of body, mind, and soul. Such an investment is never taken lightly, and whether it costs one dollar or years of devotion, perspective provides a narrow focus.

As Bren, Paul, Derek and I set out for a bike ride through the Austrian Alps, we agreed that we would require such harmony to make it home alive, and paid a rare visit to the habitually unaffordable grocery store on our rented mountain bikes.

"Paul, man," I said, "we'll throw these bad boys in your bag and when we stop for a break, we'll close our eyes, eat chocolate, and be wherever we want to be."

"Sounds good to me," Paul said with a chuckle.

In a rueful stage of temporary self-denial, we stowed the bars away in Paul's backpack amongst a bunch of other crap that we wouldn't be requiring during the course of our trip.

"Let's stop by the *pension* on our way out so that I can get rid of some of this other crap that we're not gonna need," Paul proposed. Bren sighed at the thought of extra pedaling. Based on the not-so-clear directions we'd received from Brigitte, the Grandma-like host of the pension where we were staying, we expected the trip to take a couple of hours.

"Yeah, I'd like to grab my camera," Derek said, his eyes on the camera case that was tied to the back of my seat post.

We rode through Salzburg like young boys, racing around corners and calling ourselves the Red Barons, as our bikes were the appropriate color. By the time we arrived at Brigitte's place, the late morning was growing steadily warmer. The clouds had burnt away and heat waves were visible across the central canal.

"Make sure you leave the chocolate bars in there," I said to Paul as he dismounted his bike. He returned a look that told me I was not giving him enough credit, and rushed inside. Derek followed hastily.

Bren turned to me as we waited in the garden where we'd eaten a Brigitte-provided breakfast that morning. That may sound luxurious, and although the setting could not be improved, the breakfast itself had involved dry bread and old jam, which we had devoured as if it would be our last meal for days.

"How long do you think this ride will take?" he asked.

"Tough to estimate based on Brigitte's directions," I replied.

"Sounded like we just follow the canal to the next town, and then we'll start to see some signs."

"That's what I gathered also. I'm sure if it was gonna be longer than a couple of hours she'd have warned us."

"Good call," Bren said, looking questioningly over his shoulder at the canal that stretched out of sight as it wound its way between the old town and the new town.

"Let's bust," Paul said, as he and Derek came outside.

We hopped on our bikes and began pedaling with more energy than we would have throughout the remainder of the day. We were anxious to see the salt mines that Brigitte had described as something "not to be missed," and the relentless competition to hold the title as the "leader of the pack" motivated us to maintain a good pace.

We followed the canal on the old town side, glancing back and forth at the new town across the water and the old buildings on our side, built into the side of the rocks and overlooked by a fortress; such a wonderful contrast. At first, we passed numerous people along our path. Gradually, these people thinned out, and we began to enjoy the solitude of our ride. Our voices and laughter grew louder as we began to own our path.

We kept an eye out for any signs mentioning the neighboring town, but came across no evidence of such a town's existence. An hour or so into the ride, we decided to pull over for a snack.

"It's time to refuel, guys," I said.

"Yeah, those chocolate bars will be awesome," Derek agreed, applying his brakes and looking at Paul anxiously.

We pulled our bikes off to the side of the path. Bren and I sat down on a bench as Paul took off his pack and began shuffling around for the chocolate treasure. We all watched anxiously, but our excitement died fairly quickly as Paul's face gave an expression of "oops."

"Dude," I said, with a lengthy hesitation, "Don't ... tell ... me. ..."

"I must have taken them out by accident. ..."

"You've got to be kidding," Derek said. In our case, as I believe would be the case for most, hunger always thinned the ice. We were usually hungry. My stretch band boxers had been loose around my hips for days and I'd been dreaming of chocolate all morning. Obviously pissed off, Derek said nothing more, mounted his bike, and started pedaling. I hesitated and followed, as did Bren and eventually Paul, solemnly accepting the fact that if we got lost in the woods, he would inescapably be eaten first.

No matter how frustrated the four of us got with one another at times, no matter how much we were tempted to offer threats of forceful secession, we always managed to respect the indestructibility of our friendship. Our anger was quickly transformed into playful aggression. This playful aggression resulted in a two-hour Red Baron demolition derby. It began with my ramming Bren so that he had to steer into a ditch. Paul and Derek turned back when they heard my cheering, and laughed as Bren picked his bike up and came rushing toward me for a counterattack. The sky was clear, and the afternoon was hot, but we were in a contest that allowed no surrender. We became completely immersed in our attempts to out-maneuver one another and come out the victor in each of our individual battles. Alliances were formed and divided. Superficial bonds were respected and ignored. Rims were bent and reflectors were broken.

When sufficient damage had been done to our bikes and our bodies, it became time for practicality and sensibility to set in.

"Hey, Davis, man," Bren said while picking his bike up off of some gravel and studying the rear wheel. "Didn't you have to give them your passport number to rent these things?"

My reply came quickly and halted:

"I — shit."

We decided to call a universal truce, although Derek and I, who happened to be allies at the time, exchanged discreet winks in affirmation of our victory.

We then propped my camera on the gravel path and captured one of my favorite moments of the trip: the four of us holding our bikes, our shirts off, the hot sun on our backs, and our arms around each others' shoulders, with nothing on our minds but that we were together and that it was a good day.

As we gathered our things, we finally saw another group of bikers, and after a brief conversation realized that we had ridden far off course during the heated battle. We managed to retrace our path to the junction, and then continued in the direction that the other riders had assured us would lead to the nearest town.

When we arrived, we found no evidence of any salt mines. No signs or tour buses or even tourist-information centers. We agreed that our long-lost chocolate bars and the resulting violence of our morning provided sufficient justification for lunch-time indulgence.

"It's necessary for our safety and survival," Bren concluded.

"Especially Paul's," Derek added.

We entered the first restaurant we came across and studied our menus scrupulously, as if our chosen dish would be served to us for every meal of every day for the rest of our lives. We all shared in the debate that ensued as efforts were made to translate the menu into English. Derek, Paul, and I found pizza on the menu and felt that this would hit the spot. Bren, on the other hand, was taking a gamble at some of the less decipherable words in an attempt to track down a classic — spaghetti and meatballs.

"Because the portion will be huge and it feels like I haven't eaten spaghetti in years," he explained when we questioned the difficulty he was making for himself.

"It's gotta be the most expensive one," he deduced. "Yeah, 'Krake' sounds like a term that could mean meat."

"Whatever," we replied through expression, wanting him to order so that the food would arrive.

The waiter took our orders with no comment and whisked the menus away on his way to the kitchen. We talked of nothing but food until our plates arrived. How great the pizza would taste, how big the portion of spaghetti was going to be, how full we would finally feel, how much we'd earned this meal...

The pizzas came first. They were set down in front of us and we made no comment. We simply began to eat, moaning satisfaction between mouthful deliveries.

Bren became anxious as he waited for his turn to defeat the hunger he'd been battling.

I'm hard pressed to think of a comparable expression to the one that came across Bren's face as the plate was set down in front of him. The small, unappetizing-looking portion of octopus tentacle spaghetti caused his face to contort into an ugly glare of disappointment, confusion, and rage. His eyes narrowed, his brow furrowed, and his mouth drew open slightly. He cursed enough to embarrass his three 18-year-old male companions.

When he was through, we urged him to at least give it a taste. This taste was followed by the expulsion of half-chewed octopus parts from his mouth. He then slapped his money down on the table and stormed out of the restaurant, leaving the three of us alone, with large platefuls of pizza and small stomachs devoid of any kind of nourishment. We debated going to get him and offering to share our pizza, but we were eighteen, selfish, poor, and starving, and we comforted each other out of any kind of guilt with expressions like,

"We warned him!"

"He should have asked the server," and

"If he were really that hungry he'd eat it anyhow."

I'd like to think that had it been nearer to the end of the trip the three of us would have chipped in and brought him out a pizza of his own. At that point, however, I must shamefully admit that we offered no such aid, and later found Bren outside on a park bench, sharing a dry footlong baguette sparingly with some local pigeons.

"Hey man," Paul said as we approached him. Bren looked frustrated almost to the point of tears.

"Hey," he replied, softly enough so that it sounded like "uhn."

"Dude, you know you'll be laughing about this in a few hours," I said.

Once again Bren volunteered a lengthy series of curse words.

"OK ... maybe it'll take a few days," I muttered to the others as we packed up our things and got ready to continue our ride.

Although this small town presented us with no salt mines, it did present us with some mountains on the far side. Our path grew steep enough so that at times we were coaxed off of our bikes and onto our feet. The rigorous travel, as well as the hot sun, resulted in a gradually intensifying thirst, and we were reminded of delusional desert travelers when we came across a mountaintop pub.

When we were asked to pay for our cokes with deutschemarks, we were taken aback. Brigitte had failed to mention that we would be leaving the country and traveling back into Germany that afternoon. As a result, we were not prepared, but luckily the bartender accepted Austrian currency and also helped out with some vague directions as to how we could reach the salt mines.

"I wonder if these are even the same mines that Brigitte was telling us about," Derek questioned as we left the pub squinting, and exposed ourselves to the penetrating rays of the hot sun.

"Something tells me that we'll never know," I replied. And so we continued our ride.

The hours drew on, and the sun grew larger, closer, brighter, hotter, with every push on the pedals. We began to wonder where we would be sleeping that night. The landscape was breathtaking, and it kept us in the moment and out of the approaching tide of worries and concerns.

Finally, after close to six hours since our departure, we arrived at the salt mines. From the outside, they did not appear as rewarding as we'd hoped, but this was due solely to expectations clouded by hours of arduous travel. We approached the ticket booth with a sense of pride at our accomplishment. We were smiling and walking as if we'd just woken up and found the booth next door to our bedrooms.

The satisfaction of our triumph was momentarily defeated at the clerk's greeting.

"Eight deutschemarks each," he said.

I was at the front of the line. I paused, turned to my friends, turned back to the ticket booth, took out my wallet, looked inside, looked at the ground, looked back up at the clerk with hopeful eyes, and asked as if I was asking for a day off on my first day of work at a new job, "Do you accept shillings?"

His frown offered little promise.

"No, sorry. No shillings."

I was about to follow suit with Bren's earlier display of frustration when a friendly voice with an American accent rose up from behind.

"No worries, guys," the young gentleman behind us said, "I'll take care of it for ya." He had already pulled out his wallet and was shuffling through it. We were speechless.

"No, no," said the ticket clerk. "You boys go ahead. It sounds as if you've earned it."

We thanked both of the men repeatedly, and proceeded excitedly towards the entrance of the mines.

I don't remember much about being in the salt mines. I recall being huddled around small AM-radio-quality speakers that spoke to us inaudibly in our native language throughout the tour with all of the other "English-speakers." I remember going down some wooden slides that were pretty cool. We also crossed an underwater saltwater lake in rafts. The tour was summed up with one of the few circumstances in life under which you are given a free shaker of salt. It was almost food, so we were appreciative, and may have snatched a couple of extras. Hopefully the industry is still flourishing in spite of our selfish act.

I do recall the ride home clearly: We found the highway, with the help of some tourists who were more familiar with the area, and enjoyed a two-hour, downhill ride through country sides and between mountains, as the sun dropped low in the sky and spread its warm red glow along the rocky cliffs of the mountains behind us. The breeze was warm, and my friends were there.

I have since tried unsuccessfully to recapture the splendor in drawings and stories, not unlike this one, but I find some things simply too difficult to describe with any kind of writing utensil. Some things simply have to be experienced firsthand.

Davis Bawtinheimer is a third-year commerce student at the University of Victoria, in British Columbia, Canada. He is currently running a painting business in order to save up for a trip around the world. He has always enjoyed writing and has taken some creative writing courses at the university. Davis is looking forward to the beautiful surfing that he will next enjoy in Indonesia.

The People You Meet

Salzburg, Austria

LINDA SANDS

I WAS SITTING ON A BUNK BED IN A MOUNTAINTOP HOSTEL IN Salzburg debating whether I should try to find a market in town or pay for a dinner of questionable quality right here, when I heard someone say, "Switzerland."

Eavesdropping is a great backpacker tool. It helped me choose Bruges over Brussels, convinced me to take an Amsterdam detour, and warned me about the Spaghetti Bolognese in Stuttgart. So, when I heard the girl say she was headed to Interlaken, I introduced myself as Linda from San Diego, on my way to be married in Florence. Her eyes widened in a that's-really-interesting way, said she was Debbie from British Columbia, traveling with a guy friend from work, and meeting up with her high-school pal in Turkey. Then she said, "Have you met Cynthia?" Cynthia was from the other side of Canada, Quebec, where she had some boring insurance job, made a bunch of money, then four months ago ditched it all to travel around the world — the backpacker's dream. My heroine.

Debbie said, "Cynthia's roommate, Cathy, knows the way to the Secret Beer Garden." Now, *that*, I thought, was interesting.

We found Cynthia on the patio with Dennis, Debbie's co-worker, and Spi, a young blonde dude from California. They were talking Ireland, but seemed equally intrigued with the prospect of a Secret Garden, so when Cathy stumbled from her room an hour later, we were waiting. She told us with beer breath and wild arm motions, "Yeah, I know where it is. C'mon, I'll take you."

All the way down the winding, tree-lined, mountain road into the streets of Salzburg, I never once doubted my new companions. I didn't know their last names, but I trusted them with my life. There is a bond among backpackers that people with suitcases and taxis and reservations will never understand.

When Cathy walked up the church steps, I thought she was joking, until she said, "Shhh," with one finger near her lips and swaying just a little. We looked at each other, shrugged and followed her inside the church.

The Catholic in me felt a little uneasy, like the feeling you'd get as a kid slipping out the window at midnight, or now, when you make long-distance calls on the company dime. I went last, right down the middle aisle, past kneeling nuns fingering rosary beads and the bowed heads of penitent locals. We followed Cathy behind the altar and, like some cheap detective novel, through a hidden door to a damp, yet well-lit stone staircase. The walls were cool to the touch and the steps curved away and down. I hurried to keep up, following the slap and echo of shoes hurrying toward beer. At the bottom of the stairwell was another door, faint sounds filtered through the thick wood, a deep rolling laugh, a high-pitched squeal. Cathy said, "Ready?" then pushed it open.

The first thing that hit me was the smell — pure brew. Brown-robed monks straight from a Friar Tuck book of stereotypes were laughing and hefting large ceramic steins.

From what I remember, there was more beer than garden. Sure, some plastic tables and chairs sat under a sad-looking tree, and there appeared to be a few trampled flowerbeds in the shadows, but the focus of this garden was the keg. We paid the chunky monk at the head of the table, selected a heavy stein and filled it to the brim. "Do like this," another well-fed Brother told us. So we did. We slammed our steins, "Prost!" and sloshed beer all over ourselves until the keg was spent. Then a tall, thin monk rolled out another oak barrel and the rest gets kinda fuzzy. I remember a mallet and a poky tool, and the chunky monk asking for a volunteer. I remember singing *Waltzing Matilda* and *Frere Jacques* and I remember those plastic chairs weren't all that sturdy. But mostly I remember the long dark walk back up the mountain, and how perfect Salzburg looked, like a painted movie backdrop.

In the morning, my new pals invited me to join them on The Sound of Music bus tour. I really didn't feel up to noxious fumes or the Trapp Family; instead, my plan was to really depress myself with a trip to Dachau.

When I returned that evening, we sat around the hostel with maps of Switzerland, bright orange guidebooks and cold beers.

We left in the morning. There's a lot more waiting around when you travel with a group. Not everyone eats or rests or needs a bathroom at the same time, and there's the polite open-ended questions — "Should we take this train, or. ..."

I could almost hear the groans of Austrians when they saw us coming, six young travelers in wrinkled clothes with sneakers tied to overloaded backpacks. Luckily, we found an empty compartment and were able to close the door. We talked all the way to Zurich, sang rock-n-roll with busty 15-year-old boarding-school students in Bern, and by the time we reached Interlaken, we knew who wanted to live in Florida and who had a butt-cheek tattoo.

We hiked our raggedy parade through town right up to the doors of Balmer's Hostel, past the TV room and laundry facilities to the wood-paneled dorm rooms, which separated boys and girls and required sharing three-high bunk beds. But, since we were here to play and not sleep, it didn't matter. We met up with the boys on the patio for pretzels and wine. Deb made friends with a Balmer's employee who laughed at our jokes, and after a few more glasses of wine, led us to the Hotel Interlaken for dinner.

We spent the evening going bar to bar, dance floor to dance

floor, and rearranging garden furniture in the yards we passed. By the time we flagged down the Balmer's van in the street, I was holding a Swiss license plate and speaking with an Australian accent. We could have been going home to a bed of concrete and it wouldn't have mattered. Although, I think our Spanish roommates would have disagreed. They found no humor in our late night arrival or our drunken whispers and giggles. They were all business, and Spanish curses.

The next morning, Spi and Cynthia had to leave, one to seek a rich relative, the other, a mountain. We kissed and hugged and promised to stay in touch, then Dennis, Deb, Cathy and I moved to a private room.

We hung our wet laundry from a makeshift clothesline, played poker using green beans as chips and drank red Swiss wine like water. Dennis drew tattoos on our ankles and the best mural on the bathroom wall. We swam in the freezing water of Lake Brienz, hiked the Geissbach Falls and made late night sundaes in the employee kitchen. I found the perfect dress for my wedding in a second-hand shop, and my friends pitched in to buy it. They would be at my wedding, after all.

Ten years later, we still keep in touch. Dennis is an animator in LA, Spi is a computer geek in Germany, Cathy is a married nurse living in Florida, and Deb is a single mom in B.C., looking for the perfect man. I'm still trying to find Cynthia. Last I heard, she was filming a travel documentary in a remote area of Mexico and would be unreachable for a while. She's still my hero.

Linda Sands loves travel wandering, but now limits her backpacking to trips to the grocery store with her two children, and long walks in the woods with her dog. Settled in a small Georgia town where pickup trucks and barbequed pork reign, Linda dreams of the day her family will set off with matching packs to explore Portugal, Spain and Africa. In the meantime, she tries to sit still long enough to complete her novel, Simple Intentions.

Switzerland

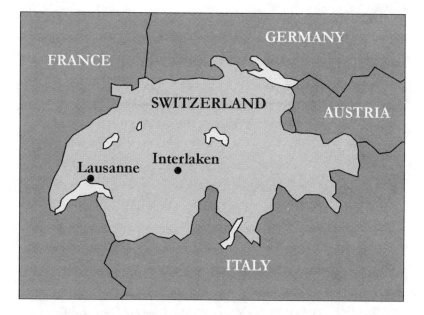

We Were Going to Kill Each Other

Interlaken, Switzerland

KASE JOHNSTUN

WE WERE GOING TO KILL EACH OTHER. BRANDON WANTED TO KILL Jason. Craig wanted to kill John. John wanted to kill Brandon. And I figure one or all of them wanted to kill me. We woke up tired this morning, just like every morning, because we never got enough sleep at night. Every night a different bed, and every morning a train to catch. This morning John was late. The morning before it was me. We usually took turns being late so things wouldn't get boring. In Berlin two weeks ago, John was late and so we missed the train to Poland. Everyone wanted to kill John that morning. This morning John was late again, and we almost missed the train to Interlaken, Switzerland. Thank God we didn't or John wouldn't be with us now.

In our separate and unique ways we were annoying. None of us shared annoying traits. We all had a patent on our own. John, as noted, was always late. He could not get out of bed, get into the shower, and get dressed in less than 45 minutes. He wouldn't wake up earlier than the rest of us. He would just promise that the next morning he would be faster. And the next morning it was the same thing. He never had a second gear. His freckled six-foot, five-inch body crept through the mornings like a toy running out of batteries.

Brandon never showered and he stunk. I would ask him why he rarely showered. He always stuck with the answer, "If I shower, then I can't sleep as long." I think he truly believed this, because I lived with him for four years before our trip, and he averaged 16 hours of sleep a day. It was a pain just to be near him at times. He gloated that he fit in more with the Europeans because they didn't

234

shower either. He was right, but I never saw that as something to gloat about.

Jason talked about his girlfriend every second of the day. Walker this and Walker that. When he returned home his phone bill was over 4,000 dollars. All it took was one beer, and we couldn't shut him up. At one point, somewhere in Eastern Europe, I would provoke him to call her just so I didn't have to hear anymore about her. Jason kind of stunk too. But more importantly, he wouldn't shut up about Walker.

Craig thought that he was smarter than everyone. No one could read a map better than he could. And no one could question his navigational skills. If someone did (me), they would get a glance of pure stupidity from Craig. That someone was usually right and internally smiled when we got lost.

I am sure they had a list of things about me that annoyed them all. I will take a shot at it now. I probably annoyed them with weight bands that I worked out with every morning in the hostel, and pushups and sit-ups on the train. I would annoy myself. I, like John, but not as severely, moved like a snail in the morning. At least I didn't stink. Well, I don't think I did. You know what they say: *Pigs don't know pigs stink*. But with this logic I couldn't have stunk, because I knew Brandon stunk.

That morning I could see it in all of our eyes. We wanted to kill each other. The train pulled into Interlaken. We jumped out and began our typical search for a place to sleep. Our options were limited since we were living on 42 dollars a day. We had to pay for shelter, eat and travel with this money. We were only halfway through our trip and we were over budget.

We spent the two previous nights playing cards in our hostel in Vienna because everything there was too expensive to enjoy. Craig and I walked down to the grocery store and bought cheese and bread for dinner. I would tear off one end of the bread and slide a piece of cheese in my mouth. I did this several times; it made it seem like there was more that way. Brandon chose Vienna to eat out. He was the most broke of us all, and he chose to eat out there. He found a Chinese buffet near our hotel. All the way to Vienna to eat Chinese buffet. He never had money when we needed to do our laundry or to tip someone, but he had it when we were eating bread and cheese.

In Interlaken we found a cheap place, 20 dollars a night, downtown. Five bunks in a small room. It was perfect. Running water and all. This was a great benefit since we spent two nights in a circus tent in Munich. We didn't sleep much those two nights because of the wooden floor. We stayed up around the campfire and swapped stories with hundreds of other backpackers. That was how we found out about Interlaken. The backpacking community is informative, friendly, and always helpful. We started our trip in Belgium and headed eastward to Eastern Europe and then downward through the eastern part of Western Europe. We planned on circling the continent and then ending back in Belgium. A lot of the packers took our same route, but many took the opposite route. Every one of them said, "You have to go to Interlaken." It wasn't on our original itinerary, but when we left the cold, rainy nights of Munich we were convinced.

The town was small and enclosed by the Alps. The tall, earthquake-born white peaks shot straight up above the little town between the two lakes. Interlaken was a tiny town with high prices. After finding our place to stay, we moved on to the second part of our ritual in a new city — finding food. Pizza 10 dollars. Beer four dollars. Everything else was 15 dollars or more. We scarfed down our pizza and beer. We ate pizza and drank beer in every town. Pizza was the cheapest food. Well, beer wasn't the cheapest drink, but it was beer. We had spent our budget for the day. We had to go to the room.

We walked back to our room under the quiet night of the Swiss sky. The lakes held us tightly in their liquid arms. The gigantic peaks hid the moon behind their marvelous faces, and high clouds hid the faces of the giant peaks behind their breath.

Brandon selfishly slid into the shower before any of us could request it. He strolled out of the shower 25 minutes later. My emotions were torn. I was happy because he finally showered, and I was pissed because he took so damn long. The rest of us took showers with cold water and a hair-clogged tub full of water.

John took off out the door in search of something. He always just took off with no warning or real known destination. In Italy he took off for a day without telling any of us, and returned with a coin from Monte Carlo. "I need a coin from every country," he would say.

"Then go to the bank in the states, dumbass," Craig would say. They loved each other deeply.

But tonight John returned with a large bucket of ice cream for us all. We were excited. We all sat down close to the ice cream. Our eyes bulged toward the treat. We hadn't had a treat like this in days. Beer and pizza. Our golden calf sat nicely in John's hands. Jason was gone down the road on the phone with Walker. The ice cream wouldn't survive until he returned. Brandon scooped in first and layered one third of the cup onto his plate. John, Craig, and I didn't feel that it was too fair, since there were four of us.

"Hey you took too much before all of us had a chance," Craig yelled.

John, knowing that Brandon worried about his weight at times muttered, "Yep, fat people tend to do that kind of stuff." Craig and I fell off our seats laughing. Brandon shrugged his shoulders and ate his load of ice cream. We continued to laugh.

"Well, John snores all night," Brandon retorted as he shoved a large scoop of ice cream in his mouth.

"I don't snore. You guys are high."

"You snore like a train."

"Yeah, but Brandon chokes in his sleep."

Jason came in the room, returning from his phone call and holding his belly. "Oh, I am gaining weight. It was Germany that did it to me. The beer was cheaper than water, and there are a lot of calories in that beer."

I took the opportunity to slam: "So, you gained twenty pounds in two days? Hah."

"Oh Kase, are you gonna use your rubber bands tonight?"

Over the last week, coalitions had started to form. Craig and Brandon ragged John behind his back. John and Jason ragged on Brandon and Craig. For some reason, I got to hear all of it.

We woke up late today, happy to stay in the same town for two nights. We jumped on a train heading up to a small town named Grutschalp. The coalitions were intact. J and J sat at one end of the train, and B and C sat on the other end. The little trolley train climbed slowly up the base of Monch. My eyes were stuck to the green feet of mountains. Their weeded phalanges tickled the ground near the train. The train scooted along the edge of Lake Thun, and the early-morning sun skied along the water, jumping each ripple on the surface. The tension between my friends was gone for a moment. I looked around the train. John was filming the scene. Jason was writing a letter to Walker. Craig and Brandon were talking about something. I returned to the lake. Lake Brienz came up quickly on the right side of the train. Eiger shaded this lake from the sun, and the base of the mountain, its trees, snow and grass were reflected in the lake. Jason wrote Walker a letter. John filmed. Brandon and Craig talked. I left.

The train slowed beside a town that stretched the length of the train. There were two shops, a restaurant, and six houses nuzzled between two cliffs of the canyon wall. Jason lit a smoke. John took off somewhere.

"Where ya going?"

"Up here to see stuff," John said.

"I could tell you what's up there without you going up there. It's a mountain," Jason said, cigarette in mouth. John was gone. Craig, with his lanky tan body and dark hair, and Brandon, with his stubby body and long greasy hair, watched John head up the hill. The four of us went into the restaurant to look at the menu. The only thing in our price range was beer and pizza, so I dug into my pack, grabbed a power bar and dipped it into peanut butter.

John came storming into the restaurant. "There's a city up the mountain we can hike to."

"Let's go," I said, peanut butter and powerbar stuck to my mouth.

"How long is it?" Jason asked with smoke in hand.

"It can't be that far."

Within moments on the trail, we lost sight of all that was human. The concrete trail ended. The dirt trail ascended in front of us until the green brush consumed it.

For a while we all stuck together, laughing, joking, planning, and bickering. As the hike went on, we started to split off from each other just like every other stop on our trip. The split usually occurred along the lines of moods and who could deal with whom on what day. But today the split appeared along the lines of lungs. The smokers were in the back, mainly Jason. Brandon didn't smoke, but he fell behind, too. Craig, John and I shot up the mountainside, stopping to let the spray from the waterfalls mist our faces and cool our backs. Brandon and Jason cursed us every time they caught us. We spent the time lying on the grass until they came, and when they hoisted their feet up the trail beside us, we jumped and took off again because we were rested.

"You bastards, slow down."

Sarcastically we responded, tone of voice whiny and shallow:

"We aren't moving fast. You're moving slow." Annoyed with us, Jason lit up another cigarette. I couldn't understand it. How could he inhale that stuff when the mountains were giving him a fresh, alive scent?

We fought the mountain — foot against face. For some of us, the trail cushioned our feet, held our legs softly against its ground, and grounded us as we slanted like the trees and the spiny blades of grass. Others, the mountain wailed on them. They battled against it, pushed on it, with anger rebelled against it. Their lungs hurt from the thin breath of the mountain sky.

I began to tire, and I could see Craig's and John's faces blushed from the wind and the stretch up the trail. We decided to stop and wait. A rock looked up at me and I at it. We became friends quickly as he hosted my rear for a moment. Sitting, gazing, wondering, dreaming, creating, drifting, resting, we lounged facing the giant Jungfrau peak that stood proudly away from us across the canyon abyss. Below us were clouds, beside us trees, and within us thoughts. As Gretel Erlich depicts, we have two landscapes — one outside of us and one within us. My landscapes were starting to join together when I heard:

"You fuckers are going way too fast." Brandon and Jason's heads bobbed in the lower distance, coming closer to us with every slow, concentrated step. Their sweat created halos below their necks, and their arms shifted unbalanced as they walked. Shift, walk, bitch, shift, walk, bitch. They came closer. They sat. They complained. We complained about their complaining. A horrid cycle. We left them again.

We climbed, angered by them, and they followed, fed up with us; the creek beside us whispered lightly as it passed the rocks on its journey downward to the pair of shining lakes.

The top came quickly for the three of us. Train tracks held the ground tightly to the earth; we skipped over them. Murren was a quiet little town: a few restaurants, hotels, and little mountain cottages scattered around its center, accompanied by miles of mountainside. The inconceivably large mountain face flattened to give Murren a place to settle, and Murren settled nicely below the rocky cliffs and above the clouds.

We waited for the other two to walk with us into the village. Jason started to laugh a little. I saw the left side of his cheek curl up like he was going to say something. And then he did. "I'm fucking quitting smoking." (He didn't.) Everyone laughed hysterically. Just when I thought it was going to get worse, it all changed. Instead of us killing each other, the mountain almost killed us. I feigned being perfectly comfortable, but I was tired, too — exhausted. We all were. On the way into Murren on the flattened train track, a song crept up out of nowhere. "Everybody cut, everybody cut."

Within moments we all were bellowing, "Kick off your Sunday shoes. Everybody cut Footloose." Our feet began to skip along the trail. Laughter filled the thin mountain air. A cable car carried tourists up to Murren, and when we were drudging up the mountain, we had discussed taking it down, resorting to the proficiencies of technology, returning to our naturally lazy tendencies; we walked right past it. We had no idea where the trail led us but we followed it.

John pulled out his video camera and we stood on the winding, descending trail, clueless to where it led. A bridge connected the two giant mountains, a bridge of light bowing above the canyon — a rainbow. Our eyes and John's camera crossed the bridge of refracted light. Our feet nailed to bumpy trail, our eyes wide and drifting, trying to capture the moment forever. An almost horizontal waterfall stretched across the side of giant Jungfrau, and my inner landscape melted into my outer landscape merging thoughts with visions, relieving stresses, joining beauty with exhilaration — melting. Silence, admiration, bonds. We stood. The green mountainside waited solemnly for us to capture it with the curve of our eyes, and it lay sturdy beneath our feet. Up high, I felt more grounded than any time on our trip. Alone, together, we stood, like vagrants feeding off the vision above the clouds. A momentary realization drifted between us, creating a rope-like bond placed in our palms and wrapped out around the rainbow.

John: "The camera just can't capture how beautiful this is."

"Painter Bob couldn't capture this," Jason said. We all used to sit around, drink, and watch Painter Bob on PBS in amazement. Now we just laughed. But Painter Bob meant something to us.

We began to run down the narrow trail. We placed each foot carefully and quickly between rock and twig. The rain started to pour heavily upon us but it didn't matter. We ran, creating tunnels between trees, whisping along side streams, and laughing at how we acted. We ran singing and chanting, darting and giggling. The hike, the view, the rainbow, the clouds, the rain, all ran with us away from the petty things we said to each other, away from the tram, away from the cold wooden floors of a Munich tent. We ran like boys, arms spread, trying to catch the wind beneath, not tempting fate like Icarus but holding fate's hand. We climbed. Not too high, but high enough to ascend above late mornings and missed trains.

Two hours later the water drifted over us. Wet from the rain, we lost all inhibitions and sat calmly in the middle of a stream. The water sifted through our fingers, ran over the slope of the rocks and then gently over the slopes of our necks.

John was late the next morning, so we missed the train. No one said a word.

Our spirits are high from the exercise and experience. It gave us what we needed to keep traveling. This line still baffles me after the story has been written and reflected on, after the words that fill in the gaps of the journal have made it to the keyboard of my computer. I sit and I wonder. What was the last line of my friends' journals? Was it as epiphanical or was it brief with no hope? I am sure their journals outline the same events, but would their story between the lines share the same memory and feeling? Even if they filled in the lines with a different tone and maybe even a different ending, I know that they could fill in the lines. There are many pages of my journal I could flip through and find the plot of a day. But I could not fill in the story as well. On this day I don't just remember timelines, but I remember moments, and my heart remembers that moment on the mountain when we all became brothers again.

Kase Johnstun is currently a staff writer for a small paper in Salt Lake City. He received a master's degree in creative writing and wrote for Consumer Choice Magazine *in Dublin. Kase backpacked Europe in '99, and has been back quite a few times. His education and employment have taken him to South America, Europe and even the Midwest.*

The Kindness of Strangers

Switzerland

RICHARD ALDERTON

WE TWO HITCHHIKERS SPED OFF THE HARD SHOULDER AND ON TO the N1, which hugs the shores of Lac Léman on its way from Geneva to Lausanne, driven by a young Arab who had stopped to give us the lift. His name was Mohammed. "Je m'appelle Richard, et mon ami s'appelle Jeanne," I ventured, my clearly anglophone tongue struggling to remember the contortions it had never mastered at school. It wasn't until several minutes later, after two junctions of nervous laughs and multi-lingual hand waving, that I noticed Mohammed carried a fourth passenger. Peering out from behind a small mountain of rucksacks and hastily manuvered shopping bags was his young daughter, Jasmina.

Mohammed explained that he had just picked up Jasmina from the airport, when he saw us on the road with our scrawled cardboard sign for Lausanne. The only reason he stopped to pick us up, he said, was that he knew no one else would.

Over the next day or so, our lifts would vary widely: the elderly widower on a 120-mile round-trip to buy apricots ("because Martigny's apricots are the sweetest in the world"); the bunch of army cadets on 36-hour leave who had me worried when they put Jean in a different car and disappeared out of sight; the Genevan artist who, on learning that I was from London, exclaimed with inexplicable delight: "Oh really? I've been to Helsinki." Then there was the Florentine businessman who hesitated a couple of seconds too long at our junction and found us, and our ice axes, sprawled across his leather seats before he could find first gear (sorry about the upholstery, mate). None of these, though, would be quite as memorable as Mohammed and Jasmina.

One never knows how much conversation is polite when hitching — some drivers stop because they want someone to talk to; others would rather get on with whatever they were doing before they picked you up — but within minutes of getting into the car, Jean and I knew we had made two friends. Mohammed was a Ph.D. student in Geneva, separated from his wife. Jasmina, it was clear, loved spending time with her dad.

Of all the nine-year-olds I have met, whom I could probably count on one hand, Jasmina was by far the oldest. Having just jetted in from Rabat, she told us of her cousins in Morocco, and corrected every grammatical *faux-pas* I dared to make. Jasmina was also learning English, and she counted to ten to prove it.

I told Jasmina and Mohammed of our plans. We were heading for the Dolomites 200 miles or so to the East, in Northern Italy, to meet a friend of ours for two weeks' climbing. We hoped to reach the Italian border before the end of the day, and Bolzano some time the next.

Somewhere along the road, the sun grew nearer to the horizon and the prospect of finding somewhere suitable to bed down for the night more distant. "You must come and eat with us," said Mohammed. Jean and I looked at each other and a quick nod was sufficient to indicate that we were both happy to take the chance; the pair didn't look like serial killers. We would love to accept their hospitality, but I was still concerned that we wouldn't find anywhere to sleep. "And they can stay at our house, can't they Dad?"

Their flat was dark, and very small, but was obviously well looked after and very homey. Jasmina set about preparing something for us to eat while Jean and I had a hushed conference in the corner of the room. What did we have to offer them in return? Food? I looked in my overstuffed rucksack and found two cheese

and pickle sandwiches and a melted bar of supermarket chocolate — an insult itself in the confectionery capital of the world,
and not exactly a fair swap for the generosity they'd shown.

We needn't have worried. Soon Jasmina had grown bored
of the kitchen and came over to join us, wide-eyed with incredu-
lity at the ridiculous amount of equipment a two-week climbing
trip necessitates. She loved my plastic mountaineering boots, like
moon boots on her, and spent the next half-hour stomping around
the apartment in them, giggling with glee every time she fell over.

We sat down to a meal of couscous and vegetable stew and
chatted, in stilted French and rather better English, about
Mohammed's life since moving to Lausanne, Jasmina's school
project, and more about our plans. Jasmina wanted to know why
we would do something so foolish as fly to Geneva when we
wanted to be in Bolzano. I had no answer to that, which seemed
to fire her imagination even more. Mohammed asked why we
weren't staying longer in Lausanne. There was a lot to see, he
said: the Gothic Cathedral, the beautiful lakeside town of
Montreux, and some breathtaking hiking — this was the Alps,
after all. Jean and I glanced at one another. The one thing we
could offer them as a thank you for their kindness would be to
stay longer, to allow our hosts to show us their town, and that
was the one thing we couldn't do — we had promised to meet
Simon on the steps of the Bolzano train station at midday the
next day. We both felt a little ungrateful at taking all of this
hospitality and offering so little in return. We would just have to
make this evening worth it. Maybe a game of travel backgammon.

No such luck. Ten minutes later, we were back in Mohammed's
car and speeding up the N1 again toward the town of Vevey, which,
if I had understood correctly, was holding some sort of festival.

This was no ordinary festival. The two-week-long *Fete des*

Vignerons is held roughly every 22 years to honor the region's wine growers. The *fete* has a long pedigree: Its history can be traced to the 13th century. Among the singing, the dancing, the street pageants and the plays, spectators also have the chance to taste a dizzying array of local wines. We had no tickets for the entertainment, but Mohammed and Jasmina led us on a walk through the town to catch the evening buzz. We passed locals in traditional dress and saw impromptu street performances. At one point we stood silent as we watched a herd of colorfully dressed cattle, reared especially for the festival, being driven past with their own musical accompaniment.

Mohammed suggested we go for a drink and waved us toward a small pavement cafe just off the main square. I was unsure. I knew that Muslims didn't drink alcohol, but was it polite for others to do so in their presence? "It's OK" he said, "have a glass if you want to — I'll just have a small coffee." I did, and had a hard job persuading him to let me pay for the round.

The next morning Jasmina brought us breakfast in bed. Coffee and croissants. We sat in dappled sunlight on the balcony for our second and third cups of coffee, but too soon it was time to leave. Having swapped e-mail addresses, we found ourselves once again in the back of Mohammed's car.

As our new friends dropped us at the end of the slip-road that would lead us, eventually, to the Dolomites, we smiled and said our profuse thank yous. I asked Mohammed where they were going to next. "I will drop Jasmina at her mother's house." He had less than a day with his daughter, and he had chosen to spend it with us. *That* was hospitality.

After two and a half years working in an office, Richard Alderton realized he needed to get out more. He has written for High *Magazine, CitiWiz and* Real World *Magazine, and, as you read this, is probably looking on the Internet for a cheap flight.*

Italy

Anticipation

Somewhere between Munich and Venice

Ben Ingram

Looking out the train window, I saw the first faint glow of morning light. It was light long in coming to one who hadn't slept all night; a dawning that made me feel as though something had been both accomplished and lost.

I was sitting on a padded seat that folded down from the corridor wall of the train. I hadn't slept since Verona. There were six of us traveling together, and, as we planned the trip at the last minute, two had had to find seats elsewhere.

After crossing the Austrian border into Italy, the porter had taken a look at our passports and tickets, and told the four of us who were together that we needed to get on a different train in Verona. We tried to SMS the other two while simultaneously finding out which train we needed to get on. When that didn't work, we tried the old-fashioned way: opening up compartments, rousing people from their sleep, and being scolded in several tongues. At this point we could see why Shakespeare set his greatest tragedy in this fair city. What could we do? The only possibility was that we had missed them while searching the train.

With only minutes before our train left for Venice, we gave up on our friends. It may seem harsh, but it was four in the morning, and we had tried our best. They had a train pass and modern communication. We would eventually meet up with them.

As we boarded our new train, downtrodden and beaten, a familiar face popped out of a compartment.

"Did you just try to SMS me?" our friend asked, yawning and rubbing her eyes. We all looked at each other. How did she end up on the right train without waking up? Soon one of us remembered that, like discontented lovers, trains in Europe often split during the night.

There were only two empty seats in the compartment, so I volunteered myself and my girlfriend to sit in the hallway. I have to confess it wasn't pure altruism on my part. We were still new to each other, and I had convinced her to come with us less than 48 hours before our departure.

Most of us were exchange students in Germany, taking advantage of a break between a language class and the start of the semester. We had stumbled onto the night train after spending the day in a certain southern German city, at that most famous of beer fests. We decided to take the night train from Munich to Venice after being told there was no way we would find a room during Oktoberfest. The trick was to drink enough Oktoberfest brew so that a seat on the train was "sleepable" (all the *couchettes* were taken), while not drinking too much to forget about the train.

After the singing and dancing and uncontrolled festivities, I wanted to be alone with my new girlfriend, even if it cost me a little comfort and sleep. She lay with her head in my lap, and I stroked her hair as I looked out into the darkness.

I have found that travel is at times most enjoyable during the periods of anticipation and memory. At that moment my head was filled with both. I thought back to my first visit to Venice, during a seven-week Eurail trip three years earlier. I traveled mostly with a friend from high school and his girlfriend. For the Italy portion they had wanted to be alone to appreciate the full romance of the place. Therefore, I had spent my time in Venice with a friendly guy from Ohio.

As the Italian countryside whisked by our train, I decided that we should find the hostel where I had stayed then. It wasn't that impressive, but it was memorable. We stayed in a large room full of bunk beds. As we rested in the warm afternoon, a cool breeze and the singing of gondoliers floated through the window.

Although Italy had impressed me enough to want to come back, I thought it would be much more powerful when romance was involved, no offense to the guy from Ohio.

To be in Venice is to be lost. In my book, staying near the train station or taking the water taxi to the San Marco Piazza should be considered poor style. Every traveler in Venice should have the experience of making a turn that they are certain leads to their destination, only to find the Grand Canal in front of them with no recognizable landmarks in sight.

As I was daydreaming I realized that we were now surrounded by water, which meant we were very close to Venice. As the sun rose, a golden, shimmering band of light streaked across the lagoon toward the train. I felt I should go wake the others, but I wanted to appreciate the moment, quiet and peaceful as it was.

Soon they would be up. Soon we would get to the station. Soon we would put our packs on our backs, making sure we didn't leave anything important. Soon we would climb down the stairs onto the platform, feeling slightly uncomfortable in our public display of grubbiness. We would try to orient ourselves. Our lives would soon be about direction and priorities. "Does anybody need a bathroom? Something to drink? Eat?" someone would say. "Let's just find our hostel first," another would plead.

But for that moment I wanted to sit and fully appreciate the smell of the sea, the feeling of the chill wind coming through the window, and the anticipation of arriving at a city that has captured the imagination of people for centuries.

Ben Ingram is finishing a M.S. in Psychology from San Diego State University. He is thankful for his memories, and continually searches for experiences worthy of anticipation.

Bums in Venice

Venice, Italy

STEVEN SIMICICH

I ARRIVED IN VENICE AFTER TWO MONTHS OF VISITING TWELVE CITIES in eight European countries. Urban similarities blurred together in my mind until I hit Venice, where I expected more car-crammed streets but instead found boat-filled canals. Venice is a picturesque dreamscape, an interactive work of art.

When my fellow travelers and I decided we had to visit this former hub of the Venetian Empire, we made a pact to do it without spending precious funds on a hotel room. In our plan, we would arrive at noon in Venice, party through the night and leave on next morning's six o'clock train. We were confident in our ability to entertain ourselves because we had made marathon nights commonplace on this trip.

Our first priority was to stow our backpacks at the train station. The information-desk person informed us about a long-term luggage checkroom, but knowing that no guards would be watching our bags, I proceeded to sift through my backpack for precious cargo. Call it my "New York City mindset." I prioritized my possessions in a separate little knapsack. All the essentials I needed to return home — passport, credit card, plane tickets, rail pass, and money — were already in there. I added to them my camera, 15 irreplaceable rolls of used film and my contact lenses. Bringing my camera and securing my eyesight were obvious, since I was in the most photographed city in the world. Now the luggage attendants could incinerate my entire backpack, and I would still be able to leave this city safely and at ease.

As we exited the *Santa Lucia* train station, passengers were boarding a waterbus nearby. I couldn't help but admire these locals. They strolled through their neighborhoods without ever expecting cars to turn the corner before them. Walking past street vendors, I saw intricately decorated *Carnevale* masks for the ten-day celebration before Ash Wednesday. I thought about feasting and remembered that we hadn't eaten during the whole nine-hour train ride.

My friends and I immediately searched for a restaurant in the *Cannaregio* district. Hunger wasn't the only motivation. People-watching with an available bathroom close by was appealing, too. We quickly choose a prix fix menu in our budget and were seated. My choices were *antipasto di pesce* (assorted fish appetizer), *spaghetti al vongole* (pasta with fresh clams and spicy vegetables), and *insalate tre colore* (three-color salad). Immediately after ordering, I took advantage of the men's room to wash my face and hands, put in my contacts and brush my hair. My antipasto was waiting as I exited the restroom, reborn.

The meal provided nourishment for the rest of the day, and cost only ten American dollars after tip. The ambiance was grand, enjoying my fresh plate of pasta as I watched gondoliers row past. The only item that would have made this moment more perfect was a loved one sitting across from me. This was the reason we left ourselves such a small window of time to see Venice: My friends and I anticipated that we'd find it frustrating to stay more than a day in such a romantic city without a wife, girlfriend, or even some woman we met on the train. When I'm asked whether I took a gondola ride, I explain this. My friends and I didn't take horse-and-buggy rides across Central Park, so we sure as hell weren't going to board a gondola together.

After the delicious three-course meal, we headed for the *Piazza di San Marco*. Our waiter offered directions, but I couldn't keep up. My mind drifted as he spoke, and before I realized it we had walked away. Finding a waterbus stop and figuring out which boat to take was relatively simple. These *vaporetti* are the only form of public transportation. This poor man's gondola ride costs 3 euro, and operates all day. All aboard, we properly observed Venice's breathtaking grandeur as the boat made all local stops.

The city consists of 118 bodies of land, varying in shape and size, crisscrossed with mazes of narrow winding streets. The one exception is the wide-open *Piazza di San Marco,* which is the only official piazza. The confusion induced from touring this town is contrasted with this glorious spread of radiance and space. Dominating the piazza is the recently renovated *Basilica di San Marco,* whose fusions of 13th-century Byzantine and 16th-century Renaissance architectural styles and interior mosaics embodies Venice's historic linking of east and west.

The *Piazza di San Marco* was once a bustling epicenter of international commerce. Now it is a beehive for tourists. My friends and I made our way through the massive, camera-touting crowds. At every turn, pigeons were eating from travelers' outstretched hands, and I, for one, didn't share their desire to imitate a bronze statute. New York or Venice, to me they were still filthy pigeons. We stumbled upon the *Basilica di Santa Maria dei Frari.* (St. Mary of the Friars), a Renaissance church that housed stunning works by Titian, and the tomb of the master himself. Soft, angelic music played as we walked around inside.

Then we went shopping to supply the next leg of our journey. The 6 a.m. train we planned to catch was headed for the southern Italian port city of Brindisi, from which we'd board a ship to Corfu, Greece. At a nearby grocery store, we found three plastic gallon jugs of wine for $5 American each. Such a cost-effective purchase! But now we had to carry them around until we caught our train.

We continued our wandering, sitting near some docks of the *Canale di San Marco* and resting as enormous cumulous clouds drifted by overhead. We could see the *Isola di San Giorgio Maggiore,* and in the water beyond, replica Renaissance ships and high-powered speed-boats. This meshing of past and present was breathtaking, and we reflected on our last months of traveling as the sunset began.

Night settled and the sea winds increased. We started to make our way back toward the train station, and settled on the stairs of the *Ponte Scalzi* (the Scalzi bridge) to watch people and take in the atmosphere. A crescent moon showed between the clouds as street performers gathered audiences. One middle-aged hippie playing an amazing version of Stairway to Heaven.

We spotted a group of three cute females sitting by themselves. A single giant light bulb went on over our heads. Maybe we could find a little shelter before our train. Conversation began rather smoothly as all six of us circled around. They were from California, and touring Italy for the summer. The surfer girl nearest me was named Wendy. She had medium-cut platinum hair, crystal blue eyes and smooth bronze skin. All of us sat and spoke for hours before the topic of sleep arose. They felt sympathetic about our plight and invited us to hang out in their room. Everything seemed to fall together perfectly as we made our way to the hotel. Then it started to drizzle.

The rain had increased by the time we reached the hotel's block. Wendy told us to wait as she went ahead and checked the lobby. I sensed the ease of this situation turning and we learned the catch: The hotel didn't allow visitors. In hindsight we should have just walked with them like fellow guests, but I offered to speak to the man working the front desk. My Italian had gotten better on this trip, and I enjoyed showing it off. The three girls walked toward the stairs and I approached the desk to explain our situation. As soon as he realized I didn't have a room, the man began yelling. My friends and I were rushed out, left standing under the girls' third-story window. Wendy appeared and waved goodbye, closing the shades. As if on cue from a film director, thunder clapped and the rain turned into a downpour.

We scurried in the cold rain, finding that most establishments had closed. Anything still open was in the process of dying out and would require money anyway. It was time to admit defeat and head for the train station waiting room. The walk was quick as all three of us vented about the possibilities halted at that front desk. Approaching the station, we noticed people sitting on the sidewalk near the doors. Chains were wrapped around the handles, and a sign said that the train station was locked until 4:30 a.m. At this moment, we fully realized the stupidity of my attempted courtesy at the hotel. We decided we had no other option than to sit out of the rain near the doors.

Then, I remembered our wine. I poured three glasses of red and proposed a toast to our destitute state. Then yet again another stupid maneuver became apparent. A chain reaction of disheveled faces began looking in our direction. We realized we were surrounded by homeless people and had just revealed our supply of alcohol. One man rolled toward us in a wheelchair. He had no legs, and he smelled worse than burning rubber tires. He began mumbling to us, calmly dumped his begged change onto his lap and extended his paper cup to me. Words weren't needed. I gently filled his cup and watched a smile appear. The sound of that sweet elixir pouring seemed better to him than any clink of coins. I was taken by this warm moment, but the stench kicked me back to reality. We realized he wouldn't leave us, which meant it was time for us to venture back into the rain.

We said goodbye to our foul-smelling friend and walked down the stairs. Quickly surveying the situation, my friends and I saw that the only available shelter was the nearby waterbus station where we had stood earlier. Under its covering, we were relieved to be out of the rain, but becoming increasingly aware of the wind. Noticing an empty ticket counter, we each squeezed into a separate compartment. Desperately looking at our watches, we realized it was still hours before the station would open. As I sat there, with my body contorted to avoid the elements, gulping cheap red wine for warmth, something occurred to me. Most tourists leave this city with memories of being consumed by pigeons in *Piazza di San Marco,* and enjoying romantic gondola rides through the vast network of canals. I, on the other hand, experienced Venice's sunny splendor by day like a well-healed tourist — I had the roll of film to prove it. Now, by night, I was seeing it like a bum. What I'll always remember is, concrete isn't nearly as comfortable as a restaurant chair.

Steven Simicich graduated from S.U.N.Y. Albany in 2000 with a B.A. in Political Science and Communication. He has spent two summer's backpacking around Europe, visiting twenty cities in ten countries. Steven is a recent graduate of St. John's University Law School and plans to pursue his writing along side a legal career, and hopes to one-day work in Italy.

The San Lorenzo Market

Florence, Italy

CHRISTOPHER FELTON

IT ALL BEGAN, OF COURSE, WITH THE STORIES. STORIES OF LEATHER shops surrounding entire squares — stories from parents about the affordability — and of course stories of the loquacious, charming, pestering men and women who sell their goods.

I knew once I hit Florence that I would be on the lookout for the perfect leather jacket at the perfect price – but what I didn't truly realize was the effort it would take.

Young people in America have grown up in such a commercialized consumer market, we've been completely deprived of the old-world way of acquiring goods. When we go to the mall and see a price on something we want, we know that price is the price we must pay to obtain our dearly beloved. But Europe and most other countries are less rigid regarding purchases, and they have developed a sort of bohemian avant-garde means of bargaining and interaction that has grown more and more popular with Americans seeking the ultimate travel experiences.

And such was the case with me, as I meandered through the leather district after a day with Leonardo, Tiziano, and Sandro exploring gods and goddesses of antiquity. This labyrinthine locale deep in the heart of Florence can feel a bit overwhelming. All of the shops appear identical, but the siren songs of the ultimate deal lure you into nearly each and every one. The problem, however, is that once you are inside, you become center stage for the salesmen — and they won't let you go without a fight.

As a result I chose to start out speaking very little, and only in broken Japanese that I hoped they wouldn't understand. It worked — I soon found myself popping in and out of different stores, viewing everything with much less aggravation than some of my comrades.

It didn't take long, though, to find something I liked. Allow me to set the scene:

...Inside, the smell of leather — well, outside, the smell of leather too, but more so once you step in. Lingering in the back is a dark figure on the phone carrying a Corleone-esque shadow. Around him, two worker bees eagerly anticipating any customer entering the shop. I am immediately approached by a slender Italian salesman who is a tourist veteran. He knows what I'm going to say, and I know what he is going to say.

"I ave di perfect jacket for chu. Lemme show you dis one over ere. Yeeees it look purfect. You gotta get dis one. Nobody in America ave dis one. I tellju Armani bring dis style out in two-three month."

This time, I've already heard anything and everything a salesman may use, so I brush him off and continue to peruse the shop. He persists: "So tell me ... 'ow much you willing to spend?"

Now I highly recommend having an answer to this question, or feel the oncoming pressure of making a split-second decision.

"Me?" I say innocently. "Well, I'm not sure. I'm just lookin' around."

It doesn't impede him; he continues to bring me jackets from all over the store, some chic, some burly, others plain ugly, and all in varying colors. Finally I feel it's time to give the guy a little help. I tell him I'm looking for a black leather one that hits just below the hips and isn't too heavy. He pauses for a moment, not long enough to breathe, and races around the store picking up more jackets. I narrow it down to two coats, both similar, but one a little softer and a little smoother, and naturally, pricier.

So here comes the fun.

Me: "Well, I'm interested in both jackets. They both have the look that I like, but this one is more expensive. Can you tell me why I should even consider it?"

He looks at me annoyed. Like I've insulted his intelligence more than anyone ever has before.

Him: "C'mon man you gotta look at dis one closely and you can tell ees a much bedder quality." Look at dat steetching on de arm and shoulder. Feel dis material ees a much smoother to feel."

I proceed to feel and examine, knowing already this is the one I want. I remain outwardly stubborn, though, and continue to appear hesitant to buy it.

Suddenly he whips out a lighter from his pocket and brings it up to the sleeve of the jacket.

"Look at dis. Look dis jacket is smooth but is also water-proof, and look at dis…" He proceeds to ignite the flame and hold it against the jacket for a good 4 seconds. "…man! Ees a fireproof also. This the best quality jacket I got in dis place."

True or not, I am bound to get this jacket. So I tell him I like it, which means, "Ring it up."

As he walks to the register, I follow him and add that I think it is too expensive. He freezes (and I can just imagine his dis-gruntled face), turns around and tries to shake me a bit with some more salesmanship. It doesn't work; I know there is no way I'm about to spend 300 euro. He knows it, too, and drops the price to 200 euro without much angst.

Now, 200 euro — not a bad price for a quality leather jacket in the U.S. But I feel I can squeeze a little more out of him, so I say no thanks and start to walk away.

"Ey man I think you like a dis one?" questioning my desire for the jacket.

I brush him off and tell him I like it, but I'm sure I can find another one somewhere else for a better price. So once again he counters with that sure-fire question:

"So you gotta tell me 'ow much you wanna spend?"

I tell him now that 150 euro is the most I'm willing to go.

"Aww, amico, 150 euro? I doan know if mi capo can let mi give you dis one for 300."

I say 150 is all I'm willing to do as I drift closer and closer to the front exit. He becomes nervous and excited all at once, spins to the back and stomps heavily to the rear of the shop, where the capo sits ear-to-phone mumbling Italian lingo.

A pensive second and quick nod affirm the price as the salesman rushes back to me, offering congratulations on such an amazing jacket and indefatigably relaying how lucky I am to get *this* jacket at such a low price. I smile and brush it off, following closely behind him to the counter. The deal was closed …

… or so I thought.

In America, we get so accustomed to using credit cards, we seldom carry around ample cash. But in order to use an American credit card, a small charge is applied to the vendor, and after such laborious bargaining, my salesbee is not in the mood to see me whip out my gold VISA. His smile flips to frown.

"Amico, you gotta use cash in here for d'price mi capo ees a givin' you. You know if we take di card from you, we lose money."

I look back at him slyly and wait a moment before I respond, even though I know there is no way I'm going to use cash to cover the full 150 euro. I may feel a little sorry for the guy because he's spent a good deal of time with me and in his mind he's made the sale, but I simply do not have the cash on me to pay him, so I say so, hoping it'll slide.

Unfortunately, he is quite reluctant and tells me I have to up it to about 160 euro in order to use my plastic.

Now, normally I wouldn't really mind, seeing as it's only 10 bucks, but I am so proud of my bargaining job, I didn't want to ease up and let him have the upper hand. So I get tough again, and tell him it's 150 euro on the card or I'm leaving. He looks back at me and says he can't do it, so I turn around and head out the door.

I had had it. It was in my hands, it was on my shoulders. It smelled amazing, felt even better and at a price Americans in America would adore. But I didn't take it over a measly 10 euro! What was I thinking?

"I totally should have gotten tha—" my line of thought is interrupted by my salesbee tapping on my shoulder.

Slightly short of breath but glowing nonetheless, he looks up at me with a smile.

"Mi capo ees being a very strange tuday but he says I geeve you dis jacket for di 150 euro on credit card. Me? I think hees a goin a little crazy, but I know juws gonna love dis jacket so I think ees a okay for me to give you dis price."

I was surprised, to say the least, but beamed from the inside after my moment's hesitation turned out for the best.

I still wear that jacket and love it because of its feel and smell, but more so for the story I can tell behind its purchase.

So go to Italy. And go to Florence. And plan on getting a leather jacket.

Christopher S. Felton was born in Pasadena, California, and attended Flintridge Preparatory School before attending Vassar College in New York. He graduated with a bachelor's in film in 2002. He currently lives in Japan, teaching English.

Il Palio

Siena, Italy

CHELSEA BAUCH

It is a celebration of centuries-old rivalry and ageless pride, of tradition and honor. It is a testament to social virtues and social failings, religion and ritual. It is the Italian character and the universal spirit, all building, twice each summer, to the rush of ten bareback riders frantically racing around a lopsided dirt track.

Il Palio draws locals and tourists from around the world to Siena, Italy, for its July 2 and August 16 festivals and horse races, held in honor of the Virgin Mary. This medieval-style celebration dates from the 13th century, when horse races were common in towns throughout Italy. It is named for the *palio*, a banner or cloth that is awarded to the *contrada* (neighborhood) whose horse wins the race.

Over the years, *Il Palio* has become the symbol of the city of Siena itself, of the race and of the celebrations and rituals surrounding it. Much more than a horserace, *Il Palio* pits Siena's seventeen *contrade* in fierce competition against each other. Each spends weeks on preparation, staging elaborate festivities and a final, wild horserace around the dirt-paved *Piazza del Campo* in the center of town. The local rivalries have become legendary, and an elaborate web of bribery is standard. Although the race itself is achingly brief — less than three minutes — and the related festivities last only a few weeks, the spirit of the *Palio* is ever present in Siena.

I came down from Florence the week before the race, drawn by stories of these events. From my arrival, I found myself caught up in the momentum of a city in excited anticipation, preparing for grand events. Everywhere, people displayed scarves bearing the colors and emblem that represented their *contrada*. I lost myself in the sloping, labyrinth-like cobblestone streets, watched people gather in excited parades and start impatient fights. In the midst of all this, I also felt something else — an intense expectation, as if everyone in Siena was awaiting something, but what, I couldn't yet tell.

On the afternoon that I arrived, I walked down to the city's main square, *Piazza del Campo*, and watched workmen bringing in soil to surface what would become the racetrack. I sat in front of a restaurant and watched trucks dump load after load of soft, brown dirt. In only a few hours the square would be filled with eager Sienese, coming to joyfully begin the ritual *pestare la terra*, literally, to tread the earth. For now, the square was almost peaceful with its newly laid soil.

In a city of fewer than 60,000, people identify first with their *contrada* and second with Siena. This may also have originated in the Middle Ages, a period characterized by deeply rooted rivalries, violence, treachery, and deceit, when one depended more on one's close family and neighbors than on the nobles and administrators of the city. At points in Siena's history, there may have been as many as forty different *contrade*, but the Sienese rulers designated the current seventeen by geographic boundary decrees in 1729. Each *contrada* is considered to be an independent city-state, complete with its own flag, seat of government, constitution, church, museum, saint, emblem and colors, and animal totem, including *Istrice*, the porcupine, *Aquila*, the two-headed eagle, *Bruco*, the caterpillar, *Pantera*, the panther, *Oca*, the goose, and *Leocorno*, the unicorn.

The fierce loyalty and exclusivity that accompany residence in a neighborhood is extraordinary. When one *contrada* wins the horse race, for example, its traditional rival is considered to have lost, even if it did not compete. So, should *Aquila* win the *Palio,* then its traditional rival *Pantera* is considered the loser, even if its horse did not run the race. A person is born into a *contrada*. Even after decades of living there, without the proper birth claim one is not considered a true member of the neighborhood. Immigration into a *contrada*, until modern times, was unheard of. Husbands in "mixed marriages" were even known to carry their laboring wives across neighborhood boundaries to secure *contrada* citizenship for their newborn children.

Understandably, the selection of horses and jockeys for *Il Palio* is complex. Only ten of the city's seventeen *contrade* compete in each event. Of those ten, seven will be ones that did not compete in the previous race, and the remaining three will be decided by a lottery held three weeks before the race. The horses are then irrevocably assigned to each competing *contrada* by a lottery. It is when these ten competitors have been determined that the intricate diplomacy of the *Palio* truly begins.

Once chosen, the *contrada*'s horse is guarded 24 hours a day by strong young men of the neighborhood. Drugging, kidnapping and even maiming of horses are not unknown. The main reason is that the winner of the race is the *contrada*'s horse, not its rider. Jockeys are often thrown, by horses or body blocks from other jockeys, so all bets lie on the neighborhood's horse. On the Sunday before the race, the devout lead the horse into church for the priest's blessing. The ruthlessness of these extremes evokes the bloody vendettas of past centuries between rival *contrade*. The *Palio* is, after all, a form of ritualized warfare, a ceremonial focal point for the rivalries, aggression, and emotion between the city's neighborhoods.

Bribery is also deeply embedded in the contest: the *contrada* is free to select its own jockey, or *fantino,* but to confound the oppositions' attempts to subvert its champion, a *contrada* may hire several jockeys, and a *fantino* may compete for rival *contrada* from one *Palio* to the next. Deals are made among *contrade*, jockeys and individual patrons in an elaborate web spun to secure the *fantino*'s ultimate loyalty during the race.

Three days before the race, the first of six *prova*, or trial races, is held. I stood pressed against the fence to watch them at the *Piazza del Campo*, surrounded by other eager spectators. The center of the square had been fenced off as a place for public viewing, while the perimeter of the track was reserved for paid seating in stands called *palchi*. The anthems and chants of various *contrade* suddenly burst from all around me, inharmoniously competing with one another and happily contributing to a general cacophony. The air pulsed with song and excitement.

The day after the first *prova*, a parade of ornately costumed figures from each *contrada* climbed their way up the streets from the main square to *Santa Maria di Provenzano* where the *palio*, the banner, was blessed. The area surrounding the church was too crowded, so I watched the procession pass by before wandering back through the city. Within a few minutes, I heard drumming ahead of me. As I came around a corner I saw a small square where three young men in pale blue costumes stood laughing. The first had a drum strapped around his chest and two drumsticks in his hands. The other two held large flags, depicting the crown-wearing dolphin of the *Onda contrada*, the neighborhood of the wave. Standing just out of sight, I watched as the three practiced an elaborate routine. The first man began a steady beat on his drum as the two others effortlessly fell into a synchronized routine of tosses, leaps, and waving with their banners. After countless attempts, the trio was finally satisfied, and breathing heavily from the exertion, they happily left the square.

The day of the race I hurried to the center of the *Campo* to find a place to watch. I had been warned that the square would be hot, crowded, and unpleasant. It was hot and crowded, but the view and the energy made it far form unpleasant. Before long, I could hear the distant drums, chants, and cheers of the *corteo storico*, the historic procession, as it made its way down from Siena's main cathedral, the *Duomo*. Medieval-costumed men and women in brilliantly colored and patterned clothing soon entered the *piazza*, mingling in a loud and colorful parade. As the pale blue and white *ondaioli* passed by, I saw the drummer and the two flag bearing *alfieri* whom I had watched two days earlier. Their performance was flawless, and as they proudly grinned at one another during the applause, I secretly shared their joy.

Twilight brought an end to the parade; the crowd pulsed with energy and expectation. The air hummed, as though the city was waiting in suspense. Suddenly the doors of the *cortile*, where the horses and jockeys were eagerly waiting, opened. After several attempts to properly assemble nine prancing horses and their nervous jockeys, the tenth horse, known as the *rincorsa*, was signaled to start the race.

They were gone before I could even see the lineup. The crowd spun, dragging me along, as the horses tore through the first of three laps around the *Campo*. A yell went up at the bend of *San Martino*, notoriously the most perilous turn of the race. A jockey fell from his horse, but I could not see which it had been. Again the horses sped past me, beginning their second lap. I tried to watch but saw only a fleeting mass of color and hooves. The intensity of the crowd reached a feverish pitch as the horses came around for their final lap. I pushed forward so that I could watch the finish. The crowd yielded for a moment and I was suddenly pinned against the barricade, trapped beneath centuries of expectation. The horses sprinted toward the finish line and for a moment I held my breath, without knowing why.

At the last moment I saw the green and white flash of *Oca*, the goose, gallop into the lead. The crowd lost all control, but amidst the chaos it felt oppressively silent, too. I dared not breathe. The once ubiquitous anticipation dissipated, the hum subsided; the expectation could no longer sustain itself. As the emblem of the crowned goose finally crossed the finish line, it seemed as though the entire city finally let out its breath.

Born and raised in Northern California, Chelsea Bauch now lives in New York City, where she is a student at NYU and continues her writing. She is interested in studying human migration, from pilgrims to immigrants, to better understand her own itchy feet.

The City of Beautiful Towers

San Gimignano, Italy

Maria Ivkovic

Jennie and I left the bus stop in San Gimignano with no clue of the beauty beyond the stone walls. We went there on a whim, eager to go anywhere but Florence, Venice, and Rome, cities that in June were too packed with tourists, lines, cramped hostels, and the stress that we had originally wanted to escape when planning our summer. We picked a city that neither of us had heard of, reasoning that if nobody else had heard of it either, it would be fairly empty of tourists. As soon as we passed through its stone-arch entrance, I realized we had discovered a magical place.

San Gimignano is one of the United Nation's World Heritage Sites, an ancient town perched atop a hill in the Elsa Valley of Tuscany. The city, often referred to as "San Gimignano delle belle Torri," is a city "of beautiful towers" built by patrician families in the 11th and 13th centuries. The families who controlled the city built some 72 tower-houses (up to 50 meters tall) as symbols of their wealth and power. Only 14 have survived, but the city has retained its feudal appearance. To a limited extent, tourism had reached this old town — the occasional shop features San Gimignano T-shirts and postcards of the famous towers. However, the old charm of the city remains untouched.

Walking down the narrow cobblestone streets, I reached out my hand to touch the stone walls, smooth and slick like sea-glass, on either side of me. Jennie and I followed the Via San Giovanni past the black-and-white-striped façade of a monastery turned wine cellar. One magnificent plaza led us to another, past gothic stone arches. In the main square, the Piazza della Cisterna, named after its moss-covered well, we caught sight of the main cathedral, pigeons circling the sky above. Flowers sprang up everywhere — in ceramic pots in windows; between the cracks of stone.

Our first stop in this central piazza was the tourist office, which, we were told, could find us a room. Jennie approached the man behind the desk, who was sitting at the computer, playing a computer game. He had a boy's face, a playfully mischievous air, even though he was an older man. When he looked at Jennie, his face lit up. She is a beautiful woman, with a small ballerina build and big blue eyes also filled with mischief, should the right person present himself to her.

"So you come here for a room?" His Italian accent had a jovial, staccato quality.

"Yes, can you help us find one?"

"Of course! Come with me; I have just the room for you."

Surprised by the ease of this exchange, and by the cheap price he stated en route to the room, Jennie and I were a bit nervous about how the room would look. After all, our latest hostel experience in Florence was twice as expensive and extremely dirty, with a blue neon light flickering annoyingly into the room.

He took us into a quaint stone building sitting in the corner of yet another plaza. As soon as he shut the door behind us, I was overcome by the welcome coolness that rushed over us. The old stone provided natural air conditioning. We climbed a short flight of steps to the door of our room. When he pushed the door open, Jennie and I let out a soft gasp of surprise. The room was rustically romantic, like an ad from *Country Living* magazine. The bed sat on an ornate stand of wrought iron, its sheets a pristine pink, and a large window looked out onto a quiet street. Fresh flowers adorned a small table in the corner. Soft jazz music hovered in the air, rising from the classy, quiet bar in the narrow street below.

Jennie and I chuckled when we looked at each other. The room was very romantic; it would have been a couple's paradise, a honeymoon suite.

The jovial man introduced himself as Mauricio. His English was very poor, but he energetically persisted in speaking to us, asking if the room was adequate and if we would accompany him back to the tourist office so that we could give him our passports.

There was no question about our opinion of the room. It was godsend, a respite from the stream of bad luck with hostels elsewhere in Italy. Back at the tourist office, Mauricio introduced us to a good-looking, slender man named Davide, who was, unlike Mauricio, wearing a tourist office pin on his shirt. Davide's black hair was cut very short, and his green eyes contrasted with his tanned olive skin. He laughed as soon as Mauricio entered the room, and it occurred to me that they looked more like friends than coworkers.

Mauricio asked Davide to take care of our paperwork as he dramatically put on his sunglasses and opened the door to leave. "And Davide, show them the tower tomorrow. You have my keys."

Jen and I had wanted to spend the next day quietly contemplating and writing in our journals. But we were intrigued by the tower and would have felt rude turning down the offer for a personal tour by the very friendly San Gimignano tourist office. Besides, we figured the tour would not take too long.

I woke up the next morning to the happy chirping of birds. For the first time during our trip in Italy, I felt fully rested, having slept quietly and soundly in a comfortable bed. Jennie was already gone. She left a note on the table informing me that she was out by the cathedral steps, writing in her journal. When I found her, she was chatting with Davide, who was animatedly pointing over to one of San Gimignano's towers.

"Ah, you come finally, sleepyhead! I was just telling Jennie which tower I was going to take you to."

Jennie was laughing as he said this. She and I were both rather amused and surprised by the eagerness of our Italian hosts. We were used to the guarded private lives of our fellow Americans, and in truth were most comfortable guarding our own personal space, wary of strangers. At that moment, I was uncomfortably aware of our cultural differences. Mauricio was absent at that moment, but I thought of him then. At his old age, he maintained a more youthful and carefree approach to life than I had in my early twenties.

Davide led us through a few stone arches to the plaza beside which the tower stood. Many of the towers are not accessible by the public, and this was one of them, privately owned.

Davide dramatically took a set of keys from out of his pocket and jangled them around until he found the one that would let us in. In my periphery I caught sight of a small American tourist group about to enter one of the public towers. A woman in the group yelled after us: "Why do THEY get to go up in that tower?"

I was embarrassed by this loud question, and yet I couldn't help but wonder the same.

Upon passing through the doorway of the tower, I again felt the coolness of the stone space. We entered a small room, the bottom portion of the tower. Immediately to our right was a spiral staircase that led up to the next level. Davide led the way upward through the tower, and I couldn't believe my eyes as we went. I felt as if Jennie and I had stumbled onto the set of an old James bond movie, passing luxurious rooms as we climbed upward — a small bedroom, a living room with couches and a television set, a kitchen with modern amenities and futuristic décor. The kitchen even had impressive natural lighting coming through the narrow slit window in the stone tower. We paused there, and I noticed that Davide had worked up a considerable sweat. However, ever the enthusiastic host, he kept pushing upward through the tower. When we got to the top, Davide punched a code into a panel on the wall. Jennie and I stood back, amazed, as a glass panel in the ceiling moved aside. We continued to climb the stairs until we stepped into the bright daylight, on top of this private tower in San Gimignano. The view was spectacular. Jennie and I were the spoiled voyeurs, blessed with a panorama that I could have only dreamed of. All around us was the soft green of the Tuscan countryside. Wildflowers dotted the divine canvas, and the other towers stood nearby. As a subtle breeze kissed my face, I thought for a moment that this was heaven. I couldn't shake the feeling that this beauty had a surreal quality to it, that a fairy-tale landscape extending as far as the eye could see could not be real. This natural splendor reminded me of a few lines from a Wordsworth poem: "Enough of Science and of Art; close up those barren leaves. ... Come forth into the light of things, let nature be your teacher." My last four years had been spent at an Ivy League school. Most of my time there involved pouring over such barren leaves. And while I valued my education, I realized then that I had missed the intoxication provided by a breeze and a view.

Davide's energetic voice interrupted my introspection: "Can I get you ladies an espresso? Cappuccino? We go back down the tower, to the main square, and we sit in Mauricio's café."

Though it was difficult for us to leave the view, several minutes later we were sitting in the plaza below, under the shade of a sun umbrella, sipping cappuccinos and watching passerbys. Davide asked us questions about our studies, about our social lives.

"Do you like Italy?" he asked.

"Yes, especially San Gimignano," I replied sincerely.

"Mauricio likes to meet nice young people like you, to show

them our beautiful city. He is a good friend for you to have here
— he knows everybody and owns the tourist office and many of
the cafes."

"Does he own that tower as well?"

"Well, to be honest, I'm not sure. But I wouldn't be surprised. You see, Mauricio's family has been here for centuries,
perhaps the oldest family in San Gimignano."

As Davide paused to take a sip of his cappuccino, we heard
Mauricio call out to us:

"Davide! You talk to Jennie and her friend!"

He promptly joined us, filled with energy, smiling from ear
to ear. Davide turned to him and said: "Mauricio, I was just telling them that your family has been here for centuries and owns
much of the city." Mauricio did not understand what Davide
was saying to him, and so they lapsed into Italian.

Davide translated for Mauricio: "Mauricio says his family
has been here since 1355. He says he could never, never imagine
leaving." To this, Mauricio shook his head, looking at Jennie.

"Jennie, Jennie — do you have a boyfriend?"

Jennie and I both laughed at this question, amused by the
forwardness of our new friend. Jennie's face flushed as she
shrugged her shoulders; I knew that she was flattered by Mauricio's
attention.

While Davide was finishing up his cappuccino, he asked us
what our plans were for the day.

"Well, we would like to visit nearby Siena. We've read that
the architects who built this city were schooled there."

At this Mauricio's face broke into yet another grin. "Davide
and I will take you there. The bus, it is no fun."

Still rather reluctant to spend so much time with strangers, I
hesitated. So did Jennie, who was somewhat alarmed by Mauricio's
transparent attraction to her. And yet we could not say no to

Mauricio's excited expression when he offered to personally take us to Siena. Before we knew it, we were in his little European car, speeding across the Tuscan countryside, through fields of sunflowers. Mauricio had offered Jennie the front passenger seat; I was in back with Davide, peering out the window at the scenes around me. Confused by Mauricio's decision not to take the highway to Siena, and aware of the remoteness in which we were finding ourselves, I started to panic, wondering if I was wrong to let my guard down with these strangers. There were no signs of Siena — just flowers, fields and the blue sky. I stared at the back of Jennie's head, wishing Davide didn't understand English so that we could discuss an escape plan.

Suddenly Mauricio pointed up at a small plane landing nearby. The car rounded a bend in the road, and into our view came a large garage sheltering a variety of four-seater planes.

"We are here. Bonjourno, Flying Club of Tuscany! I take you up in my plane!"

Alarmed by the prospect of putting my life in the hands of Mauricio, and annoyed at his executive decision not to take us to Sienna, I told him that I didn't want to go. Besides, I had been up in a Piper plane once before, and distinctly remembered suffering severe motion sickness. Still, I was intrigued — I wondered if there was anything this man didn't do.

Jennie persuaded me to come onto the plane. I discovered then that Jennie was more of a risk-taker than I; she had a twinkle in her eye at this adventure ahead, and didn't seem at all bothered by the idea of letting Mauricio take us into the sky.

Again, Davide and I sat in the two back seats, with Jennie and Mauricio in front. I felt that Davide and I were officially Mauricio's and Jennie's respective sidekicks, in the back, along for the ride, and yet inevitably part of it.

I rolled my eyes at the flimsy seatbelts, not bothering to put mine on. Davide tightened his across his lap, a horrified expression on his face. My mistrust or paranoia about these assertive strangers dissolved as I looked at him, also terrified. The engine sputtered and roared, Mauricio flicked a couple of switches, and suddenly we were up in the air, soaring over Tuscany. Mauricio energetically told us about his love for flying, with Davide interpreting from time to time. Jennie, her eyes still sparkling, asked Mauricio if she could take over the controls of the plane. Davide looked sick as he translated this for Mauricio, who dramatically reached over and kissed her forehead. "Of course you can, Jennie! You can do anything, Jennie!"

The countryside of Tuscany was stunningly vivid from our height. I felt we were flying through a fairy tale, and Mauricio's words echoed through my head: "You can do anything!" I had a feeling that Mauricio approached life that way, embracing every opportunity to experience adventure, including welcoming strangers into his life. Though I may not have realized it then, I decided up there in the plane over Tuscany that I would try to live my life more like Mauricio.

Jennie was in control of the plane, which started fluctuating in altitude, making me feel sick. Davide was clutching his stomach and grimacing, beads of sweat on his upper lip. He gave me a weak smile: "It is fun, no?" And then he pointed to what lay ahead, now in our field of vision: Siena. Jennie exclaimed, "Look, there it is!" as she and Maurico together dipped the plane's wings for a better view. As we swooped over Siena's famous central plaza, Mauricio exclaimed, "Look, Jennie, you dip the plane! Jennie! I love you Jennie!"

Davide and I were laughing in the back seats, which provided the perfect vantage point from which to appreciate the scene before us: Siena's wonderful plaza, Mauricio's boyish grin, and Jennie's amused reaction to his words. It was giddy and wonderful, as if we were all drunk on life. Soaring through the air like that, I felt we were on top of the world and that anything was possible. I even thought of my high-school Latin teacher, who always ended class with his trademark "carpe diem" — seize the day. Jennie caught my eye, and we gave each other a look that said we would never forget this moment with our Italian friends.

Jennie and I sat for dinner that night at a small restaurant just outside the center of San Gimignano. While we missed the laughter and spontaneity of Mauricio and Davide, we were excited to be on our own and celebrate the day. The restaurant tables were elegantly set with linen and goblets, and the menu offered a wide range of meat and game. As we waited for the wine, we giddily recounted our favorite moments of the day, often laughing to the point of tears. When the wine arrived, we raised our glasses for a toast. For the first time in my life, it came naturally: "To San Gimignano," we said in unison. Jennie added, "To Mauricio. To Davide. To living each day like it's your last. To letting go and embracing spontaneity."

In this magical town, I had taken risks that changed what I expected of people and places, and that now colored my life with wonderful memories. Browsing through the menu, I decided to try something I'd never eaten before, too. How about "Pasta with wild boar sauce"?

Maria Ivkovic took her first writing class at Brown University, where she received her bachelor's in Spanish literature and international relations. She has traveled her whole life, spending childhood summers on the Croatian coast, which few people know to be the origin of the Dalmatian dog. She is currently writing her first novel.

All Roads Lead to Rome

En route to Rome, Italy

Michelle Tay

"Platform 3, platform 3," I keep muttering to myself, as I frantically dart my eyes between the platforms and the minute hand on my watch. It is rush hour, and all around me whistles sound as trains arrive and depart every other minute.

I see platform 3. I run for it.

"*Aspettami!* (Wait for me!)" I yell out, as I see the doors begin to close. Fortunately, the controller hears me and motions for the conductor to hold the train.

"*Questo treno va a Roma, è vero?* (This train is going to Rome, yes?)" I shout out rhetorically in the conductor's general direction. He shouts back a reply I cannot hear, so I clamber onto the train just before the doors close, and set my backpack down to catch my breath.

Phew. Close shave. I fumble for my cell phone to call my friends, who were already waiting for me at the station. I had just finished an exam 20 minutes before my train to Rome was due to leave, so I was in a taxi where I had to practically beg the driver to race through the medieval streets of Florence to get me on my train. Racing through streets about as wide as five horses is virtually impossible, but my driver miraculously succeeded.

As I dial Melissa's phone number, I muse to myself about how this is my fourth time almost missing my train altogether, and I smirk at my consummate professionalism and adeptness at "traveling dangerously."

"Hello? Meliss? I'm on the train. Where are you guys?"

"I don't know our cabin number, but we got you a meal and

279

a seat."

"Well, are you near the front or the back of the train? ... Hello? ... Are we moving? ... Hello?"

There is only static on the other end. Reception is bad, the train is completely packed with people, and I do not know where to start looking for my friends. I dial Melissa's number again.

"Hey, are we moving?"

There is a pregnant pause.

"Are we?"

"We're moving ... tell me we just started moving!" I plead, only just realizing the train I am on is pulling out — out of platform 2 *and* three minutes ahead of schedule.

"No, we didn't," Melissa says, at which point our cell-phone connection dies. I start to panic, not knowing where my train is headed, how far it will go before stopping, and how far I will be from my friends when it does.

At once despondent and sick to my stomach, I slump against the train doors in a weak attempt to gather my thoughts. Inspired by a sudden spark of hope, I turn to the passenger in front of me and ask her where the train is going. She tells me *"Genova,"* which means I am heading in the complete opposite direction. Hope dashed. I start to animatedly relate my predicament to her in the best Italian I can muster in such a frantic disposition. She listens, first intently, as do some others in the vicinity, then rather amusedly, and assures me that every train out of Santa Maria Novella (the main station in Florence) stops at Campo Di Marte (the station on the outskirts of Florence) before heading full-speed toward its final destination. This means that I can get off the wrong train and get on the right one when it comes along. Joy!

I thank the lady by wishing her a thousand graces (*"mille grazie")* and waste no time hopping off the train. Within the next five minutes I am able to identify the approaching train as mine because I see four heads sticking out of one window — the heads of my friends — all scanning the platform for any sign of me.

"Michelle!!!" They scream in unison as soon as they spot me weighed down under my blue backpack, sheer delight on my face. Looks of amusement on the locals' faces abound, as does general chatter about "silly, overexcited tourists." I receive many a smile as I sheepishly board the train, and I smile back, somewhat apologetically for the grand commotion.

The first ten minutes of the ride that follows features endless jokes about my haste, carelessness and near-status as an unwilling Genoan tourist. As soon as those die down, my friends confess that the McDonald's value meal they were saving for me was now resting in five equal parts in each of their stomachs, in addition to the meals they'd already had (living and eating in Italy expands one's gastronomic capacity).

"We didn't think you were going to make it!" Nancy blurts out in all earnestness. I am at first disappointed with the idea of going without dinner for the next three hours, but soon I realize that after the adrenaline rush, hunger is the least of my worries.

It takes me no time to curl up in my seat and listen to my favorite songs on my minidisc player. I look out the window and keep a mental count of the number of towns we pass, but my mind soon drifts to memories of Rome.

I recall my first visit to the Eternal City — the grandeur of the Vittoriana, the Trevi fountain, the Coliseum, the Roman Forum. I think about my first exasperating attempt at conversing with Italian youths. I wonder if the Coliseum will have changed its façade, because the last I heard, they were going to build a wooden platform right across the center of the gladiator arena. The incongruity of that ancient-modern image perturbs me, and I turn my attention instead to the things I look forward to doing in the city this time around.

I want to revisit the Trevi fountain. Its cool, clear, light blue water always offers hope that my wishes will come true when I throw a coin into it. I want to admire the magnificence of the white marble that makes the sculpture of Triton so popular. I want to see locals working and living and witness the first-time joys of giggly tourists throwing coins over their shoulders.

Then I want more of that divine gelato from San Crispino, the famous gelateria round the corner from the Trevi. I even decide which flavors I want to get — *miele* (honey), *cioccolato bianco* (white chocolate) and their house special. I almost start to drool.

I also set my mind on having *pasta all'amatriciana* at least once. The sweet tomato-and-bacon sauce is a specialty of the region and a must-try for savoring a true taste of Roman cuisine.

Soon my mind wanders to what I have learned about Italian culture by living in Italy for four months. Memories immediately turn to those late mornings in downtown Florence where I tried to order a *cappuccino* near noon and got puzzled looks, sometimes little frowns, while being served. It took me three weeks to figure out that *cappuccino* is traditionally never taken after 10:30 in the morning, *espresso* is taken any time of the day (though a favorite after meals), and *caffe Americano* is generally considered bad coffee — an American-invented anomaly, and too diluted. *Macchiato* means a drop of alcohol is served with your caffeine fix, *lungo* means a little less concentrated than *espresso*, and *latte* means an extra large dose of milk. Rules on when it is acceptable to partake in the drinking of the last three kinds of coffee remain unclear, but most will forgive and humor all sorts of coffee requests from those who are clearly foreign.

I also recall how a meeting with my former Italian professor, Francesca, taught me that the Italians are culturally obsessed with "*fare una bella figura*," or making a good impression. I giggle quietly as I replay the scene at a sidewalk café: She was profusely apologetic about not knowing what the Pantheon is now used for and lamented to her friend that she was making *"una figura di merda"* (a most horrible impression) on me.

I miss her. I call her and tell her I am on my way to Rome.

"Ah!" she exclaims, and orders me to call her once I arrive so we can meet up for a meal.

"Pasta all'amatriciana?" I state my request.

"Certo! (Certainly!)" she beams back.

Ahh. Italian hospitality.

Ouch. Hunger pangs.

I finally decide to get up to try to find the food cart. Just then, I notice people getting out of their seats and reaching overhead to grab their baggage. I realize the three hours have passed in a flash and we are about to roll into Roma Termini. I gently wake my friends and announce our arrival. We can hardly contain our excitement, and as the train screeches to a halt, a couple of us look like we are about to break into a dance routine.

The doors open. We filter out. There is a fresh, cool breeze — a more-than-welcome change from the smell of dingy leather seats — and my hunger dissipates again.

We cannot resist running toward the bus station. The sooner we get to check into our hostel, the sooner we will get to paint the town red.

Roma, la città eterna, here we come!

Michelle Tay is a senior at New York University, majoring in international relations and minoring in journalism and Italian. She aspires to further her studies at the London School of Economics in the following year, then become a travel writer, a foreign correspondent, a boutique owner and designer, or an ambassador of her native Singapore to an European country. She also hopes to live for some time in Paris and Rome, preferably while serving as an ambassador.

Sneaking in

Rome, Italy

TYLER TOBY

IT WAS A VERY HOT DAY. BUT I DIDN'T GIVE A DAMN. AS THE TRAIN rolled into the Rome station, I was delighted to finally enter the city of Caesar. Here I was at last, standing where the gods of ancient Rome once stood. I could only imagine what the Roman streets had in store for me.

My first stop was McDonald's to pick up a map. As a seasoned traveler, I knew where the best (and free) maps were to be found. Yes indeed, American capitalism was serving another excellent market — the far-from-home American backpacker. After consuming a Big Mac, I followed my Mickey D's map to the nearest hostel, which happened to be outside of the center of town, by the Olympic stadium. When one gets off the sweaty train, one always heads to the hostel to wash up and get some general bearings (unless you are in Amsterdam, where you go straight to the cafe).

I was cruising on my own and knew that, down at the hostel, I could probably hook up with some other cool single travelers like myself. I made my way through the front-door bureaucracy and was able to find an open bed in the communal room of sleep. Just at that moment, people were congregating around the center row of bunk beds, talking about what to do that evening. I overheard the word "Coliseum" and knew that a journey was in the making. Perfect timing. I soon found my way into the group and got myself signed up to venture out with this band of Canadians, Americans and Australians. After chow, we were all going to meet up outside the hostel. This was a chance of a lifetime, to join a group of trekkers on their way to sneak into one of the most revered and sacred places on earth. We cruised into the city center; the town was buzzing on this hot July night. We finally made our way through the center of town and soon could see the nightlights encircling a beautiful oval shape. This structure had been standing since 80 A.D. It had been through countless wars and battles. It had weathered the test of time. Now I would walk in the footsteps of Caesar.

The leader of our group was a tall Canadian guy with a goatee. He had gone on this journey before. Only he knew how to guide us to the inner sanctum of the Coliseum. We would not merely slip through the gates where the public walked in the daytime. We would drop over several tall iron gates that would lead us deep into the heart of this beast. We would go where the lions and Christians were kept before their fateful meetings. We would go into the pits where men would contemplate their fate. The average tourist would only be able to look over the edge and see down into the pits. We would go into the pits and look up at the sky and see things that only archaeologists and Romans would see. Everyone was excited when we reached the first gate. The gates were very high and took a great deal of effort to climb. Yet, slowly and surely, each of us made our way over each gate. We helped each other as much we could, but ultimately each of us was involved in his or her own struggle. This was a small price to pay to set foot on sacred ground. Each of us knew the significance of the moment.

Finally, we made it to the pits, to stand in the very heart of this wonderful place. Once there, we looked around at each other and smiled with glee. We had done it. We had crept into the bowels of "The" Coliseum. This was a story for the ages (and for the party scene back home). This would be my lead into countless drunken conversations, knowing that no one listening could say, "me too." At that moment, I came down to earth and realized that we hadn't just set foot on the top of Everest. Some people were sitting on a ledge above us, beer bottles in hand, and when they saw us emerge into the Coliseum, they made whistling sounds as if to say, "Bravo, you made it!" This made us feel welcome and somewhat at ease in these awesome surroundings. Cool. We looked at this place as sacred. They saw this significant landmark as their Saturday night hangout place. That thought suddenly put everything in perspective for me. I now saw myself hanging out in my local historical site back home, drinking a few beers with my buddies. This scene before me in the Coliseum was no different.

We proceeded off in our own little groups to explore the history of this place. Every corner seemed to tell another story. In one area you could envision the lions and tigers chained up, ready to be released on the helpless Christians. In another area, you could see benches in rooms that must have been where the gladiators and victims said their final prayers before the slaughter. We were walking in the footsteps of men and women from almost 2000 years ago.

After an hour or so, we went back the way we came, leaving everything the way we found it. To disrupt even the slightest pebble would have been sacrilegious. We knew that preserving the moment in our minds was good enough. To celebrate our victorious journey back at the hostel, we opened a few beers. As we toasted the rest of the night away, we listened to each other's experience from the trip. It was clear that this had been a special night for all. The next morning I bid my farewell to the group and set out to explore the rest of the city on my own. One stop I made was the Coliseum. I wanted to see how lucky we were and how unlucky the rest of the tourists were. Going down into the pits, as we had done, was out of the question for them. Even to go up a few levels, you had to pay a few extra bob. When I managed to get to the edge and look down to where we had ventured, I pointed down and said to the guy standing next to me, "I was down there last night." With a face of disbelief, he looked at me and laughed. I walked away, thinking about what my next adventure was going to be. Topping this one would be a thrill and a challenge. But I was prepared.

Tyler Toby is an adjunct history professor at Emmanuel College and a marketing director for an Internet startup. Previously, he was a Boston public school teacher for four years, lived in Ireland for a year and traveled all over Europe. Toby is working on a book called Visions From A Treadmill.

Upon These Jagged Cliffs

Amalfi Coast, Italy

Peter Hallinan

I CLUNG WITH DESPERATE DETERMINATION TO THE CLIFF FACE ABOVE
the Amalfi Coast. The mountain goats hundreds of feet above me
also struggled, dislodging rocks. Unlike them, if one of my
handholds crumbled, a bit of vegetation pulled loose, or I made a
misstep, I could plunge a thousand feet into the turquoise Mediterranean below.

I paused for a moment to catch my breath, watching clouds
swirl fluidly around me. I tasted water vapor on my tongue, felt cool
cloud mist surround my body. Minutes later, the clouds had disappeared and the fiery rays of the sun baked my body instead. The
weather shifted constantly on these jagged cliffs.

Three days earlier and 50 kilometers north of here, I had stepped
off the night train in the Stazione Centrale of Naples, Italy. Dozens
of homeless people slept on the sidewalk outside, huddled together
for warmth. Vagabonds and drug dealers drifted by, to be replaced
after sunrise by pickpockets and conmen. A few early-rising hobos
across the street were cooking food over a fire inside the shell of a
brick building. Still sleepy from my ride, I waded through scattered
trash, found a bar and ordered a cappuccino.

Away from the train station, down by the sea after sunrise, I
found Naples delightful. Castles, cathedrals and statues tower above
the bustle of pedestrians and honking vehicle traffic, shops, pizze-
rias selling hand-tossed dough, and open-air markets. I had to show
courage in order to cross each busy street: no Napoletano, on foot
or behind a wheel, obeys the traffic lights. While I was warming to
the city, I couldn't stay: my goal was to see the Amalfi Coast, and I

headed back to hop a Circumvesuviana train for Sorrento. In ancient times, this was the reputed haunt of the sirens, those drop-dead gorgeous maiden-monsters whose irresistible songs sailors could not resist, as they sailed to shipwreck and doom on the faces of Sorrento's cliffs.

So when I arrived in Sorrento, I asked some locals if any sirens had been spotted that day. Sirens sounded good; being lured to my doom — I just needed to avoid that. No sirens, signore. I decided, then, to take a bus ride along the coast, on the narrow, cliff-hugging, twisting road that connects the Amalfi Coast's Mediterranean towns.

I gave myself a respite from the careening bus ride at Positano, a town wedged between sea and mountain peak. Its streets zigzag their way up from the water, sometimes narrowing into paths or abruptly turning into winding staircases toward the top. Flowers weave themselves into the architecture and rockeries, and an occasional orange tree grows within easy reach, so that you can pick an orange if no one is looking. Most of the trendy shops and tourists are down by the coarse sand beach, and if you go up you quickly ascend the green mountains of Amalfi and can see the Mediterranean spread out below.

I caught a boat back to Sorrento that evening and stood on the rocking deck, entranced by the majesty of the Amalfi cliffs. I felt as if they were gently tugging at me, as the moon pulls the oceans. I wanted to explore those cliffs, but, I had decided to spend my last day on the Isle of Capri, so turned away reluctantly.

The Sorrento-Capri hydrofoil the next day was packed, as was the Isle itself. I wandered listlessly, finding one stunning view from the island lookout, but otherwise, mobs of tourists buying trinkets at stunning prices. I couldn't shake the feeling that I was witnessing the death of an island, choking upon tourists and vendors. Beauty attracts tourists and tourists destroy beauty. That night I decided I needed to escape this consumer madness, and I found myself staring at those cliffs again. I asked some locals if there were any trails in the area, perhaps between Sorrento and Positano. "There are no trails -- you must walk on the road or take a bus." So I bought a map, and found I could indeed hike between Positano and Sorrento, if I just followed the dotted red line.

That night, over dinner with a woman named Amy whom I had met in the youth hostel, I explained how I wished I had gone hiking along the Amalfi Coast. She agreed that would have been exciting. By my fourth glass of Chianti, I decided that I was going hiking, and *to hell* with tomorrow's train ticket. It took Amy five to decide she was going, too. So at dawn the next day, wine still pulsing through our veins, Amy and I caught a bus to Positano, bought sticky pastries at a *pasticceria,* and then set about finding the trail back to Sorrento. After six inquiries, we found it.

The trail begins with a switchback staircase that rapidly ascends the mountain. It is a difficult climb, but it soon enters the forest, where the shade of the trees and the sound of chirping birds is a refreshing change from the clamor of cash registers back in town. Uphill from there, we came upon a rickety hand-operated tram, attached to a rope line that stretched hundreds of feet over a valley to a derelict shack on the other side. The tram still worked, but I looked at its rusted metal and envisioned squatters living in the shack, so we stayed off. Twenty minutes up the trail, I saw another tramline strung across the valley. By then I was sweating profusely and found it hard to imagine people packing supplies to such remote homes.

Beyond that was an intersection of the trail, in an area which the map described as "sometimes marked." With increasing frequency, we had found ourselves backtracking to determine where the trail had disappeared, and now we had reached another intersection that was not marked on the map.

"I think we should take the left branch," I said.

"Are you sure?" Amy asked. "The other path looks better kept."

"True, but it's heading inland and back in the direction that we came from. This way looks more direct. We'll be okay as long as we keep the Mediterranean to our left."

"I dunno, all I see is cliffs in that direction."

"We'll be fine, trust me." *I hope.*

The path we followed gradually faded until it was indistinguishable from the rocks and scrubby bushes. We weren't lost yet — we just didn't know where we were. We hiked slowly across the steep terrain for the rest of that morning and well into the afternoon, picking our way through prickly bushes until I found a bramble-laced goat path. We kept an eye out for trails but found none, because clouds swallowed the cliffs below. At least I couldn't look down — that is, until a narrow ledge that we had been inching along abruptly ended in a vertical drop. We couldn't continue; and neither of us wanted to turn around and spend hours hacking through brambles; so that left going UP. Not the steep but manageable sort of "up" that leaves one feeling sore the next day, but the kind of white-knuckled UP that reminds me why I never go rock climbing. We stared at the wall of layered shale above us. It towered into the sky and disappeared inside a swirling cloudbank. There were frequent handholds but the loose shale pulled free when I tested one. I handed the rock to Amy. She glared at me.

"I'll buy gelato when we get back," I promised.

"If we make it back," she replied.

As I stood staring, I asked myself, should I make an assault on this mountain fortress? My optimistic side said it might be possible, while the rest of me screamed *No!*, this was ludicrously dangerous. Then my ego asked if I was going to make a cowardly retreat. I reluctantly began climbing, handhold after foothold, and Amy followed. Rocks gave way and tumbled down in speedy silence, vanishing from sight. The clouds pressed down while whitecaps broke far beneath. Higher, higher.

Suddenly, I heard a great clattering of rocks from above us. Uh oh, was a landslide starting? I looked up and spotted the source: a family of mountain goats, ambling along the cliff. I watched them walk above me, wishing I had a free hand for my camera. Amy and I continued climbing, sweating and cursing until abruptly we reached a sizable ledge. With shaking arms, we hauled ourselves onto level rock. When we were ready to continue, we found that the eight-inch-wide ledge slanted up the rock wall, and we followed it until the cliff was below us and the land became a steep slope rising to the peak. Amy and I scrambled up the final stretch and gleefully leapt onto the highest boulder, panting, enjoying the rushes of adrenaline, euphoria and exhaustion. The clouds to the west had parted momentarily, and we saw a passenger ferry out at sea. Then they shifted so that a harbor came into view. Sorrento shimmered in front of our eyes. Now we could see the other side of the mountain, and the trail that we had lost six hours before. Again the clouds shifted, obscuring Sorrento, but we'd come alive with anticipation of a hot shower and cold gelato.

It took us two hours tumbling down the mountain to rejoin the tourist hordes. With silly grins plastered on our faces and dirt, blood and sweat coating our bodies, Amy and I strolled down the main promenade, past elegant restaurants and expensive boutiques, content at last.

Born and raised in Alaska, Peter Hallinan attends the University of Oregon, where he studies journalism and viola performance. He studied for six months in Siena, Italy. Plans include scuba diving in Lake Titicaca, Peru, in search of Inca ruins, and hunting for dinosaur bones in the Arctic.

Cinque Terre

Cinque Terre, Italy

BRADLEY FINK

FROM VENICE WE HEADED EAST BY TRAIN FOR THE LIGURIAN COAST. It was a late night ride through dark country for eight miserable hours, during which we passed in and out of sleep. My friend Shade and I were painfully cramped in a coach crowded with four little Italians. In the Venice station we had been warned of gypsy thieves who prowl the trains while passengers sleep, sneaking into cars to steal whatever they can find. Suspicious of everyone, we sat with our packs clutched tightly to our chests. Once I woke to find the man opposite me peering at us with one eye open. Shade noticed it too, so we shouldered our packs and set out for the dining car, where, in the dim ivory glow of nicotine-coated incandescent lights, men sat smoking cigarettes and drinking coffee. The only thing served was a ham and mayonnaise sandwich, hot or cold, by a portly chef behind a small window at the back of the car. So we sat for the next few hours with our heads resting stiffly against the stuffed nylon of our packs, our eyes half-cocked in drowsy wariness. The train came to a halt not long after sunrise glowed through our window, and the conductor announced that we had finally arrived in La Spezia.

From there, it was a twenty-minute train ride to Cinque Terre, a collection of five small fishing villages terraced into the cliffs at the northern crook of the Ligurian sea. Only one train serves each of the five towns. Not many roads lead there, and passage between them is managed on foot by a series of ancient, winding, cliff-hugging goat paths that become dangerous at the narrower passes. Our train arrived at Monterosso, the principal of the five villages, and Shade and I walked to the tourist office just below the station to inquire about accommodations. While waiting in line, we struck up a conversation with a backpacker named John, traveling from Ohio through Europe on his own. To save money, the three of us took a single room with two beds.

Along the main street, small stores sold fresh vegetables and meats and wine, as well as towels, beach mats, sunglasses, and sunscreen. Just below the street was a beautiful pebbled beach, and to the south stretched the sea. As we walked up the steep road to our *pension*, we exchanged travel stories. John spoke mostly of Interlaken, Switzerland, the most beautiful place he had ever been, and the next place Shade and I planned to see. At the *pension*, a middle-aged woman in a garden dress led us up a staircase through her house, and gave us the key to our room. Inside were two twin beds, a private bathroom with a shower, and a window looking down on the garden below. Beside the garden was a swimming pool that was off-limits to guests, and in the back yard was a chicken coop that housed an obnoxious rooster. Throwing off our packs, we quickly crawled into bed for some much-needed sleep.

The rooster woke us up around noon with its crowing. John got out of bed first. He had a thin, six-foot-three frame, a moppish blonde haircut, a clean face and some marijuana he had bought in Switzerland. After showering, he stood on the bed in his towel and smoked a pipeful, blowing the smoke out the window. Shade showered next, while I lay in bed listening to music on his disc player. After my shower we all put on shorts and went with our towels down to the beach.

That day we relaxed by the water, swam, talked and watched girls. We ate an early dinner and by sunset were back in the *pension* showering again, putting on our jeans and shoes to walk to the bars and cafes. In the newer section of town, just beyond a long tunnel that cut through a cliff at the end of the old main street, was a tavern where many of the summer travelers had gathered. We stayed there most of the night, talking to different people and drinking bottles of beer. One fellow from Canada had tried to hike to the next town just before midnight and had fallen twenty feet down the side of a cliff. He was bruised and bleeding and quite proud of his adventure. By the time the place shut down at 2 a.m., we were awfully tired and drunk. Making our way back through the tunnel, we trudged up the steep street to the old woman's house, and inside our room Shade and I each took a puff of John's pipe before falling into bed to sleep.

The rooster woke us the next morning at nine. By nine-thirty, John was at the window with his pipe. After a small break-fast of focaccia with fresh cheese, tomatoes and ham, we set out on our hike to Vernazza, the first of the four villages east of Monterrosso. It was a grueling climb. Beginning at sea level and rising steeply through a landscape of magnificent stone walls and terraced vineyards, we were able to view the coastline from high within the cliffs. At some places the trail grew so narrow that two people would have been unable to pass. Along the way we stopped many times to take pictures of the coastline, and after a ninety-minute jaunt we came to Vernazza, where we explored the laby-rinths of steep cobble-stoned streets and stone-carved stairways, then sat for awhile to rest and watch the blue, red and yellow boats bobbing in the harbor.

"What do people do, living in a place like this?" John won-dered as we sat and rested. "It's beautiful, but look, it's just cliffs and the sea. No roads, no office buildings, no shopping malls. Really, what the hell do they do?"

"They fish," said Shade. "And they grow vegetables and make wine. They do what they need to live."

Across the square was an old man selling shoes from a pushcart. As we rested, I watched him and wondered at the simplicity of the life he must live. In the Cinque Terre there were no cars or corporate centers or celebrity gossip magazines, and it appeared that life had little to do with the prestige of wealth, and much to do with the simple pleasure of living. Admiringly, I watched the old man, imagining that he had a cottage up the cliff much like that of the old woman with which we were staying, with a garden of fresh vegetables and perhaps a small pool and a workshop where he mended his shoes. Sitting there for a short while, looking around the square at the happy vendors and the outdoor cafés and little shops, and at the fishing boats in the harbor with their nets hung to dry, it all seemed very remarkable to me. The things that mattered to the people here were the things that seemed to make sense.

It was an arduous two-hour climb from Vernazza to the next town, Corniglia. After resting in a tiny piazza filled with restaurants and shops, we decided against the final two hikes and hopped the train back to Monterosso. Walking through the tunnel to the newer part of town after lunch, we noticed a small cove that cut into the cliffs, where two Italian boys had climbed to a precipice and were jumping from the rocks into the sea. From where we stood it looked awfully dangerous. We decided to make our way to the jagged shelf where the two boys sat resting. It was a hard climb down, inching our way along the steep slope of the bluff, carefully placing one foot in front of the other. When we arrived, they looked up at us and smiled.

"There's no way I'm doing that," Shade said.

The cove was wide enough for three people to swim, but only deep at the middle, so that whoever jumped had to throw himself accurately. Any misjudgment would have meant landing on the sharp shallow rocks. While the two boys jumped, the three of us stood and debated whether we would do it, then who would go first. I jumped first, then John. Finally, Shade had no choice but to follow. After the first few jumps, we got the hang of it, and the Italian boys began showing off. One did a somersault over the ledge and splashed safely with his feet. The second boy went next, inching his heels over the cliff and falling perfectly backward. Soon, a young American couple arrived, and then there were six of us sitting on the ledge talking and waiting for the next person to jump. After my last jump, I felt tired, so I just sat on the shallow rocks in the water, enjoying the coolness that felt so nice after hiking all morning in the sun.

Again that night we went to the tavern beyond the tunnel. There we met two American girls who had just come west from Budapest. One of them was a very pretty brunette named Shauna, who looked like a gypsy with her deep-set brown eyes and dark skin. Shauna and I moved outside with our drinks and sat on a stone step by the tavern to talk. She had a sweet face and I was in love with her, more in love than I had been with my beautiful tour guide at the Vatican in Rome.

"We're leaving in the morning for Paris," she told me.

My heart broke immediately, and I frowned at my luck. Traveling was a lousy way to fall in love. Everyone was always coming or going. I stayed out with Shauna all of that night, talking about our lives back home, telling of the things we had seen, what we had learned, and the plans we had made for when the traveling was done. She had received an internship with a financial firm in the States. I still had to finish another year of school.

"What do you want to do?" she asked me.

Taking her hand, we walked to the harbor and sat on the seawall, staring out where the moon shone full on the surface. "Nothing, really."

"Haven't you got any plans?"

I shook my head.

"Well, what are you studying exactly?"

I told her that I wanted to be a writer, that I wanted to travel, to see wonderful places and be adventurous, to have money and meet interesting people and fall in love while I put it all down into books. She smiled out at the harbor and said it all sounded very nice. But that was a difficult thing to do.

"Nearly impossible," I agreed, sadly.

"Why don't work with your father in the mortgage business?"

Suddenly I imagined myself sitting cramped behind a small desk in an office building wearing brown socks and a shirt and a tie. In that instant my life became monotonous.

"I would rather not pay for my money with time," I told her. "Somehow it doesn't seem like such a fair exchange."

Shortly after dawn Shauna met her friend and I walked them to the train station. She gave me her e-mail address, as well as a telephone number I might reach when I returned home from our trip. After the train rolled away, I walked sad and alone along the empty main street, up the steep road to the *pension*, and, nudging Shade over to one side of the mattress, I crawled sleepily into bed.

After studying creative writing at NYU, Bradley Fink recieved his bachelor's in writing from Florida State University. Having traveled exten-sively throughout Europe and the Americas, he began his professional ca-reer freelancing reviews and travel articles for the Pasadena Weekly *in California and several Florida publications. He is currently the founder and editor of* Venezia Magazine, *a high-end fashion, culture, and lifestyle magazine for the South Florida region.*

To my mind, the greatest reward and luxury of travel is to be able to experience everyday things as if for the first time, to be in a position in which almost nothing is so familiar it is taken for granted.

BILL BRYSON

Greece

The Transition

Somewhere in the Adriatic Sea

TRACY SHAR

I TOOK ONE LAST NOSTALGIC LOOK AT THE WATER-FILLED CITY, filled my lungs one last time with the glorious Venice air, and stepped aboard the ferryboat for the voyage to my next destination, Patras, Greece. It would take some work for me to let go of Venice, and it looked like 36 hours on the water might be just the ticket.

The boat was more like an enormous cruise ship than a ferry, with casinos, a disco, a couple of restaurants and gift shops. I walked up to customs, where the officials laughed and pointed at my scrawny, over-traveled self sporting a backpack the size of Canada. They stamped my passport, and barely checked that it was valid. Grinning back at them, I collected my passport and made my way to the Eurail section of the ferry. This is the seating lounge for all the Eurail pass people who either don't realize that the Eurail pass doesn't get you a bed on a ferry, or knew but couldn't afford an upgrade, like myself. We would spend the next day and a half trying desperately to sleep in upright chairs.

I dumped my pack in the not-really-storage section that the guards had told me I could use, (ah, sometimes being female really *does* come in handy; thanks, boys!) and made my way to some small tables I had seen next to some large windows, where I could enjoy our departure and watch the water as we floated away. Over the past couple of weeks, I had been traveling with an Australian girlfriend I had met along the way, so I hadn't been alone much. I realized that I was glad to be back to just me again, and happy I had decided to take this trip alone. The possibilities of traveling around Europe alone are endless, and I was going to start by giving myself time to transition between Italy and Greece.

I picked up my book and started to read. After about 15 minutes, I began to sense a presence watching me. I looked up, and there at my table stood a total Fabio-looking guy, complete with Greek god shoulders, long blond locks, the orange "wifebeater" and baggy hippie pants. He motioned to the chair opposite me. I waved him into it and continued reading, figuring that whatever ethnicity he was, he most likely did not speak my language. I also really just wanted some time alone, to read and ponder my journeys up until this point. But alas, Fabio suddenly grabbed my book right out of my hands, took a good look at it, and grunted, "Ah! English."

"Yes." I said. "English." He didn't speak a word of it, just as I thought, but we began communicating anyway. I learned that he was Greek and had been traveling with his friend. He couldn't pronounce my name, so after a while he commenced to calling me Jessica, which I suppose was the only English female name that he knew and could also pronounce.

"Jessica!" he said, "I hungry. You?" We made our way into one of the cafeteria-type restaurants, where we met his friend, who spoke slightly more English. Through talking with him, I learned that they'd been all over Europe together, and we started comparing countries we'd visited, and when I got through my list to Amsterdam, they both breathed in sharply. They told me they *loved* Amsterdam, and made it very clear why when I was suddenly invited back to their room to partake in some leftovers they had brought from that very city. I assessed the situation, decided they were harmless, and went along.

As we entered the room, I looked behind me and realized that Fabio's friend had not followed. Fabio locked the door behind me and immediately covered me with his hands, trying to get me to kiss him. "No." I repeated over and over. "Why no?" he demanded. "Why no?" I replied. "Maybe, Fabio, because you don't understand a single word that I'm saying, and you think my name is Jessica, and I'm never gonna see you again after this ferry ride. Maybe *that's* 'why no'." He looked at me in bewilderment, then slammed his hand down on the desk. I remember that was the only moment in my entire trip where I actually felt scared, like maybe my instincts had been wrong and I had just walked into a potentially violent situation. I held my breath and waited for what was to come next. "Fine!" Fabio bellowed. "We smoke drugs." I looked at him, astonished, as he opened the door to find the long lost friend, and together, they began rolling a joint of hashish.

In the humorous hours that followed, I learned all the Greek curse words, the days of the week, and a few basic sentences. They learned all the English and Russian curse words, and we all had a pretty fine time. I can remember laughing so hard, while screwing up Monday with Saturday and mispronouncing things so that suddenly I was accidentally cursing. There's something truly wonderful about communicating with people who don't speak your native language. Even though you can't get across each thought you have, the things that matter get through. And it makes those relationships more special. I have no doubt that if I ever went back to Greece and looked these two guys up (I *do* have their real names and address' floating around somewhere), they would not only remember me, but invite me into their homes with open arms. It's a big difference between American and European culture. Americans don't bond with you and invite you home like the Europeans do. You can't get this kind of hospitality in America, and it's too bad, because it's something pretty amazing.

Before I knew it, the night was over, the day was over, and

the boat was pulling in to Patras. There was a sign-up line for the bus to Athens, where I planned to meet a friend I'd worked with in a hotel in Amsterdam. As I started to queue up, Fabio stopped me, asked what I was doing, and after I explained, he told me that no, he and his friend would take me to Athens. So I stepped out of the line, and after 30 minutes of waiting for Fabio and friend, and wondering if I had made a huge mistake, and thinking I would end up hitching to Athens alone after all, they appeared. Not in a car, but in a huge 18-wheeler. They hadn't told me they were Greek truck drivers. They popped open the cab door and invited me to climb in.

So I took the four-hour ride to Athens in their truck, learned we had very similar tastes in music, and while Fabio tried to grope me by the side of the road a few times, I knew I could handle it, and that he was mostly harmless. If anything, he'd probably just whip out another joint. Plus, I was getting the story of a lifetime out of this, and some good smoke, and no way was I going to miss out. About an hour outside of Athens, we drove into a small town to make a delivery. I waited for them, interested in seeing a small Greek town, but also tired and ready to reach Athens, check in to my hostel, and meet my friend.

They got back in the truck, we drove another few miles, and then they pointed down a street and told me that the center of Athens was just a couple of blocks that way, and that they had to run — their next delivery was in the opposite direction. To this day I still don't know what, exactly, they were delivering, but it was something small and packaged. They wrote down for me in Greek the name of the street where I was going, we swapped music tapes and said our goodbyes.

I began walking, and continued walking, and walking. Every few blocks, I would see someone, show them my piece of paper, point straight ahead, and say "Ney?" ("yes?"). "Ney," they would tell me. I walked another hour, a blister had formed on the ball of my foot, I was carrying a backpack the size of Canada, I hadn't showered in about 45 hours, and I started getting upset at Fabio and friend for dumping me in the middle of Nowhere, Greece.

Just then, a bus pulled up in front of me. I handed my piece of paper to a gentleman boarding the bus, said my usual "ney," and he nodded, took one look at me, laughed and handed me a bus ticket. "Ney" he told me. He pushed me off the bus when it arrived at my stop, and I had four hours to spare before I had to meet my friend. I checked into my hostel, dropped the pack off my aching back, nursed my enormous foot blister, and fell onto the bed. Venice was just a memory now. I knew I was in Athens, and my transition was complete.

Tracy Shar has spent her life thus far hoping to travel constantly. And she's done pretty well on that front, studying theater in countries like Russia and Scotland, and taking advantage of the opportunity to continue traveling around the world once she was there. Her main ambition in life is to create an international festival of theater that travels from country to country, and encourages diversity and cultural enrichment for everyone involved. She hopes her stories will inspire others to "catch the travel bug" — the world is an incredible place.

Escaping Ios

Ios, Greece

Jo Shuttleworth

It was hard to move on from Paros. As much as hopping from place to place was the name of the game, it seemed like so much work to uproot that first time, find a ferry, catch a ferry, find another place to stay, find a beach spot to call our own. Without wheels of our own to navigate the roads, the travel joys of Paros were limited to us, and the ferry was our best carrier to new destinations. We bought a backgammon board as a travel incentive, and finally got ourselves on the move. At the dock, we sat on our backpacks, waiting for the ferry and playing our new game, trying to imitate the high-speed play of the Greek men we'd watched.

The boat carried us to our next stop, Ios, the party-island. Word on the backpack circuit was, 'People only stay here a few days, and then they have to move on due to the excesses', Tors and I couldn't wait to dive right into that scene. We found the beach first — long, sandy and filled with the people we wanted to be — then a campsite to call home. Tentless, we laid our sleeping bags on the dust under a bamboo shelter and went to make friends.

Our campsite was not the best: overwhelmingly beige, a couple of plants to try to squeeze shade out of, dirty facilities that encouraged sandal-wearing in the shower. The molded concrete outdoor restaurant was run by a dark, greasy-haired guy, sporting a perfect sphere of a belly and a cigarette attached to his bottom lip. Let the ash fall where it may. He smiled at us as we wandered in, his cigarette hanging. We sweetly smiled back, knowing from previous experience that you should *always* be on your best behavior with the chef, acting like a puppy so you get fed extra tidbits.

The restaurant was full of our new camp mates. It had a perfect view over the quiet road to the tempting, fat sandy beach and deep blue waves of the Mediterranean Sea. We sat on a concrete bench, made friends over ouzo slammers and backgammon boards, and were told of work opportunities in the heaving bars and clubs at the top of the hill.

If there's an opportunity to gain some cash whilst having fun, Tors was on it, with determination. In short order, we found ourselves standing outside Homer's Cave Disco Bar, tempting people in from the cobbled streets. We got paid a pittance, plus more for each person that we brought into the club, and we had the perfect excuse to chat the night away to any stranger we desired.

The nightlife was everything we had been told of and warned about, and we were ready. As soon as the sun went down, the disco lights dawned all over. The tanned bodies donned glad rags, there were people to meet round every corner, and the town got louder and louder, music blaring and mixing from building to building, raising the excitement level to a fever pitch. It was cocktails here, there and everywhere — and "they don't import it," we were informed. We didn't understand the significance of this until we were told of the Ios Cough.

The Cough comes from overstaying the few days' party limit that is all most travelers can take. The strength of the Ios Cough is directly proportional to the number of cocktails imbibed during this period. These cocktails are concocted from locally made spirits, which Tors and I decided meant the stuff that you normally use to clean paintbrushes. The spirits slowly but surely strip the hairs and layers off your throat until you cough like a donkey — a nasty, guttural cough that rips you apart.

Regardless, we drank through our working hours, and our smooth chat worked very well. We had fun. We made friends. Unfortunately, we didn't influence people. No one was interested in the empty red interior of Homer's Cave. In the end, we cheated. "Just walk in, have a look around, walk out and we get paid." (Cue Tors' sweet, beautiful "please" look.) The passersby did it. We earned bonuses. It was a dream ... until the owner caught on. And, like that, we were fired.

But now we had tasted the fun of earning money on vacation. The campsite had turned into home, and suddenly we were no longer nervous backpackers on a pretend health drive. We knew what we were doing. We had surpassed the "few day" limit with ease.

We tried working with Antonio, the cigarette-lipped chef, but our behind-the-scenes initiation into the realities of what goes on in a Greek kitchen was too much, even for our newly hardened attitudes. We just felt that even if the salad couldn't be refrigerated, maybe the meat could. It was nearly the end of our addiction to the lamb souvlakis that oozed hummus. But not quite — it takes a lot to ruin our taste for food.

Eventually fate decided we deserved a treat. We met two girls who worked in the Red Lion Pub — the dream location for the English abroad, a pub just like home that stays open until 2 a.m. The girls worked every day, but wanted to work every other day. Would we, could we work alternate days with them? Would we, could we say no to this job? Qualifications: First, walk along the beach of beautiful people during the day, dispensing leaflets to tempt viewers for that evening's films; must be a good communicator. Second, get to the pub for the 9 p.m. opening and dance the night away; must be a good mover and shaker. Rewards: free drinks, half-priced meals, pittance of pay.

We made our own rules as to who deserved sunbathing interruption to receive our colorful pieces of paper — basically, boys. Boys we wouldn't run from on the dance floor. We loved this job, strolling down the beach in carefully chosen beachwear, so obviously old timers of the Ios party, handing out fliers. We knew people.

We chatted, and best of all we were dancers. Yeah, baby, yeah.

We were addicted. We were Ios queens. We worked the beach, but knew that the real daytime hangout was away from soft sand and round the corner, a clamber over rocks. When the backgammon and ouzo in the campsite got too much for us, off we would go to lie on the rocks, where we chatted to whomever, or laughingly slide into the clear water, pretending to our audience that we were Olympic synchronized swimmers.

Every other evening, we would make our way to our dancing job. It was simple. Just drink and dance. No costumes, no podiums, no poles, donkeys or chickens, just a bit of smiling at customers to try and make them feel comfy about hitting the dance floor. If we were lucky, our preferred beach males would appear. Any unfavorable males were hauled away by our own personal bouncers. At the 2 a.m. pub close, we would go and meet our fellow campers to dance the rest of the darkness away in sweaty packed clubs with podiums and a fading starry sky peeking through. Mad holiday nightlife with people from all over the world, a sense of mayhem in a world without adults or young kids. However, as the ugly reality of the early morning hit, we would take our leave and stumble and sway down the steep, dusty donkey path to the rocks and a refreshing skinny dip in the sea. Tors and I, drunken and proud of our holiday lives, would try to come up with some answer to the meaning of life. After all, that's what we had given our friends and families as the reason for our trip. One morning we found it: "It's all a question of relativity and perspective." Our new philosophy worked with everything. We had achieved our goal.

After philosophizing came the wander down the beach road to our now-tempting beds. It took a lot to make a sleeping bag on hard, dusty ground desirable in any way, but by 8 a.m., it would seem like a fairytale double-bed. That was until noon, when the spell would be broken by the heat of the midday sun, and it would trans-form into a sticky piece of dirt. Only the shade of the concrete restaurant could save us from the unbearable shriveling of skin under the intense sun. Unfortunately, that shelter from the sun also meant another round of backgammon and ouzo slammers.

Our lives became routine. We had made our point about beating the Ios few days' stay. Now it was becoming a joke, and we realized that if you hadn't managed to leave Ios within a few days, you would be stuck there for all eternity. We couldn't get away. The ferry left in the morning and we could never manage to climb out of our fairytale beds. We were stuck in a never-ending cycle of backgammon, ouzo, dancing and swimming. There was no escape.

One night after we had danced our hearts out, I began to feel the effects of the Ios life. "My leg hurts," I whined, more drunk than usual as the stars faded.

"OK, OK," Tors eventually replied, her mind on other things — mainly a boy who was accompanying us toward our donkey path. I was the last thing she needed.

"I think it's my knee," I said.

People were passing me. Age was catching up to me. This life had to change. I sat down on a low stone wall and scrunched up my face, trying to work out what the pain was and where it had come from.

"All right, just a minute" came the exasperated reply. A few minutes passed, and Tors returned excitedly, leading a dark stranger on a moped. "Here, quick, jump on."

"What?" I said, confused.

"Get on here. Here ... get on," Tors said, indicating the back seat in a voice that defied me to question it.

I climbed on, wrapped my arms around him, and came to my senses. I was on a moped, helmetless, in the early hours, speeding away down winding roads. Tors stood on the path grinning and waving, growing smaller, arms linked with her boy. "Hey!" I shouted.

My driver turned round. "No, don't turn round," I screamed. He smiled. "No, look at the road." Confused from all my ranting, he returned to his biking skills while I prayed — silently, of course, so as not to distract him.

This was the one thing I had feared — after all the bloody scraped arms and legs and bodies we had seen, the mad drivers on the curving unmarked roads, the grinning girls clinging to Greek companions piloting mopeds — our one rule of the trip was *not* to ride a moped. Tors and I agreed we weren't going there. Here I was, doing the one thing we had agreed to avoid, and she was on her way there, too.

It was not far down to the campsite; strangely, my Greek driver knew where to go. Tors had used her determined skills to get me straight home. I jumped off with a quiet *efharisto* (thank you) and walked without any trace of knee pain to my dirt bed, pleased to be alive. But I could not believe that our one and only rule had been broken.

The next day I found my own determination. I hauled my ranting friend Tors up out of the fairy tale and onto a bus to the port. We made our escape from our favorite rule-breaking island once and for all.

Jo should be an investment banker but instead travels, writes and takes photographs. Her parents hope she settles down soon. Unbeknownst to them, she plans to write her book and enjoy more of the world instead. Her most recent adventure was an 8-month solo trip around South America.

The Greek Goddess

Athens, Greece

Christopher Ruth

She took a long drag of her cigarette and exhaled. The smoke hung in the air like the silk of her dress hung on her breasts: gently. Wetting her lips with the golden liquid in her glass, she pressed her mouth to the lobe of my ear. One day in Athens and I was in the dark corner of a bar making friends with the locals.

All day I had wandered the littered streets of Athens, making my way between various archeological sites. The streets were crowded with beggars, dogs, and garbage, and, like the garbage, the beggars and dogs are often kicked out of the way by vendors and tourists. Scattered throughout the city are archeological sites such as the crumbling Parthenon. Athens is a combination of the worst of modernity and the best of the classical world. The sites act as a cemetery commemorating the once-great Greek people. Hundred-foot pillars, twenty feet around, are now dead on their sides, broken into hundreds of cross-sectioned pieces. Decaying statues of goddesses and beautiful maidens stand headless, their femininity now solely located in their marble breasts.

Friends told me that there are two things to do in Athens: visit the ruins and drink. The morning was spent snapping pictures of fallen temples and palaces. In the afternoon I decided to take the latter advice — drink. Even in late October, the heat was enough that I needed to change and drop off my backpack at the hostel before exploring the social life. While walking the broken cobblestone streets back to my hostel, I was approached by a man with white hair, a glowing cigarette butt, and a Greek tongue.

"I'm sorry, but I don't know what you are saying."

"Oh, my friend, you are American! What are you doing in my beautiful country?" He flicked the butt out in the street and extended his dark, wrinkled hand. I hesitantly took it. Once a hold of my hand, he shook it furiously between both of his and would not relinquish possession.

"Visiting," I replied.

"And you like? Of course you do. Who no like Greece?" Finally released, my hand fell alongside me and sought security in my pocket. "Tell me my American friend, from where are you?"

"Chicago."

"Chicago! That is by Texas no? My son is in Texas. He is tall like you. Big tall boy just like you. He play basketball. You play basketball? Of course you do." Placing a hand on my shoulder, "Forgive me, my name is Georges." I offered my name and he baptized me Greek and changed it to Xristos, pronounced *Christos*.

"Come Xristos, we go have a drink together. I pay."

Page 134 of Rick Steves' Greek Travel Guide states: "The Greeks are extremely friendly people."

I accepted the invitation. Before I knew it, I found myself being led by the hand through a maze of streets and alleys, wishing I had Theseus' ball of twine to mark my path. The appeal of a free drink was too great to turn back. Each time we passed an outdoor café, I asked why not here? Georges' response: "I know good place."

Finally we reached a staircase leading down to a basement bar. Walking through the door, I was temporarily struck blind as my eyes tried to adjust to the absence of light. Slowly focused, I found myself in the midst of a dimly lit bar, the air heavy with smoke. The few patrons inside curiously eyed me. I stopped, unsure about whether to stay.

Georges grabbed my arm and led me to the bar where he

proudly pronounced in English, "A drink for me and my American friend!" The heavyset woman behind the bar smiled at me and asked what I wanted. My slight hesitation allowed Georges to jump in. "Give my friend Xristos the best drink Greece has to offer. Ouzo!" Georges then ordered a vodka and orange juice for himself.

Sitting down at the bar, I took off my backpack and dropped it on the floor, sliding one of my feet through the straps. Then I slyly allowed my arm to brush my front pocket to reaffirm the place of my wallet. The Greeks might be nice people, but I wasn't going to take any chances. I had heard about tourist traps too often.

Placed before me was a tall, thin glass containing ice cubes and a cloudy white drink. The bartender joined Georges and me in a toast. "To America." My throat burned as I swallowed the licorice alcohol. The bartender said her name was Maria and asked about me. The few other people sitting at the bar moved closer to listen. Aware of my audience, I tried to make my story as interesting and as far from the Midwestern truth as possible. To the people of that small bar in Athens, I was Xristos, the ex-American basketball player now wandering the world trying to find the meaning of life. My repertoire of adventures included a retelling of an actual event that happened to me earlier in the day. "So, I was eating in a park where there were hundreds of pigeons around a fountain. Feeling generous, I broke off a piece of bread and threw it into the center of the flock. Now, apparently Greek pigeons are more skittish than their American cousins because the entire flock took off in a panicked flight, crapping all over a group of German tourists nearby. As the eyes of the angry Germans started to focus on me, I decided that lunchtime was over. I took off running to the angry shouts of 'Scheiß!'" The story was at least good enough for Georges to order me another glass of ouzo and two more for himself.

Looking around, I noticed that the bar was similar to those lounges in old black-and-white movies. The walls, ceiling, and floor were all dark red and black. The spaced-out, low, circular tables each had a lone lamp, shaded with a green cover. The light was only enough to illuminate the table itself. Soft music and smoke filled the void between each table. I was Humphrey Bogart, the star and center of attention. The only thing missing was my femme fatale.

I smelled her before my eyes found her. My nose was intoxicated by the aroma of peaches. On my left, Georges was still ranting on about America. Looking to my right, I saw her — a woman delivered from the heights of Mount Olympias down to the bar stool next to me.

"Do you mind if I sit with you and have a drink?" Her voice warmed me almost as much as the ouzo. I did not know if she meant for me to buy the drink or if she just wanted the pleasure of my American company. I did not care. Having the undivided attention of a bunch of old people was pleasant, but to have drawn the interest of a beautiful foreign woman was a fantasy made real. I called Maria over in an unsteady voice and allowed the beauty to order what she wanted.

Her dark hair flowed down her head until it melted into her black dress. The dress stopped just past the curve of her bottom. The edge of the dress was lined with an inch of lace, which gave way to the olive skin of her legs. Her curves were as perfect as any Greek statue. The dark hair and olive skin pleasantly contrasted with her large, blue eyes, and heightened the effect they had on me. It was as if her eyes spoke the words, "My name is Helena."

"And this is Xristos," Georges' hands ran through my hair as he petted my head, "my friend." Suddenly I became extremely uncomfortable around Georges. Sizing up the scene, Maria offered Georges another drink and told him to let us kids alone.

Putting her hand on the nape of my neck, Helena leaned in and whispered, "Let us go to the back."

She put an arm around my waist and led me to a scarlet cushioned couch. As she lowered herself to sit, her dress slowly slid up her smooth skin until there were only a couple of inches left for her to sit on. Trying to be a gentleman, I left a bit of space between the two of us when I sat down. She quickly moved closer.

"Do you not like?" Helena wrapped her hands around my bicep.

"No, I like a lot. So … are you from around here?"

"I tell you, but first we have another drink." She placed a cigarette loosely between her lips and handed me her lighter.

The whole time I talked with Helena she was pressed against my side. Our eyes were drawn together and our hands all over each other. I had experience with girls but this was my first time with a woman. The difference between girls and women is not physical — a woman does not have to be taller or have bigger breasts. The difference is in the way the eyes look at you. A girl's eyes have innocence; a woman's are filled with determined purpose. Everything about Helena was sexy: the gentle cross of her legs, her tongue licking the rim of her glass, even her subtle puffs of smoke. We talked about everything. I learned that she was taking classes part time at a local university in hopes of pursuing her dream of biology. She was sexy, foreign, and intelligent. I was not sure if Helena understood all that I told her, but I did not care. Our connection was more than just words.

Time disappeared and so did our drinks. I continued the small talk only to keep up respectable appearances while in the bar, but I was getting ready to ask her back to my room. A few sips of alcohol remained in each of our glasses and so I decided to ask Helena if she had a job. One more question to give us time to finish our drinks and depart.

"Job?"

"Yes. You said that you only go to school part-time, so do you work the rest of the time?"

"Oh yes, I work."

"Where?"

"I work here."

"Here? Why aren't you working now?"

"I am."

Those two words hit me harder than a fist. Suddenly I noticed her leopard patterned coat and it all made sense.

"I need to go," is all I was able to stutter.

"Oh. Are you sure?" Her hand rubbed my pants.

"Yes."

"I have one more drink?"

"No, I really think I should go. I'm really tired."

"OK, I get you the check."

The sway of her hips was mesmerizing.

Maria came over to the table with Helena. Helena slid next to my rigid body, seemingly not sensing my discomfort. Maria handed over the paper check and my heart stopped. A rush of pain hit me in the abdomen and I could feel the sweat accumulating under my arms and in my palms. The total was for 125 euros. One euro equaled one dollar.

I struggled for breath and demanded how this could be. Maria pointed out that my drinks totaled 25 euros. I looked toward Georges' empty place at the bar for help. My first mistake. Maria then showed that Helena's five drinks were each 20 euros. She pointed the drink out in the menu, but all the words were fuzzy. I could not think. I turned my attention to the door. Somehow the distance to the door kept growing. Besides, I could not even feel my legs to be able and run. My hand trembled as I took the money out of my cleverly hidden wallet and gave it to Maria. I then turned to Helena.

"It was really cool to meet you, but I have to go now."

"Oh. You buy me one more drink?"

"No!"

Cool air exploded on my face as I rushed through the door into the street and the setting sun. Gagging, I bent and rested my hands on my legs, trying to catch my breath. With my back to the sun, I began to walk in the direction I hoped my hostel was. The shadows of the buildings stretched out before me, melting together in the middle of the street, darkening the city and my path. A blue uniformed street sweeper stopped collecting steel cans and paper advertisements with his broom and stared at me. A stump-legged beggar picked his bowed forehead off the concrete and stared at me. A child, face and fingers sticky with brown, raised his eyes and stared at me. Anger welled inside me and my pace quickened. Did they all know? Was the whole city in on my misfortune? Abruptly stopping, I turned around to confront the leering stares. Shielding my eyes, I saw that no one was looking at me. Laughter welled up inside me until it exploded out of my throat. I started back toward the hostel, unable to keep the laughter from bringing tears to my eyes.

The publication of this story enabled Christopher Ruth to pay off his bar tab. Chris is a recent creative-writing graduate from the University of Illiniois in Urbana-Champaign. He is a starving screenwriter currently working on his first screenplays. Not liking to stay in one place too long, Chris has traveled all over Europe as well as the United States in search of inspiration and good times. Some good times are more expensive than others.

Not all those who wander are lost.

J.R.R. TOLKIEN

Off the Beaten Path

Baby Blue Underwear

Northern Portugal

Mike Riley

Northern Portugal is a very romantic place to visit when you are in good health, have packed carefully, a beautiful lady has her arm wrapped in yours and you have adequate toilet facilities. I had none of the above. Instead, I had stomach problems so intense, disemboweling myself with my travel penknife seemed like a good idea.

It felt like a nuclear bomb pushed against the walls of my stomach and intestine. The pressure in my abdomen mounted slowly, as a side note, when I left that morning in a hired car from Vigo, Spain. As we drove south on a narrow route paralleling the Atlantic coast, gastric juices sloshed and foamed like the rough ocean waves slapping the rocks to the right of the road. My stomach twisted and shivered with every pothole our Portuguese driver hit. He seemed to be of the driving school that says, "The faster you drive over them, the less you feel them." I belong to the school that says, "If the jarring that occurs because of the way you drive over these potholes causes me to soil my only pair of pants, I will single-handedly follow you the rest of my days and torture your soul," and I told him so in no uncertain terms, though he did not understand my Portuguese.

To my right sat an overweight Spanish mother. On my left sat a middle-aged British man with a thick red beard and stringy hair. He talked incessantly about why he married a Spanish woman, elbowing me in my bloated side every time he made a reference to her excellent cooking, and smiling at me with tobacco-stained teeth. I made a mental note to smother him with my backpack and bury him in one of the car-long potholes our driver sailed over.

By the time we crossed the muddy Minho River into Portugal, my intestines were screaming with pain and I was sweating profusely. I looked out the window and tried to distract my mind from my dilemma as the passport control officer stuck his head in the car window and began what seemed like a State of the Union speech to each passenger, complete with pauses for applause and standing ovations.

The officer's speech and questioning dragged on, and as I cursed the Spanish hands that made the meat dish that caused my sickness, I resorted to the ultimate, last resource in the book of travelers diarrhea: cheek pinching. Cheek pinching is the art of tightening your gluteus maximus muscles in order to block "the exit." It is a precise art. If you pinch too late you may find you only "pushed things ahead." If you pinch too early you run the risk of cramping cheek muscles that, due to fatigue, do not allow you to pinch when you need it most. At best, it is a reckless method sometimes known to further the problem, but when the intestinal gods are angry, a cramped muscle is a small price to pay.

So with pinched cheeks, we rolled past passport control, back onto the road and toward Valensa do Castelo. Valensa do Castelo is a small castle sitting on a high hill overlooking the Minho and Portugal's northern neighbor, Spain. Its granite walls surround a medieval town unchanged through the centuries. Within the small town, cobblestone roads weave, intersecting each other in two or three places. Locals eat at one-room cafes with tiled floors covered in sawdust, and whose drinking bar is made of a single slab of dark wood, stained by years of spilled Port wine. Valensa do Castelo has a market place in the heart of town. Loud gypsy women promote their copper wares, yelling, "Beautiful, buy my copper!" or "King, I am the cheapest you will find!" The smell of fresh carnations fill the air in the northern section of the market; they're squeezed together in the flower stands like a live and colorful mosaic. On the southern side, red and raw meat dangles from hooks over shiny fish and other seafood. Large blocks of cheese with samples to be cut for anyone line the stands nearest to the city walls. Mixed within the entire market are Gypsy clothing stands whose cheap products are often stained or already ripped. The market is truly the lifeline in Valensa do Castelo. It fills the town and spreads through the castle gates, over the moat and drawbridge, and into the surrounding fields.

Our driver parked the car like all Portuguese drivers do: as if they have just had a seizure. I nudged the British man out of the car and tried the near impossible task of sliding my six-foot, two-hundred-and-forty-pound body frame out of a European car the size of a shower stall without relaxing my pinched cheeks.

Immediately I walked away, looking for the closest café with a restroom. My walk was awkward. Cramped cheeks in the pinched position seldom allow for anything more graceful than a waddle similar to that of a drunken duck with only one leg. The locals stared at me in amusement and a bit of fear. When asked for a bathroom they smirked and pointed down alleyways so dark and uninhabited one would bet they hadn't seen human life since the Renaissance.

My desperation grew. I was considering gracing a local field of tall weeds with a lifetime supply of fertilizer when I turned a corner and saw, shrouded in a brilliant light of glory, a public restroom. I shuffled across the street and into the plaza, then down the stairs to the filthy restroom. The restroom was empty and I slammed open the green door to the first stall. I considered lining the toilet seat but decided my shaking hand would have done a poor job. Besides, if any bacteria could survive the fumes of what I was about to "deposit in the bank," they deserved to use my body as a home, and I would show Portuguese hospitality and welcome them as sons and daughters of mine.

I released and filled the restroom with a magnificent audio display rivaling the best Fourth of July firework show in any town. Immediately, my abdomen shrunk to its normal size and a heavy cloud of despair and worry was lifted from my brow. I relaxed for a second, wondered aloud how many calories I had burned per minute of cheek pinching, then turned to grab some toilet paper. Imagine, if you will, my despair when I saw nothing but an empty roll.

Tidal waves of panic and stress crashed over me as I decided my next step. I listened carefully for any signs of life, lifted myself from the toilet seat, then gently stuck my head out of the stall door to see if the coast was clear for a stall-to-stall move in search of toilet paper. Of course, it was not. Five or six men were waiting for my stall, which happened to be the only functioning one, with their eyes set on my curiously shaved head popping out from behind the door, eyes wide open in apparent shock and embarrassment, then slipping back into the stall.

I looked around the stall quickly for any scrap of paper — maybe a candy wrapper or a newspaper section had found its way into my stall. There was nothing. Slowly, my eyes found their way to my boxers. It had to be done. I pulled off my boxers, took care of business, clogged the toilet trying to flush a large pair of boxers down the drain, and walked out of the stall under the grins and snickering of the Portuguese men.

The next matter of concern was replacing the underwear. I had decided to travel light and leave my backpack in Spain. Since I was planning on spending at the most only one night in Portugal, I had brought the clothes on my back and a small backpack for souvenirs. Now, worried I would have another intestinal attack, I decided I needed a new pair of underwear more than my family needed souvenirs from Portugal.

I walked back to the market and began looking for a clothing stand. I quickly found one near the fringe of the market and close to the city walls. An old lady with no teeth and the disposition of a pitbull ran the stand. She looked like she had a million better things to do than sit in the hot noon sun and argue over the price of cheap clothing. A cigarette dangled from her chapped lip, and she watched the ash fall onto her merchandise without concern.

I scanned her stand for underwear, looking back and forth, but found none. There were skirts, thin dress shirts with buttons missing, and socks, but there was no underwear in sight. I smiled at the old lady and began walking away.

"Que?" She yelled as I was moving to the next stand, asking me what I was looking for.

I shook my head and told her I didn't need anything.

"Que?" she repeated. She was yelling loudly, so I walked back to the stand, hoping her tone of voice would lower a few thousand decibels.

"Que?" she asked again.

I knew the Spanish word for underwear, a word that once you are familiar with will not allow you to eat certain Italian food, and used it. "Calzones?"

"Calzones?" She repeated back to me with a confused look on her face.

"Calzones." I affirmed.

She still looked confused, so she turned to the man working at the cheese stand next to hers and recruited his expert help.

"Calzones?" she said to him.

"Calzones?" He responded.

"Calzones." I affirmed again.

He looked at her, then looked at me, shrugged his shoulders

and yelled "Calzones?!" across the lane crowded with shoppers to the man working another clothing stand.

The man across the street looked pensive for a second, then shook his head in confusion. He dodged through the shoppers, across the dirt lane between the rows of stands, and joined the original clothing lady and the cheese man, forming a sort of Portuguese Translation Committee with dogged determination to figure out what I needed.

"Calzones?" he asked.

I mumbled to myself and decided to invest in toilet paper stock as soon as I returned to the United States.

It was obvious to me what my next step had to be. I had to use hand signals as a means of communication. My cheeks reddened and I smiled as I began pointing at my midsection with two hands, one in front and one in back.

My Portuguese friends looked at me with disapproving frowns and slowly shook their head as if to say, "You weird American, leave our country before you corrupt our children."

I giggled nervously, grabbed a sock from the stand and held it up as if I was trying to cover myself. The Portuguese trio looked at each other with shy grins. "What foreigner wears socks there?" they seemed to ask.

Suddenly, as if a lightning bolt of brilliance struck the cheese man, his face brightened and a yellow-toothed smile split his face in two.

He yelled "Ropa du baixo!" at the top of his lungs and pulled the strap of his underwear out from under his corduroy pants to affirm that he had discovered what the perverted foreigner was talking about.

"Ropa du baixo! Ropa du baixo!" began screaming the lady. I smiled in embarrassed agreement as the sound level in the marketplace miraculously lowered, as if to allow the ladies' screechy voice to echo "Ropa du baixo!" across the castle walls. Heads turned across the marketplace. Pretty Portuguese girls watched and manly men frowned as the lady ran to the back of her stand and pulled out a handful of leopardskin and baby blue underwear from a plastic bag. She ran back around and handed me one, motioning for me to hold it up to my midsection and see if it fit. Of course, the underwear was not at all like the boxers I was used to. Instead it seemed as if it was a small bathing suit flown in expressly for me from the beaches of Rio de Janeiro. I held it up and heard a general snicker across the crowds. It was a pair of feminine looking, baby blue briefs, at least two sizes too small. So … I bought them.

I ran through the narrow lanes, back to another public restroom. I would have used the one I did before, but I wasn't sure if there would be a group of men waiting to lynch me for clogging the only toilet that was functional with a pair of boxers. I snuck into the stall and gingerly and painfully began pulling the tight material up my legs. Halfway there, I took a deep breath and made the last pull till the elastic strap hung as close as it could get to my waist. Relieved, I stepped out of the restroom and began to waddle back down the streets. This time, however, I was waddling for a different reason.

Mike Riley is from Philadelphia, Pennsylvania. He has traveled extensively to 24 countries on five continents. He has had a variety of jobs, including teaching high-school English and working with brain-injured adults. His hobbies include international soccer, reading, overeating, and shaving his head. He is newly married and preparing, with his wife, to move to Asia and work for a nonprofit humanitarian organization.

The Other Side

Tangier, Morocco

BEN BACHELDER

A COUPLE OF DAYS EARLIER, I HAD NOTICED A NON-EUROPEAN country in my guidebook: Morocco. The infamous words "Why not?" came to mind instantly, and since I was already in southern Spain, it would be pretty easy to go.

So I caught a bus to the Algeciras, jumped on the ferry, where I met some fellow American backpackers, and viola, we were in Africa! We decided to stick together and tackle the country as a team. Our first day of shopping went pretty well, fending off the locals and their "My friend, you like taxi? Where is your hotel? Where are you from?" and "My friend, where are you from? What is your name? Where are you going? Tangier is a dangerous place! If you are alone, you will get hurt! I will help you, come come!"

Nothing could have prepared us for our second day, though. It started off well enough. I woke up before John and Leah, my traveling buddies, went out onto the balcony and looked over the beautiful Moroccan day. We were on a little side street, just outside the loud and busy heart of the city. I liked it. There was a man at a shop across the street, and he noticed me looking out at him.

"Hello! How are you my friend?"

"Fine, thanks."

"Come down here for a moment!"

"No no, I'm waiting for my friends"

"You are American?"

"Yeah, I am."

"Please, come down for a moment, my friend."

"No no, I am waiting for my friends."

I went back inside. They were still sleeping. Hmm. What to do. I went back out onto the balcony.

"My friend! Now what are you doing? You should come, please, I would like to talk to you!"

John and Leah didn't look like they would be stirring any time soon, so I thought why not, meet the locals. I left them a note and went downstairs.

"Ah, my friend! So you are American, from which state?"

"California."

"California! Great! I have a girlfriend, she is from Ohio. You know Ohio?"

"Of course."

"Well, my friend, I wonder if you could help me. I would like to write her a letter, but my English is not so good. I can speak okay, but I cannot write. Can you help me?"

"Sure, no problem."

"Great! We can go get some tea, you like mint tea? And we can make a letter."

"Um, well I am waiting for my friends inside."

"It will only take a moment, really. The cafe is there, up the street."

Why not? So we went. He got pots of mint tea, and I let him drink his first, just to make sure there wasn't any poison or anything (I was a bit paranoid). We began to talk, the usual getting-to-know-each-other questions. His name was Sharif. "What about the letter?" I asked. "Yes yes, the letter! 'Dear Annie. Oh how I miss you my love. I think of you every night. ...'" Man, this was the worst love letter ever written. But whatever, she wasn't my girlfriend. We finished the letter, and Sharif said that his uncle had a car, and they could take me around the city, showing me the sights and whatnot. I had helped him, so he would return the favor. Not a bad idea. But I didn't want John and Leah to miss out on it, so I asked if they could come. "Of course!" So I went back to the hostel and got them, explaining what had just taken place, and Sharif called his uncle. Within minutes, we were a group of five at the cafe, another round of tea for everyone, lots of laughs and smiles. Wonderful. I couldn't believe what was happening. We had not made any plan for the day, and now one was made for us, with locals no less.

We piled into the car and took a drive around the city, fingers pointing and explanations being given: This was the Casbah; that was the great mosque. "Would you like to see the ocean? There are some caves there as well. You must pay to see them, but it's very cheap. Three dollars, maybe." Sure, why not! We drove past a palace of the prince of Saudi Arabia, one of many. Mohammed put in a tape of traditional music and we all sang along, clapping and screaming. This was life, truly. And then the Atlantic Ocean came into view.

Oh, it was beautiful. Pictures, must take pictures! We stopped the car and out came the cameras, and along came a boy and his donkeys. Crazy! More pictures. How about pictures ON the donkey!!! Oh my goodness. More singing, more driving. Before long we were at the caves, and Mohammed did a little talking to the ticket guy while we walked in. Beautiful. There was one special spot where the holes in the rocks looked almost exactly like a reversed image of Africa, complete with the island of Madagascar, as you looked out to the sea. Amazing. Perhaps we would like something to eat? How about gong to Mohammed's place? Super! Then we hit a minor snag. The main road through the city, which we had to cross, was blocked, because the king was supposed to come. We could wait if we wanted, but the king would come maybe in ten minutes, maybe in ten hours. Never mind waiting, we were close enough to walk. Leave the car parked in traffic (!). Sure, why not? This was Morocco!

We walked to Mohammed's flat and had some sweets and more mint tea, and talked some more. I told them of my idea to see more of Morocco, and Mohammed said he had family all around the country and I could stay with them if I like. Awesome. "You know, Mohammed has a carpet shop in town. Perhaps you'd like to see it? Not to buy anything, but to see part of Moroccan culture. See here, these carpets are made here in Morocco, by women on the mountains. Let me show you one that has just arrived."

Sure, why not. Mohammed's son brought a carpet and unrolled it for us to see. Very nice indeed. It was wool and camel hair, handmade. Why not go to the shop and see more? Very well. Mohammed went to get the car, and came back looking quite distressed. Sharif explained that while we were eating, someone had broken the window and stolen the stereo. Terrible! But not to worry, we would still go to the shop. The police couldn't do anything about it, so just forget it, it's not our problem. We could also come back for dinner that night, a nice Moroccan couscous meal. Excellent idea.

On the way to the shop we tried to learn some Arabic so that the people there would be impressed by our multilingual skills, but didn't make much progress. Soon we arrived, we said "Salaam!"; there was much laughter, lots of smiles. The man there asked us the usual background questions, told us a little about the carpets, and offered us tea. John declined, but Leah and I were game. In fact, John didn't seem too interested in the carpets at all, like something was up. Curious.

The men brought out a book full of postcards and letters from people around the world, satisfied customers. How, um, nice. Perhaps we'd like to see some carpets? Yes? Wonderful. Ah, take off your shoes and socks, walk on the wonderful camel hair and wool, feel how soft it is. This one is pure silk, very nice.

Look, if you put fire to it, it will not burn. Look! Look! We can play a little game. The boy will show you a carpet, and if you like it we will put it into one pile, if you don't, we put it into another.

Leah and I played, but John just sat back and flipped through the customer book, talked a bit with Sharif and Mohammed. Mohammed had been complaining all day about a toothache, probably from all the horribly sweet mint tea. Again, John wasn't impressed. Before long we had gone through a big stack of carpets, and narrowed it down to the few that we really liked. "You know, we could give you a very good price for these. We understand you are students and don't have much money, but you will not be able to get prices like this outside of Tangier, much less Morocco. You could buy two or three, and sell the others back in America. That would easily pay for the one you keep."

I rolled the idea around in my head for a while. Perhaps he was right. They were nice carpets, and I know I had seen them for sale for really high prices back home. But how to get them back? They delivered. And how to pay for them? Credit cards are gladly accepted. Hmm. Well ... I don't know.

Idea: We go to an Internet cafe, check eBay to see if we could indeed sell the carpets for a profit, and base our decision on that. Leah concurred, and we told the guys the plan.

"My friends, you do not want to buy now? But there are many customers; your carpets may be gone tomorrow!"

"Yes yes, we'll take that chance."

And with that we left. In the car it was utter silence. Tension filled the air, thoughts of Mohammed's tooth, the stereo, the lack of a carpet sale all flew through the air, unspoken.

"Don't worry about the carpets, or anything. No problem, my friend," said Sharif.

Right.

At the Internet cafe, my suspicions were confirmed. We

would make no more than 10% profit, if we were lucky. Definitely not worth the hassle or the expense. We still had the dinner date with Mohammed and Sharif at Mohammed's place, but a couple of hours to kill beforehand. It was then that John explained his behavior. "You guys remember at lunch, when we saw the 'hand-made camel hair Moroccan rug at Mohammed's place? Well, I happened to notice a sticker on the back that said 100% acrylic, made in Indonesia. I also doubt that they actually paid for the caves. These guys are frauds. I could feel it from the moment we met them."

Yes, it did seem that way. But what about dinner? "I'm not going. I've had enough of these guys."

Okay, but Leah and I still somehow felt obligated to keep our plans, and we'd go. If they asked, we would just say that John was sick. No problem. So off we went down the street, on our way to get some food and mend up the loose ends. Before long we were greeted by Mohammed. "Look!" He showed us his car, which his son was washing, complete with a new window. He proudly showed the faceplate of the new stereo. Only it looked pretty old. I thought back to the way the car looked last time we were in it, and yes, only the faceplate of the stereo was gone. The window was definitely broken, though. Mohammed also opened his mouth and showed us the hole where his tooth had been. No more tooth, no more toothache. Wow, talk about a productive two hours for him!

Upstairs in the apartment were two Portuguese kids, a couple in their early twenties. I asked if they were friends of Sharif, and they said they had just met him on the street a little while ago and he invited them up for food. Interesting. Moroccan guys are awfully hospitable. Lots of talking, introductions and such, and then out came the hashpipe. Everybody was toking, except me. I never do, but this time I had even more reason to stay level-headed. Then Leah and the Portuguese kids were taken into the other room by Sharif, and I was left with Mohammed in the living room as he performed his daily prayer, facing Mecca, chanting and touching his head to the ground on his special prayer carpet. Wow, that was a sight to see. I'd never witnessed a Muslim praying before, and now I had it up close and personal. Cool.

I went into the other room to see what was going on, and it was a deal. The Portuguese were buying some hash. Well, that was their business, not mine, no problem. I just wanted to eat. A big bowl of couscous with chicken was brought out, and we all dove in. Mohammed and Sharif ate only a little, and the Portuguese guy said that his mom was going to call, so they left pretty early. Soon it was only Leah and me filling our faces. I felt like we were being watched. In fact, we were, by Mohammed and Sharif. I was nervous, and so was Leah. We were pinned into the room, between the wall and the table, with Mohammed on one end and Sharif on the other. Great.

"So you do not buy a carpet?"

"No, we can't afford it, really."

"And when will you leave Tangier?"

"Tomorrow, I think."

A heated conversation in Arabic ensued. Leah and I could do nothing but sit and wait, looking at each other with wonder.

"Okay. We have shown you many things today, maybe you can give us some money, twenty dollars each."

What!?!?!

"Um, I don't think so. You said you'd show us around as a favor. What happened to being friends?"

"Please, my friend. We have driven you many places, paid for the caves, given you food."

"Well, John isn't here anyway; we need to talk to him."

"You can pay for him now and get money from him later."

"We don't have any money here. It's at the hostel. We need to go."

"OK, we go to the hostel. And you give us money."

"We will pay for the caves, that is all. Let's go."

And we got out of there as fast as we could.

"We can drive you to the hostel"

"No thanks, we'll walk!"

Was he crazy? Jesus, what seemed like a dream had turned into a nightmare. We hurried back and went upstairs, found John and told him what was going on. I looked out the window, waiting for them to come up for their money. Soon the whole hostel was in an uproar. The Portuguese kids were staying there, too! The hostel owner said that this was not the first time that he'd seen this, and in fact it was a common problem in Tangier. So common, in fact, that there it was made illegal for a Moroccan to have a foreigner in their house without written permission of the foreigner. Aha! So we had the law on our side. Good to know.

And there was a knock at the door.

It was Sharif.

He wanted money.

I talked to him, calmly, and said that we would give him nothing. If anything, we would pay for the caves, but we would go to the tourist information in the morning and find the real price. He was furious. I said, "You didn't even pay for anything; go away!"

"You want me to bring Mohammed?"

Mohammed smoked A LOT of hash, so I knew he was in no state of mind to argue.

"Go ahead, bring him here."

With that he left, and we went out to unwind. The day was over.

Back at the hostel the Portuguese were sharing their hash,

and everyone stayed up until the wee hours in conversations of all sorts.

In the morning, we quickly packed our things so we could get the ferry back to Spain. I certainly wasn't going to be staying with Mohammed's family anywhere else in Morocco; I was staying with my new friends in Spain.

Another knock at the door.

Mohammed, dressed in his prayer robe and sunglasses. It wasn't over yet. Again the hostel was in an uproar. "Don't give him anything Ben!" "Call the police!" "Don't talk to him!"

"Calm down, I have it under control," I said.

Mohammed was a bit timid and a bit angry. "Why are all these people shouting? It's not their business! What is their problem? No police!"

"Don't worry about it, no police. Let's talk."

"So you don't want to give me any money?"

"We will pay for the caves only, because that is what we agreed to. However, I want to go to the tourist information to find out the actual cost."

"OK, my friend. I don't want you to have a bad impression of Morocco. Let's just say goodbye and it is finished."

"Well, it's too late for bad impressions. But yes, let's just say goodbye. Thanks for showing us around, and good luck in the future."

"OK, goodbye, my friend."

And out the door he went. A few minutes later, we went out the door as well and got onto the ferry back to Spain. We stood on the rear deck, watching Tangier grow smaller and smaller, waiting for it to disappear from sight, but never from our memory. What a trip.

I'm sure I'll be back; who knows when, but I'll certainly be more prepared. I've gained an appreciation for the order and, well, "civilization" of the western world. Don't get me wrong, though, it's a hell of a lot of fun to leave it once in a while.

Ben Bachelder was raised by hippie parents near San Francisco, schooled at UC Berkeley, and last lived in Hawaii. He hitchhiked around the world for a year, spending no more than $5 per day and loved it. To fill his pockets and his belly, Ben has been known to teach English, practice civil engineering, perform as a DJ, and even sell carpets. With experiences from sleeping in a bomb-blasted home to being molested by a Turkish truck driver, he's been around a bit. Check out some of his work on www.digihitch.com and don't be surprised if you find him at your doorstep one day (as the editor of this anthology discovered).

Terror In Tongues

Tangier, Morocco

ZENIA FRENDT

I DON'T REMEMBER RUNNING. AFTER THE DARKNESS CLOSED IN around me and the sounds of a friend's screams combined with harsh voices of Arabic speakers spiraled into my head as though through a funnel, somehow I did run. But I don't have the memory of running. Funny how the subconscious mind can keep you going after consciousness has stopped processing. I've seen this practice while driving down the street to a common location on "automatic pilot," but this time I was running for my life, so you might think that I'd remember. But I don't remember anything from the moment that I began to run until I reached the place I knew was safe. I wish I didn't remember what preceded the running, but unfortunately I remember *that* all too clearly.

I had already been staying in Morocco for months when it occurred, just enough time to feel comfortable and safe in my surroundings. My friend and I had just left a lecture on art and decided to go to the park, a habit that was not at all strange or out of the ordinary. It is true that Morocco is an African country, an Islamic country and a theocracy besides, but it is a beautiful place that can overcome the skepticism of most travelers. Even a blonde woman who is short at 5"1' and sticks out wherever she goes can begin to feel at home here among the guttural tongue and bustling souks after the amount of time that had passed. The people are kind and the atmosphere is one of acceptance once a girl gets over the cat calls on the streets of the Rabati city — and those calls are common when traveling, whether in Rabat and Marrakech, or Rome, Naples, Paris or Athens. At least for a short blonde like me.

But while a girl can sometimes use this to her advantage, there are times when a person doesn't want to stick out, and this was one of them. The man I had left the lecture with was a very good friend who came to Morocco from Great Britain. It was still daylight out and we decided to discuss the lecture and enjoy the warm fall weather. We went to a park that had become a hangout of ours; it was surrounded by beautiful trees even though we were in the middle of the city, and we had often come across interesting Moroccan businessmen there who were anxious to speak with us about our origins — the U.S. for me and England for my friend. We were always interested in this sort of discourse, for we learned a lot about the typical Moroccan through these exchanges, as well as felt ourselves beginning to become a part of the world that surrounded us.

On this particular evening, it had become dusk without us even noticing. In fact, I was just commenting to Marcus that the moon was a waning gibbous, something that a friend at home would probably notice once the moon made its way to Salt Lake City, Utah. The sky was still pink, but the air around us was becoming dark, and all of a sudden two men approached.

One of them asked Marcus for a cigarette, a common request in Morocco. You don't have to speak Arabic to understand that question. My friend thought nothing of it and was in the process of explaining in a strange mix of French, English and Arabic, that we had nothing like that to offer when suddenly I looked down to see that the man in front of me actually had an enormous knife in my ribs, something that could have come from a butcher's shop, so long, sharp and curved was its blade. An instant later it was being held at my throat. I went through a moment of disbelief, but there was no mistaking what was happening to us. The air that I had heretofore been breathing became suddenly thick, as if to choke me. The trees, once a source of beauty, seemed all at once to grasp at my throat and strangle me, and I fear that I became suddenly lightheaded, as if I would faint. I couldn't look into the eyes of the man holding the knife, could barely focus even on that. But I had a friend beside me, and some miracle of fate let me keep my senses and look to see what he made of the situation. Marcus was also looking at a long knife blade, his held directly in his ribs. He momentarily wore an expression of shock, but this was quickly replaced with something more primal.

There was no struggle between the man with a knife at my throat and myself. The experience of looking your mortality in the face is impossible to tell — my life did not flash before my eyes, rather, I felt a strange and surreal determination to get out of the situation. It was as if I was falling endlessly down the rabbit hole, in a warp without time and space, and yet still felt a conviction that I could grab a hold of a ledge and somehow pull myself up. The summers I'd spent at the lake, my dreams of travel, my boyfriend back home — none of this came to my mind until later. At the moment I knew only that I would give this dark-eyed stranger whatever he wanted in order to get the knife out from under my throat. Marcus, sitting on my right, was thinking more coherently. As the man in front of me ripped the watch off of my left wrist I turned my head to see what was happening with my friend. This moment seemed to take hours, I was so afraid to look away from the knife. Still, I felt that I had to know what my friend was doing. It is strange to tell, but the image in my mind is that of an exotic bird who seems tame until a stranger reaches out to touch it. The bird will suddenly extend all of its feathers in order to make itself look bigger. Likewise, Marcus seemed to grow. He stood up tall and unafraid, puffing out his chest and extending out his arms like some marvelous bird of prey. He told me later that he was afraid that it was rape that these men were after, and he felt a dedication to securing my safety. Moroccan friends confirmed his suspicion when told the story. At the time I knew only that I was with a friend who was incredibly brave, and yet I also feared that he was being foolish. I was of a mind to give the man with the knife whatever he wanted (the blade was an eloquent enough argument for me), but my friend may have saved me through his refusal to give in.

This refusal did not come without a price. The blood running down his face has haunted my dreams for years, as has the blood running at his sliced wrists, and the screams that accompanied the rivers of red. Who is to know in the dark what degree of injury has been sustained when the neck and the wrist are both a burning shade of crimson? The man in front of him did not hesitate to cut him, and the man in front of me finally pulled away the blade at my throat in order to help subdue my friend. But Marcus did not back down.

When his shouts and bravery at the knife had finally stunned our attackers enough to give us some space, we began to run toward the center where we had heard the art lecture. And this is where my memory finally ceases to exist. My feet pounding on the sidewalk or my heart beating in my ears? Somewhere I lost track, and it was only when they told me, for the third or fourth time, that Marcus would live, that I finally separated the two and began to breathe the breath of the alive once more. In the end, Marcus permanently lost the use of his right thumb.

The sun rose over a different woman than that upon whom it had set. Not that I had slept a wink, but there seems to be something about the dawn that brings a person a sense of change and renewal, if they are looking for it. In my case I knew I'd not be the trusting, open person that I had been, and I feared that images of the knife would haunt me forever.

In the following days, while Marcus was in the hospital having surgery on his hand, I came to at least accept what had occurred and the fact that I had been very lucky. Nothing had "happened" to me, and I had gotten my "bad travel experience" out of the way. This latter part did manage to bring some comfort to my sleepless nights — the odds of recurrence were extremely low, and I was safe. I decided not to call and tell my family about the incident, for fear that they would try to convince me to return to the States. I did end up telling my mother a few days later, but she promised to keep the information secret from the rest of my family.

Six days after the attack, I had plans to leave the city for awhile and head south into the countryside. This would be a great opportunity to mellow my mind and perhaps regain some balance. The morning of my departure, I was out of my house around six-thirty. I still hadn't really slept, other than a few nightmare-filled hours here and there in the last several days, so I figured an early start would be just as well. My plan was to catch the public bus from my house to a central location, where I would be meeting up with a small group of students and riding in a hired van down south.

The sun was in the process of rising — pink and orange filled the sky, but the fringes were already becoming blue. It was early enough that I had the streets largely to myself, giving the neighborhood where I had been living (renting out a room with a Moroccan family) a beautiful yet eerie quality. Usually shouts of greeting and haggling filled the air, along with the smells of frying fish or eggplant from various kitchens and the faint aroma of hashish. In the evenings men in long djellabas with pointy hoods sat in circles playing gambling games and drinking tea all along the streets. Baskets of small oranges would be thrust in front of me and young girls would curiously but covertly check me out from under their hijabs. The walk I was making was one that I made every day; a few winding streets took me to the main road where I could catch one of any number of buses heading to various locations in the city. This morning I would be taking the #2 bus, one that was generally filled with business people on their way to work. I was long-since accustomed to being the only white person — let alone blond person — at the bus stop or on the route. Today it was still too early for that crowd to be out, however, and I was not used to being the only person on the streets. I could almost feel the echo of the usual activity around me.

Suddenly I realized that it was not an echo I was hearing at all. My insomnia had led my mind to play tricks on me, for there were very definitely footsteps behind me, and they were getting closer. With barely a flick of my eyes to my right, where a shadow on the wall confirmed the footsteps, I knew. I just knew what was about to happen. Call it paranoia or residual fear, but I was suddenly more awake and aware than I had ever been in my entire life. Everything was humming and buzzing in my ears and I was certain that there was no time to lose. I was carrying a bag with the things I would need for the next week over my right shoulder. It was over this shoulder that I finally turned, yelling as I spun around "Qu'est-ce que vous voulez?!?" Up to that point, I hadn't actually looked at the person, and now there was no time — the knife was already extended and slashing through the air straight towards me.

But I was prepared, in a way that only experience can account for. I had known what I would see, had seen it clearly in my brain before I even turned. I swung my bag into the man while screaming for help, and I now saw that he had a huge grin on his face — the ugliest grin I've ever seen in my life and blatant with its intention. He was not expecting my reaction however, and I bought myself the time I needed to get to the main road, where, like a shining light, a policeman was waiting for the bus. I didn't ask myself until later why he never responded to the screams of "Aidez-Moi!" that were echoing off of the buildings only a minute before.

Instead I began shaking and trembling like someone going into the throes of hypothermia. I could hear my voice, strange to my ears for being in a foreign language, for its high, intense pitch and the speed of which my broken French was pouring from my mouth. I attracted the attention of another policeman around the corner, and tried to tell them both what had happened. They wanted me to describe him, but as I started to try, the hairs on the back of my neck stood up as though commanded by electricity. I slowly turned my head to the bushes and there he was. Crouching not 20 feet from where I stood he was watching me intensely with eyes that pierced my bravado. Before I could process any of this information, somebody screamed "Il est la!!" The police were dragging him out of the bushes before I even realized that the faraway and panic-stricken voice had been my own, shouting, "There he is!"

I watched in mute horror for a couple of minutes while the policemen beat him practically senseless in front of my face. He was kicked and clubbed in the knees and ribs, but the violence was not contained to lower areas. Soon his face was red with fist imprints and blood. I was pulled from my dumb-struck state when I suddenly looked at his drooping head just as he raised it to look me straight in the eyes. Through the incredible pain that he must have been feeling he found the will to hold the look for several seconds and then that ugly grin of promise spread across his face. He had just told me as clearly as if he had walked up to me in a room and spoken the English of the Queen that he was going to get me for this, and that I was going to pay.

I'm sure that the obliging policemen would have been happy

to keep pummeling away all day, but I had had enough violence. Without a backwards glance I waved at the taxi that was just passing by at that moment, as if to deliver me from this early morning terror. I jumped in, told him my destination and we were off. I did not so much as turn my head towards the scene I was departing. I was concentrating instead on holding back my sobs until I was in a more private place. I made it, but just barely.

Throughout the following week, where I was a bit distanced from what had happened in the city, I battled with newfound feelings regarding travel. I had always loved the feel of a backpack, the promise of adventure and the experience of learning something new everyday. But now I felt a bit deflated and had a fear that was alien to me. In the end I knew that I could not let those men win. I wanted to continue with my life as before to prove not only to myself but also to them that they could not beat me. In the years since, I have lived up to this. I still travel on my own and I still love the rumble of a train or the confusion of communicating in a new language. It took a lot of time, however, to come to this. In the meantime, at least in the desert countryside of Morocco, I felt a sense of security and peace.

The week in the desert did not help my sense of ease once I returned to the city, however. I continued living in the same neighborhood, for I had come to truly love the family that I was staying with. But every day as I walked to the bus, knowing that I was standing out like a wren in a flock of ravens, I wondered if my second attacker was somewhere near, watching. I had learned from my first trip to the police headquarters (when reporting the first attack) that very little, if anything, would be done. I had watched them type in the name of my father, mother, mother's mother and so forth on a typewriter that looked like an antique, while a bare, dangling bulb hung by a cord overhead, throwing light on the cracks in the ceiling. The police themselves admitted that nothing would likely come of it, and even though I had identified the second man, I hadn't stuck around to see the matter through — and anyways, that's not how things really work around there. So as I made my way to and from the stop, my mind would fill with the possibilities of what he could do to me. How easy it would be for him to watch me, unnoticed.

Furthermore, I didn't even know if I would recognize him if I walked by him in the street. There is no mistaking that I would know the smile, and most people agree that you can always tell someone by their eyes. But the truth was, I never looked up anymore. As the men continued their daily hissing and whistling, I tried to make myself as small and insignificant as possible, and walked quickly through the streets, always averting my eyes. I never looked into their faces, afraid of who I might see. And every day that I made it onto the bus, whether I was lucky enough to get a seat or just stood packed in the aisle, I would heave a huge sigh while my thoughts pounded to the rhythm of the loud diesel engine, "Was he watching me? Am I being followed? Was he watching me?"

Zenia Frendt graduated in the class of 2000 from Colby College in Waterville, Maine, where she majored in international studies and anthropology. She loves traveling and learning about different cultures, and recently completed a five-month backpacking trip through Europe. She is also an avid hiker and scuba diver. Zenia is currently teaching English in the south of France.

Trying Times in Transdniestr

Moldova

Kim Wildman

In my four years working around the world as a guidebook author, friends, family and travellers I've met have often expressed their envy of my life. While it may appear incredibly glamorous and exciting from the outside, working as a guidebook author is a tough gig. It is lonely, hard, frustrating and, as I discovered when I was almost thrown into a Soviet prison, sometimes downright dangerous.

My baptism by fire came on my first assignment for a well-known travel guidebook company when I was asked to cover Moldova, a small former Soviet country in Eastern Europe. Eager to prove my worth as a writer, I immediately accepted the assignment, despite having never heard of the country.

Assembled from pieces of both Romania and Ukraine, Moldova has struggled to stitch together its fraying cultural contradictions and forge a new national identity. Its short life as an independent nation, which began in 1991, has been marred by continuous political turmoil, simmering ethnic tensions and even a bloody civil war. Yet, Moldova is also a deliciously charming country of lush hilly plains, quaint little villages, fruit-filled orchards and bountiful vineyards.

As part of my research for the guide, I had to collect information from an area of the country called Transdniestr — a somewhat bizarre de facto republic created by Russian speaking separatists. While the rest of the Soviet Union disintegrated along with the Berlin Wall, Transdniestr, desperate to cling to its communist past, drew the Iron Curtain tightly around its deeply suspicious inhabitants. Increasingly worried about the Romanian influence in the region, Transdniestr proclaimed its independence in 1991.

Mounting ethnic hostilities, fuelled by a plentiful supply of Soviet arms, sparked a full-scale civil war in 1992 that left hundreds dead and thousands displaced. Today with its own borders, army, funny money and equally amusing nationalistic stamps — not recognized anywhere else in the world — Transdniestr is an independent state in all but name.

Shortly after I arrived, I made some friends at the Independent Journalism Centre in Chiinu, Moldova's bustling capital, and secured a driver named Mihai, and a translator named Vlad. I didn't speak a word of Russian, the official language of Transdniestr, so I was happy for the company of an 18-year-old journalism student keen to practice his English.

The morning we were to depart for Transdniestr, Mihai and Vlad arrived to pick me up more than an hour late, in a scrap heap-ready Russian Lada. Eager to make up for lost time, I jumped into the back seat next to Vlad, but as the car sluggishly putted its way through Chiinu's quiet streets and then out onto the main highway, I dismally realized that we weren't going to get anywhere an inch faster than 35 miles per hour.

After a tediously slow two-hour drive, we arrived at the unofficial border that separates Transdniestr from Moldova. The Moldovan border guards promptly processed our paperwork, and we proceeded to the side, where the Transdniestr guards were not so accommodating. After finishing our paperwork, they demanded that we leave the region by 3 p.m. Calculating quickly, I realized this gave me a mere four hours to cover Transdniestr's two major cities, Tiraspol and Tighina, each with a population of more than 140,000. Trying to disguise my annoyance, I smiled sweetly at the guards as we drove away.

We made our first stop in Tighina, where the bloodiest fighting took place during the 1992 military conflict. Here Transdniestran forces, backed by the Russia military, attacked Moldovan police on the west bank of the Dniester River, fighting their way across Tighina Bridge to take control of the city. While it had been almost eight years since the war, Tighina's scars still burned brightly — Russian "peacekeeping" troops still wandered the streets, and the strict curfew imposed on its citizens following the conflict was still stringently enforced. With little time at my disposal, I immediately set about gathering my information.

By the time we arrived in Tiraspol, the capital of Transdniestr, I had barely two hours left in which to complete my research. And if we were ever going to make our three o'clock deadline we needed at least half an hour to drive back to the border. Seemingly oblivious to this problem, Mihai took us on a leisurely driving tour through the city. As the time quickly ticked by, Vlad and I decided that the best way to complete my assignment was to get out of the car and run. We explained our plans to Mihai, who grudgingly agreed to meet us in front of the university at the far end of the city.

Vlad and I then took to the streets of Tiraspol in a race against time. In a city where Stalin, Lenin and Marx are still revered, we must have appeared a peculiar sight — a crazy foreign woman with a young Moldovan student in tow, running madly through the quiet Soviet city, making brief stops to quiz its wary locals regarding the merit of their city's hotels, restaurants and museums.

Glancing at our watches as we emerged from the city's last drab hotel, Vlad and I discovered to our surprise that we had thirty minutes to spare — the exact amount of time we needed to take us back to the border. We looked at each other, smiled and without a word started sprinting frantically down the main street towards the university.

With the car in sight, I reached out to touch it and triumphantly shouted, "We made it!" Collapsing exhausted into the back seat of the car Vlad ordered a breathless "Let's go!" in Russian.

With a knowing smile, Mihai turned the key in the ignition. The little Lada coughed and spluttered a weak reply and slowly churned its way to life. But, just as Mihai slipped the car in gear the Lada choked and stalled.

Undeterred, Mihai turned the engine over again. This time the Lada lurched forward and then just as suddenly stopped dead. Tapping the steering wheel anxiously, Mihai tried a third time. But sadly, the Lada made no reply. Sighing heavily he climbed out of the car.

"I don't believe this," I groaned impatiently, as Mihai popped the hood and began examining the car's tiny engine.

"That's Moldova for you," Vlad shrugged.

Reaching forward, Vlad gathered his daypack from the floor of the car and placed it on his lap. From it, he pulled a large plastic container which he opened to reveal a neatly packed lunch for two.

"It was my birthday yesterday," Vlad explained shyly. "So my mother packed us some of the leftovers from my party for lunch."

Surprised, I offered a weak "Happy Birthday," guiltily realizing that I had made us work right throughout the day without stopping to eat.

"Here," he said passing the container to me, "try some."

Conceding defeat, I let go of my rising panic, accepted a piece of cake and gratefully smiled, "Thank you."

A good half-hour passed before Mihai was able to revive the Lada. And so it was, that with the clock ticking dangerously close to four o'clock, we eventually made it back to the border. Being a region that is renowned for its adherence to strict rules and regulations, the Transdniestran guards were none too happy with our tardiness, and they decided to make an example of the only Westerner in our small group — me.

The burly guard posted at the gate brandished his machine gun menacingly at us, and barked angrily at Mihai. Unhappy with Mihai's excuses, he tore open my side door, and pulled me by my arm from the car. Instinctively I grabbed my daypack with my other arm and slung it over my shoulder.

As the guard marched me towards the border post's main office, Mihai began shouting hysterically at Vlad. Vlad jumped out of the car and ran to me translating, "Coins! Do you have any Australian coins?"

Unbeknownst to me, one of the guards had noticed my Australian passport that morning, and had told Mihai that he collected coins. He asked if I might have some Australian coins. In all the confusion with our paperwork, Mihai had forgotten to query me about the coins. Fortunately he remembered now.

Dazed by Vlad's question as the guard impatiently tugged at my arm, I stopped in my tracks, realizing that I did in fact have some Australian coins stashed in a small case in my daypack. Before we had left that morning for some reason, I had opted to take the case with me at the last minute.

With my free arm I struggled to open my pack. Blindly searching in panic through its contents, I managed to retrieve the elusive case, fumble with its tiny zip, and finally, open the case to dig through the assorted pens and pencils to a shiny gold Australian one dollar coin.

Relieved, I looked expectantly back at Vlad.

"It's for him," Vlad said, pointing towards a young guard standing some distance off.

"Here," I said throwing the coin to Vlad as the guard at my side hauled me up the office stairs, "give it to him."

Once inside the office, the guard let go of my arm and pushed me mercilessly towards his superior, in heated detail, apparently relating to him my crimes.

Perplexed, the senior guard turned to me and let forth with a barrage of abuse.

Unable to defend myself and not sure what to do, I silently stood my ground.

Just then the young morning guard burst into the office. Taking his superior aside he whispered to him quietly and excitedly showed him the gold coin.

The senior guard folded his arms across his chest, looked at the coin, and then eyed me warily. Having heard enough, he waved the young guard away. Stepping back towards me, he raised his hand shaking an accusing finger at me, and then pointed towards the door.

Confused, I stared at him blankly.

"You go now," my young defender urged nervously in broken English.

With my heart in my throat, I nodded at him gratefully and hastily took my leave.

As I emerged from the office, relief swept across Vlad's and Mihai's worried faces. Fearful the guard might change his mind, they hurriedly bundled me into the car. Mihai jumped in, threw the car into gear Mihai, pumped the gas and sped the Lada away from the border as quickly as it could go. But it wasn't until we had finally made it safely through to the Moldovan that I dared to look back.

Facing the front again I sneaked a sideways glance at Lad and burst out laughing.

"Let's go home," Vlad smiled.

"Da!" Mihai chorused knowingly.

I have learnt much since my first foray into guidebook authoring. But, the most important lesson is to always carry a few Australian gold one dollar coins. You never know when they will come in handy!

Kim Wildman grew up in Toowoomba, Australia, with parents who unwittingly instilled in her a desire to travel at a very young age by extending the immediate family to include 11 exchange students. After graduating from university with a bachelor's in journalism, with her feet growing evermore restless, Kim jumped at the chance to train and bus it through the lesser known regions of Eastern Europe as a guidebook author for Lonely Planet. Hooked for life, she has since worked on Lonely Planet's Athens, Eastern Europe, Europe on a Shoestring, Romania & Moldova, South Africa, Lesotho & Swaziland *and* West Africa. *Kim now lives in Cape Town, South Africa where she is studying for a master's in African studies at the University of Cape Town.*

A (Slovenian) Christmas Carol

Lublijana, Slovenia

MILLICENT BENNETT

THE SUN STAGGERED ITS WAY OVER THE SOGGY, GRAY ROOFTOPS AND in through my balcony window. The Saturday morning before our school's winter holidays, and this was the Mediterranean Italy I had contracted myself to? The city's December air hung damp with anemic chill as, twenty minutes after the alarm, I dragged myself out of bed and down to the *questura*, Trieste's local police station, to go over — for the fourth time — some issue with my student visa. My boyfriend had driven up from Florence for the weekend, and if the bureaucrats couldn't cough up my *permesso di soggiorno* we'd have to cancel our day trip to Slovenia with my roommates.

By the time the police sent me away empty-handed, it was after noon and the sky had turned a dismal, flaccid shade of gray, host to a company of morose rainclouds. The four of us stood on the steps of the courthouse and debated: without my *permesso*, crossing the border out of the EU would be illegal; without a trip out of the cheerless city, we might all go clinically insane. We piled into the car.

Trieste, where my roommates and I had moved for a year to teach English, stands as the very last outpost of northeast Italy, an industrial, backwater port crushed up against the Slovenian border. Less than an hour inland lies Slovenia's capital city, Lublijana, of which we knew tantalizingly nothing. Hungry for diversion in any form, we opted to spend our afternoon there, for better or for worse. So, after a nerve-wracking but uneventful border check, we were soon on our way. After the stresses of the morning, I quickly fell sound asleep.

And awoke to a glittering, magical world. Stepping from the

355

car, we sank several inches into the sparkling snow that lined the street alongside the city's central park. Surrounding trees hung with brightly colored columns of cloth, colossal Chinese lanterns painted with delicate winter scenes; in the park's ice rink, laughing children skated blissfully in circles. The change from the Trieste of an hour before was, to say the least, startling. We had chosen Slovenia simply for its exoticness — if for no other reason than to say we'd been there, where no one we knew had gone. We (or I at least) expected a place that fit the title "the former Yugoslavia," a town that fed my image of the war-torn state. But instead of the mildly precarious third-world environment I'd imagined, we seemed more accurately to have stepped into Victorian England, the incarnation of a Dickens novel, or a Currier and Ives postcard. The more we saw, the more I felt as if we were living out a Hollywood Christmas dream.

Having neither map nor destination, we set off towards the river, gleefully sliding hand-in-hand across the ice-touched sidewalks, still amazed by our transition from rainy, gray Trieste to this winter wonderland everywhere we looked. The colorful, majestic Austro-Hungarian architecture lay framed in white, and visible up every side street towered the huge, medieval castle, which struck us as a necessary touch of stage design. Each stretching, rambling tree seemed outlined by deliberate brushstrokes. As we crossed the three wide stone bridges at the center of town, we were greeted by wreath- and Christmas-tree sellers, rosy-cheeked in their red wool coats and fur earmuffs. Picturesque families strolled past, and, walking the streets, we seemed the only tourists, the only people out of costume, or out of character.

Reveling in the snowy scenes and homesick for New England winters, I gathered ammunition and ambushed my roommates at a crosswalk — the ensuing snowball war left us all dripping and deeply satisfied. We ducked into a nearby cafe in search of hot chocolate, but, once inside, found ourselves instead in a plush tea room, thick

with the rich scents of tea and cider and *vin brulé*. A large fire sputtered merrily at the far end of the room, and the tables were filled
with earnest students and bright-eyed young couples: to my mind,
Hollywood couldn't have air-brushed itself a more perfect atmosphere. All the tables were occupied, but, drawn in by the fire, we
simply stood helpless on the threshold, red-nosed and blue-fingered.
In a moment, two young women near us stood up and graciously
insisted we take their table, speaking a softly accented but otherwise
perfect English.

The tea was amazing, and, after more than an hour by the fire it
took a certain amount of determination to convince ourselves to
leave. Once outside, we window-shopped in snow-swept alleys amid
my growing sense that, really, we must be in a movie. Finally, I
realized that what gave me this impression was not simply the idyl-
lic Christmas scenes, not only the smiling, well-dressed people, but
the actual presence of a musical soundtrack underscoring it all. In
every street of Lublijana, Slovenian Christmas carols were being softly
piped through an elaborate outdoor sound-system, so the music
seemed to follow one throughout the city. No wonder we felt like
the extras in a holiday-movie montage!

I laughed aloud at this — what a brilliant way to sustain the
spirit, to keep peace and joy in the streets! The Slovenians had casually, magically, outdone all traditional holiday cheer I had ever known,
in life or in the movies. This strange, this perfect little city in "the
former Yugoslavia" was a living postcard, a scene one only dreamt
about in one's bleary, slush-caked, December reality. As darkness
fell, the decorations in the streets lit up, and, beyond, the castle stood
ablaze in its glory at the top of a hill sprinkled with lights; it was
floating in a sparkling, starlit sky.

What amazed me most of all, though, was not merely
Lublijana's beautiful "normalness," its expert embodiment of all
that was valued as picturesque in the world I was used to, but its

simultaneous commitment to its own strident, creative individuality. Unlike the huge, fluorescent Santas and geometric Christmas trees that hung oppressively above Trieste's thoroughfares, Lublijana's street decorations had been commissioned to a local artist, who had produced a brilliant universe of planets, suns, and shooting stars, where every street corner yielded up another shining comet...

The most memorable example of the modern spirit with which these Slovenians inhabited their fairytale world arrived in the form of an elderly gentleman we met on the riverside. We had wandered back to the water to watch the sunset, and, again unable to resist the snow, began building ourselves a miniature snowman along one of the low walls above the bank. We easily rolled three big snowballs for the body, but facial features proved a considerable obstacle; we had to scrounge around in the gutter and along the wall before we found anything we could use. Soon, though, our snowman was suitably outfitted with five pebbles (two eyes and three buttons), twig arms, a wood-sliver nose, an orange-peel mouth, and a tiny black cup that served perfectly as a top-hat; moments later, my room-mate Christine appeared gleefully bearing a tiny "fig leaf," which we placed in its appropriate location. The wooden nose, however, wouldn't stick, and as we fanned out to begin a second round of foraging, we became aware of a set of dark eyes following us watchfully from a third-story window. Christine sheepishly crept back to remove the fig leaf, and just in time — out from the building swept a tall, gray-bearded figure in a long, black trench coat and top hat, looking for all the world like a Victorian gentleman. Expecting him to stalk haughtily past, we were shocked when instead he approached my boyfriend and produced a small carrot from an inside pocket of his coat. "You may need this," he declared in broken Italian, and glided down the street with a smile.

We took the carrot gratefully, but, being kids, had soon enough resurrected the fig leaf, and the vegetable was serving a decidedly unnasal purpose. We tried carefully to shield it from any prying eyes above, all too familiar with the conservative humorlessness of Triestines, but our guard was down a few minutes later when our benefactor returned — my leap to move the carrot was futile. Without a word or a friendly glance, he hurried past us up the stairs, and was lost in the recesses of the house. Suddenly, the fun and the spirit of our game had been lost; each of us felt a certain guilt at having, even in this small way, betrayed the generosity of a kindly old man.

We were preparing to leave as the door of the house swung open a second time, and the top-hat and cloak reappeared. Grinning widely, exuberantly, with a childish joy, he slipped into my boyfriend's hand the biggest carrot we had ever seen. "This," he confided, "might serve you better."

Ultimately, it was this winkingly self-assured, youthful spirit that charmed me most about Lublijana that day. As we drove back to Italy that night, I thought about this small piece of "the former Yugoslavia" that had come proudly into its post-war, post-Communist identity on its own terms, that had taken the best visions the world's imagination had to offer and made them its own. Out here in a war-torn wilderness, it was living a postcard Christmas, written by a modernist Dickens, gently spiced with a Slovenian twist.

After a childhood spent shuttling between Tuscany and her tiny hometown in upstate New York, Millicent Bennett developed a restless instinct for travel. She has driven a camper four times across America with her mother. She has also lived as a student in Paris and as a civil volunteer in Crete and Bohemia. Having just completed a year of teaching at the International School of Trieste, she is currently settling down to pursue her Harvard fellowship as a scholar of 19th-century travel literature, and now lives in Florence, Italy with her childhood sweetheart and their cat.

Angels of the Adriatic

Badija Island, Croatia

Rebecca Kraus

As I swayed to the music of *Stari*, or "The Mostar Song", with little Amila on my shoulders, I could hear her singing about raising the spirit of Bosnia. She was joyfully waving our home-made peace flag, her voice merged with the other kids' at this last sunset of summer camp. Everyone was singing, hugging, taking pictures and declaring that love will prevail over hate. My heart was engulfed in emotion, a flood of tears rushed from my chest to my eyes and I smiled at the power of this moment and of the human spirit.

I was a volunteer then, at a peace-building camp for kids who had suffered in the Balkan wars, and I have not been the same since. Organized by the Global Children's Organization (GCO), a Los Angeles, California-based non-profit, it sits on Badija Island in the Adriatic Sea off Croatia. I'd heard stories about it, about Bosnians, Serbians and Croatians, Muslims and Christians not only sharing rooms but making friends, and I knew that waging peace would take patience and understanding.

Badija is no major tourist destination, although it is surrounded by the gorgeous aqua waters of the Dalmatian coast, across from Italy, and is a short water taxi ride from Korcula Island, the much-visited birthplace of explorer Marco Polo. The calmness of the surrounding sea and the picturesque setting inspire visitors. By day, they lounge on beaches under crisp blue skies and wispy white clouds; by night, brilliant galaxies unroll across the inky black sky, and moonlight sparkles on the water to a symphony of crickets on the island. My summer, in June 2001, the sea around Badija was busy with the usual jet skiers, windsurfers and kayakers, and island tourists were living the usual *la dolce vita* — lounging in the warm southern European sun, sipping their beer or wine and lapping up risotto and ice cream.

What most of these tourists didn't know was that there were also 100 kids and more than 50 volunteers, mostly Americans, on Badija, inhabiting most of the rooms in a converted 17th century monastery, now a quaint, albeit decaying, hotel. GCO's program mission for the camp was simple: let the children just *be*, and refill their souls with peace and compassion after being displaced by war, and suffering unimaginable terror. If they got to experience some of *la dolce vita* in luxurious settings too, with fun activities, that was bonus. At the camp, they created their own new reality, away from ethnic hatred, nationalistic politics and a crippled economy. They played, dressed up, sailed, swam, canoed, painted and imagined themselves as free, happy spirits existing in a peaceful world.

There was much contrast at camp — happiness and melancholy, youthfulness and maturity. I'd imagine my girls cowering at the sounds of bombs outside their window, wailing when they learned of their parents' deaths. Some had seen their mommies fall from running through trenches to get water, or collapse in grief at news of more massacres. Many of the kids lived amidst displaced, depressed adults in their home countries. Here on Badija, they were surrounded by beauty and comfort that it took time for them to understand. One girl at first would hustle for coins and collect extra jams at the breakfast table to hoard up in her room for some "emergency." It took her time to realize that this was a *safe* place, and she would in fact get fed the next day and the next, in great abundance, surrounded by people who loved her.

When I try to say what these two weeks truly meant to the

kids and volunteers, I realize it was a two-way street. I had come
there to contribute to the kids' peaceful reality, and I realize that
the kids' spirits nurtured me, too, and gave *me* a renewed sense of
my own humanity. They made me believe that angels do live on
earth. None of this, of course, was apparent when I first saw the
boats full of them arriving on Badija. They were from Sarajevo,
Mostar, Tuzla, Banja Luka, Dubrovnik and other parts of Bosnia
Herzegovina, Croatia and the Republic of Serbska. They wanted
to carry their bags themselves, decorate their nametags, chat and
play, right away. I got a precious bunch of girls in my "family
group": 15 of them, mostly nine-year-olds. It took a while for me
to memorize their names, from A to Z, literally, but now they slip
off my tongue.

There was Aykuna, the tempestuous, melancholy girl who
seemed more like a woman than a child; Sanela the gypsy orphan
from Dubrovnik, who was at first ostracized for her looks and
her tortured loneliness. There was Karmela, the precious, funny
spirit from war-torn Mostar who said one of the highlights of
camp was me teaching her how to "jump with her head" when
she dove into the sea. Amila was the sweet angel who made me
laugh every night at bedtime, and sang along to our goodnight
"*Laku Noć*" song. Ziyada from Sarajevo appeared to be an old
soul full of wisdom, grace and compassion most of the time, but
was just another girl who couldn't swim once we hit the beach.

As the girls roomed together, they bonded: they played tag,
sang, danced, swam, jumped with their heads and giggled. I took
great joy in teaching them new games, sharing in their joy of *skolke*
(shell) hunting around the island, and tossing them into the water
at the count of *yeden, sva, tri!* They taught me the different pro-
nunciations of "c", I taught them how to say "ice cream," and I
became obsessed with making them happy. I cheered "Bravo"
when they played volleyball well. I tickled them and played paddy

cake — simple joys lost on those whose lives have been shattered by war.

I played and connected with the children however I could. Badija had great facilities for a camp, and all the volunteers, including the bilingual ones from towns all over ex-Yugoslavia, formed an affectionate community there. We saw each other in the dining hall, smiled as we sat in the cloisters of the old monastery, laughed, frolicked in the sea. Once the kids were asleep, we adults would hold intense conversations about what it was like to be in Sarajevo during its four-year siege, to put land mines down in one's own backyard, and to see one of the most beautiful countries in Europe turn into a tinder box of frayed nations after communism fell and Milosevic gained power. Late into the night, breaking from the conversations, the ex-Yugoslavs drank, danced, and sang songs from what was once their united country. I was moved at how the inhumane experiences of the recent years in the former Yugoslavia could melt away here, that these people could create a community of people rich with humanity.

During the day, we adults focused our energy on helping give back to the children some of the joy that their wartime trauma had taken. We were blessed by the presence of the Sarajevo Drum Orchestra, a group of compassionate young men who had been in concentration camps. They taught the kids rhythm, confidence and teamwork, and also blessed our summer with our camp anthem: *Stari*, "The Mostar Song." It describes the famous Mostar bridge that had connected different ethnicities for centuries until it was bombed in the mid 1990s. Its lyrics capture Bosnia's soul:

Ja Pogoden Nisam Ni Umbro, no Pao, Samo Sam morao skociti dole. Nastavicu tacno, tamo gdje sam sto izronice Stari za one so ga vole.

I'm not hit neither died, neither fell down, I just had to jump down.
I'll continue exactly where I stopped, Old will rise for those who love it.

The kids would sing this song more and more passionately as the two-week camp neared its end. *Inglishki* or the "local languages" didn't serve us for communicating nearly as well as music, eye contact, playing, games, affection, smiles and moments of silence. Wordless communication, in fact, gave way to instances of profound emotional honesty, such as when Sanela finally got comfortable dancing with others and pulled off a perfect break-dancing move, then rushed to my side in embarrassment. Or when Miranda curled up next to me on the shore and I wrapped her in my towel so we could sit and hug for half an hour without uttering a sound. When Seydefa cut her leg, her friend Ziyada and I held her hand as we walked back to the room. As Seydefa cried, we sat, stroking her hair to show our concern. I couldn't help but think of Seydefa's tears, and how many must have been shed in moments of horror and tragedy. I felt relief that this cry was for a minor cut. As we learned about each other non-verbally, I saw how compassionate these kids were to one another, truly like angels, and I wondered, has the *pain* these kids endured enabled them to be so *loving*?

Asmira, the sullen girl whose father had been killed in Srebrenica, a town that suffered an infamous massacre of Muslim men, the worst atrocity in Europe since 1945, impressed me with her grace. She'd offer me her salad, and silently accompany me to the beach, lacking in the joyful innocence a 9-year-old girl should have. One day in the second week, she slowly took my hand for the first time, after I had taught her how to push her way through the sea. When I was taking a picture of her the last day of camp, she forced a smile so I could remember her that way. It was her way of saying thank you, *hvala*. My heart swelled as I saw her angelic image captured through the viewfinder.

The histories of these kids ran deep. I would take note of the sadness in Miranda's eyes one minute, then laugh with Amila the next. Amila liked to chew on flavored dental floss, dressed up in pretty dresses every night at our disco. One night, when some girls were crying for their mommies, Amila triumphantly announced: "I could stay here three months without my mommy. This is the best place there is!" I suspect she had never been happier in her nine years of life.

Witnessing the children's transformations were part of the power of camp. Sanela went from awkward outcast to fun-loving camper, kicking our volleyball and hiding my tape recorder. As we adults put faces and hearts to the tales of the Balkans we had seen and heard reported overseas, we watched the children grow into a joy and safety they'd never known. Many of us volunteers continued our experience after camp ended, by visiting Mostar and Sarajevo, with their abiding hatreds, bombed out buildings, cemeteries that had once been parks and cripples who'd lived through Hell. I tried to imagine what it felt like to live here. What effect might all these broken buildings, grief-stricken faces, and tombstones have on a child's psyche?

As my two week experience in the Balkans drifts away in time, I still feel a deepened connection to my own humanity. And I'll never forget the passion of song, the warmth of the hugs, and the tears in our eyes as we said goodbye to the angels of the Adriatic.

Rebecca Kraus studied psychology at the University of California, Santa Barbara and Social Policy at the University of York, England. Former managing editor of Entertainment@Home *magazine, she has contributed stories of travel and pop culture to many publications: from* Request, Rolling Stone *and* Premiere *to* Soma *and* Abroad View. *When she's not traveling around the world, she makes her living writing for the Games Design team at Mattel in Los Angeles. See www.globalchild.org.*

The Leaking Lada

Veliko Turnovo, Bulgaria

Elliott Dykes

I AM SITTING ON THE CASTLE WALLS. BULGAR KINGS RULED HERE
from Veliko Turnovo for more than 200 years before 1393. By
the looks of it, nothing much has been done since. Like all old
towns, it was built on a river in a valley, and I'm just sort of
sitting here watching the Soviet Ladas labor up the hill. All Lada
cars have tool kits in the trunk and all Lada owners are amateur
mechanics. If something breaks, Bulgarians fix it. Only if
something's irreparable do they break down and replace it. So
everything here is old. A Bulgarian once told me that the only
thing a Lada is good for is spare parts for another Lada.

The one remarkable and vibrant thing in Bulgaria is the forest. What a forest! Many things here are very old, like the castle;
the rest was built by the Soviets 50 years ago. There isn't anything else, just cracked stucco buildings of brown and gray and
the red mission tile roofs. It's like an agreement with the forest: it
swallows everything except the brown stucco buildings with red
tile roofs. It will eventually swallow this road below me. The
river on my right has no banks. The black forest grows right up to
the edge. It will be a swamp in 50 years. If they let ivy grow up
the sides of the buildings, you could camouflage the whole country. Maybe that's what the Soviets had in mind, but they lost.
The forest swallowed Communism, too. And now all that's left is
rusted iron, Ladas, empty factories, smokestacks, and railroad
tracks crisscrossing the country, leading nowhere, past stations
with no roads, harsh fluorescent lights on rusted placards naming
some desperate isolated village perched in the mountains fighting

the forest all whispering the broken promise of Communism. Perhaps the whole country is sulking.

I've heard that Communism was a good idea, just that the implementation was bad. As I watch a Peugeot taxi tow a broken Lada up the hill, I have to disagree. It is against human nature to expect a man to work harder for an abstract concept than he will for his own self interest. Any system including such an idea will eventually need a tow from a Peugeot taxi.

I initially found Bulgaria incredibly quaint and rustic, but I've changed my mind. Yesterday I visited the "traditional" village of Koprivstitsa. There they carry on in the old Bulgarian way of life — but that is true only if there is a new Bulgarian way of life. There isn't. The old and the new are the same. Koprivstitsa isn't traditional ... it's just old. It's like retro clothing. If kids rediscover old styles, it's cool. If some dude in his middle 50s is still wearing the stuff from the last time it was popular, that's just pathetic.

The only other remarkable and vibrant thing about Bulgaria is the train. Yesterday, I rode seven hours on the train for two dollars and changed at three stations. We left late because the train was broken and needed a fix. I saw the conductor/mechanic beating a rusted metal rod on the platform. Being 45 minutes late, I feared I wouldn't make my connections, which were only five minutes per station. All the other trains were late too, so it turned out not to matter.

Bulgarians nod their head for no and shake it for yes. So it happened like this: I pointed at the train, "Karlovo?" They shook their head. "Tulovo?" They shook their head. "Veliko Turnovo?" Same head shake. We are conditioned to think head shakes mean no. I couldn't help it. Every stop it was the same crisis: I'm on the wrong train, until I remembered that headshakes mean yes. Then I'd forget two minutes later and it was back to the same thing.

At 10:30 p.m. I arrived in Veliko Turnovo. It was raining a hard gray heavy Soviet rain. It was dark and the station is 5 km from town. I think the Soviet Central Planners saw the city one day growing to meet it. They had big ideas, a great vision of a coming Empire. I was cold and wet and alone with the dark and rain. All the Lada taxis were either gone or broken. My spirits were very low and I felt a little ridiculous.

I was at the station huddled under an overhang trying to stay dry. At moments like these, one thinks the worst. You have no initiative. I froze up and did what one always does in such situations: wait for something to happen.

I was wet now; it was raining thick and dark. I couldn't see anything but silhouettes. A man walked out the door with a package. "Where you go?" he asked. I told the truth, always a dangerous proposition: "I don't know." "2 lev. We go my car."

I didn't have 2 lev, only 20, which is often the same as being completely broke. No one ever has change. "OK," I shrugged, which broke every travel rule I have: Strange man approaches you at the train station carrying a large package and offers to take you for a ride ... always say no. But facing the alternative of standing in a cold rain in front of the train station for the rest of the night, — I suppose it was the lesser of two evils.

He had a Lada, which leaked badly, and there were tools everywhere. With his ten-word vocabulary, I made out that he had studied one year of English, but made a 100% effort and liked to practice. We passed into town ... a good sign. We stopped at an intersection and it was black and rainy ... a bad sign. "You sleep my house 10 lev. We go hotel, maybe 30 lev. You want my house or hotel?"

My brain lit up with every possibility in the universe and I felt lightheaded. I decided that if you're going to break rules, break them all in a grand fashion and reap the benefits. I recalled all the stories I've heard of people being drugged, robbed, kidnapped and left in the middle of nowhere. "OK, your house," I said, and we turned away from town. I experienced the euphoria one feels after making a potentially disastrous, but wickedly fun, decision. And then I became paranoid.

"Where are you from what do you do how old are you I came from Istanbul it's nice but I like Bulgaria better *(a lie)*," I said in one giddy breath eyeing his mail. Were there drugs in the package? Maybe the gun he'll use to kidnap me? I was trying to pay attention to the direction in case I had to make a run for it. Why did he keep looking in the rearview mirror? Is looking in your mirror a lot really all that suspicious, or am I just paranoid? I blurted out some more gibberish to distract myself. "I love Bulgaria the people are very nice no one speaks English I can't read the signs."

We stopped outside an apartment building. "You wait. I go talk to my woman. Maybe she not OK." I was in the car alone, but feeling good about the wife thing. I fished around his car, but found nothing suspicious except my own wandering mind.

He returned what seemed like hours later. George had a nice apartment, big by European standards, a wife named Melina, and a son, Martin. I felt good. We sat around the table and I showed them pictures from Turkey while Melina brought out some food: over-salted sliced cucumbers and a barely cooked egg. I hadn't eaten for 8 hours, so it was excellent, and I became giddier still on account of the sudden rush of nourishment. Through odd and infrequent meals, bursts of activity, long waits, noise, and no sleep, travel causes violent mood swings. I found myself caught up anyway.

"You drink alcohol?" asked George. A beer would be great before bed. "Sure," I nodded as I bounced Martin on my knee and spoke too fast for anyone to understand. Melina brought out two shot glasses and a non-descript bottle with a pale yellow liquor.

This is the part of the movie where you cringe and the dumb tourist gets drugged and robbed. Twice in Istanbul alone, I heard stories of drugged drinks and waking the next morning with nothing. He had a glass, too, and I saw her pour it, so I made a toast to our health and drank. He only took a sip and set the glass down. The mind plays tricks on you if you let it, and sometimes even when you don't. Was I feeling strange? Yeah, a little. But I took a shot of strong liquor, so maybe it's normal? Was I getting sleepy? Hmm ... I'd been sleepy anyway; it was a long day. I couldn't place anything threatening or nonthreatening, so I just imagined stuff.

Luckily, nothing odd happened. Breaking the rules doesn't always catch up with you. Risk = Reward. Big Risk = Big Reward. Breaking the Rules = Rock Star Fun and Drug Dealer Profits. Of course, there is the significant flipside to those equations, but we are preached the dogma of those from childhood until we forget that safety and caution are easy substitutes for boredom and old age. Fun and profit have a cost.

George is a civilian working with the military. "We break rockets. Last year automatics *(rifles)*." Bulgaria is meant to join NATO. Although, to me, you'd want a military ally to have rockets and guns, it seems NATO doesn't see the value of a military ally with a military. I am a simple fellow, though, and certainly not meant for politics.

George has a good job and is rich by Bulgarian standards. He counts himself lucky to have a job, but is worried about the future because they are running out of things to disassemble. His wife shared that there are several good beaches on the Black Sea. I was, according to them, the first tourist in their home and George picked me up because he felt sorry for me standing out in the rain looking lost. I even found out the contents of the mysterious package. It was a Bulgarian sweet bread sent from Melina's mother in the south. We ate some and I slept very peacefully after another shot of the homemade liquor. It turns out it's a plum brandy called *Polenca*, which is the most horrible thing I've ever tasted, including the cough medicine I used to take when I was little.

Elliott is an overeducated, idealistic, career-dodging travel junkie. He has lived abroad eight times and traveled through more than 30 countries on five continents. In search of Lord knows what, he has trekked the Himalaya, climbed glaciers in Patagonia, sailed the Mediterranean, and whiled away many happy days on the beaches of East Asia. He believes in self-development, the value of good people and work as statement of purpose. His long-term goal is to remind the developed world that people matter more than money. In fact, people are all that matters.

ACKNOWLEDGMENTS

WITH GRATEFUL ACKNOWLEDGMENT to the hundreds of travelers who contributed their stories, and my editor, Martin Westerman; to my friends who believed in the book from the beginning and devoted time to the project, Matthew Michael Manning and Justin Stuwart Rawlings; to my cousin who designed the cover, Greg Pearson (www.gregpearsondesign.com); to Mark Cutshall who offered keen counsel and the right words; to Tracy Cutchlow (SilntAsas9@hotmail.com) for proofing the final; to Joanne Snow-Smith, professor of Renaissance Art History at the University of Washington, for encouraging a business student to study art history in Rome; to Greg Gottesman, who unknowingly convinced me to write a book; to Nicolay Thomassen (http://jnt22.home.comcast.net), Andrew Schein, Kiersten Throndsen, and Katie Brown for the cover photographs; to Andréa Murphy for reading stories; to Nick Johnson for designing the Web site; to the one friend who viewed all 2,200 of my Europe photographs, Jake Ware; and to my parents, Carl and Polly Pearson, for enabling me to study abroad and backpack in Europe.

About the Editors

MARK PEARSON has a degree in business from the University of Washington. After studying art history in Rome and experiencing Europe from a backpack, he felt compelled to compile a collection of the best backpacking stories. Mark is the president of the Pearson Venture Group and the publisher of the "From a Backpack" series. He lives and works in Seattle, Washington.

MARTIN WESTERMAN, who has lived in and backpacked around Europe, is the author of *How To Flirt*, *The Business Environmental Handbook* and others, and hundreds of articles. He currently lectures on communications for the University of Washington Business School in Seattle, where he lives with his wife, two sons, and edible garden.

PLANNING THE TRIP

Now that you've read the book, it's time to go abroad. If you want to backpack around Europe, study, work or volunteer abroad, check out these resources below. From buying a railpass to booking hostels, everything you need to know is a few clicks away.

Sign-up for my E-Newsletter at **www.EuropeBackpack.com**. I'll send you the latest backpacking news, interviews with the authors of the stories, and information on the best hostels, cities, and events.

If you need some travel advice, have a story to share, or just want to chat about Europe, join my Yahoo! Group to interact with backpackers and students all over the world. Join the group at: **http://groups.yahoo.com/group/europefromabackpack/**

Now is the time to explore and discover Europe.

Happy Travels!

Mark Pearson

Rick Steves' Europe Through the Back Door
www.ricksteves.com

Rick Steves, host of the popular public television series, "Rick Steves' Europe," and author of 27 European travel books, has a Web site that can assist backpackers with country information, European Railpasses and tours. Pick-up a copy of Rick Steves' BEST OF EUROPE guidebook for a whirlwind backpacking tour of the must-see sights and cities.

GoAbroad.com
www.GoAbroad.com

GoAbroad.com is the comprehensive on-line source for travel to Europe including study abroad, language schools, overseas internships, international volunteer positions, teaching abroad, jobs abroad, and a whole lot more! You can also find great resources including discount student rail passes, embassy directories, youth hostels, travel gear and every tool you need to make the most out of your European backpacking adventure!

GuideforEurope.com
www.guideforeurope.com

The ultimate resource for backpacking and budget travelers heading to Europe. Planning your trip couldn't be easier - on-line hostel booking, photos, packing lists, travel links and hostel reviews. An active message board forum is also available, with seasoned travelers offering tips and advice.

BugEurope.com
www.bugeurope.com

This excellent resource has extensive transport and destination information plus forums where you can share travel experiences and tips with other travelers. The main feature of the BUG Web site are the hostel reviews — these allow you to post your own reviews of thousands of hostels around Europe and are regarded by many people as the best source of information about hostels online.

BootsnAll Travel Network
www.BootsnAll.com

BootsnAll's mission is to cultivate an organic community that encourages independent travel. We try to accomplish this via the BootsnAll Travel Community membership, connecting travelers, extensive resources for planning your trip (100,000+webpages), and exclusive web-only travel deals on tickets, hostels, and around the world airfare.

CanuckAbroad.com
www.canuckabroad.com

Canuck Abroad is a resource for Canadian expats abroad, or Canadians planning to travel. You'll find links and information about cheap flights and tickets, cheap trains, hostels, hotels, guide books, overseas jobs, and more.

Travelpackers.com
www.travelpackers.com

Travelpackers.com is the specialist on-line journal Web site for travellers. The service provides unlimited webspace for you to write journals, stories and post your photographs for your friends, families and contacts to share. The Travelpackers Real World Guide is a valuable source of information for anyone planning a trip. Read reviews and advice from travellers who have actually been there or post your own so travellers can be inspired by your experiences. Simply post your story or photographs and we will tell your friends that your latest news is ready and waiting, no more hassle with group e-mail from unreliable internet cafe's - and what's more, we'll do it all for free!!

Travellerspoint.com
www.travellerspoint.com

An online community from around the world, with a strong focus on individuals' experiences and adventures. For those planning a trip, there are Travel Helpers available to answer questions. Once on the road, members can keep an online travel diary to share their journey with family, friends, and other members. The travel reunion database, photography gallery, forums, and accommodation directory enables travelers to connect with new friends met abroad or start planning the next trip. Started by two brothers living on opposite sides of the world, the site is free for all to join.

Things2do.com
www.things2do.com

Things2do.com is an online store for tours and activities of every description. Featuring anything from abseiling in Cape Town to zorbing in Rotorua, this site provides users with plenty of diversion to keep them occupied.

Oldcontinent.com
www.oldcontinent.com

Get backpacking and budget travel information for Europe. Read the latest on hostels, find answer's in the FAQ section, and interact with other travelers in a forum.

STUDY ABROAD

Cultural Experiences Abroad
www.GoWithCEA.com

Expand. Explore. Experience. Study abroad is an option for you, regardless of your major, language experience or financial situation. Match your interests to one of 20 universities in Spain, France, Italy, Mexico, Costa Rica, England, Australia and Ireland. Personal enrollment advisor's help you find the right program and direct students to financial aid and scholarship opportunities. The website enables you to connect with past participants to receive firsthand information on the programs. You may contact an advisor at 1-800-266-4441 or info@GoWithCEA.com.

CIEE
www.ciee.org

CIEE is the leading U.S. non-governmental international education organization. CIEE creates and administers programs that allow high school and university students and educators to study, volunteer, work and teach abroad. CIEE has 60 study programs in over 30 host countries, 800 volunteer projects in 30 host countries, work programs in Australia, Canada, France, Germany, Ireland, and New Zealand and teaching programs in China and Thailand. Educators can participate in summer seminars in 20 countries. Call 1-800-40-STUDY or e-mail studyinfo@ciee.org to talk with an advisor.

National Registration Center for Study Abroad (NRCSA)
www.nrcsa.com

The National Registration Center for Study Abroad (NRCSA) has been a leading standards organization and study abroad registration center in the field of language and culture immersion abroad since 1968. Programs abroad for all ages in 43 countries to study any of 22 languages. Includes programs for academic credit, learning vacations, Third Age travel, internships/volunteer/teach abroad, professional development and children/teen summer camps. Go abroad for one week...or one year! Contact NRCSA at 414-278-0631 (Milwaukee) or 202-338-5927 (Washington DC). E-mail: Study@nrcsa.com

StudyAbroad.com
www.StudyAbroad.com

StudyAbroad.com is the #1 online resource for study abroad information. The site includes a comprehensive directory of programs and detailed destination information. Prospective students can easily contact programs and prepare for their travels by learning about their destination's history, politics, weather, culture, sights, and much more!

NYU Study Abroad Programs
www.nyu.edu/studyabroad

NYU study abroad combines a world-renowned faculty; bright, enthusiastic students; fully staffed sites; and academic centers that enable you to take advantage of the best that each city has to offer. Explore another culture, learn a new language, or strengthen existing language skills while you earn credit through NYU's exciting array of undergraduate courses in a wide variety of disciplines. Fall, spring, and full academic-year programs are available in Florence, London, Madrid, Paris, and Prague. For more information call 212-998-4433, or e-mail studyabroad@nyu.edu.

University Studies Abroad Consortium (USAC)
www.usac.unr.edu

Established in 1982, the University Studies Abroad Consortium (USAC) currently provides 31 quality study abroad programs in 21 countries including intensive language and full curriculum programs. Month, summer, semester and yearlong programs include field trips, university credit, small classes, numerous housing arrangements and internships. Request a catalog and apply online.

WORK AND VOLUNTEER ABROAD

CDS International
www.cdsintl.org

CDS International, now in its 35th successful year, is a non-profit organization dedicated to developing and enhancing opportunities for Americans to participate in meaningful, practical training opportunities abroad. CDS offers students, recent graduates and young professionals visa sponsorship and internship placement services, as well as study tours and seminars, in a variety of business, engineering and other technical fields in Germany, Argentina, Ecuador, Switzerland, and Turkey. Most internships are paid and last 3-18 months. While all programs contain an internship component, some have academic or language training elements as well.

AFS Intercultural Programs, Inc.
www.afs.org

AFS is a nonprofit, educational organization that offers exchanges among more than 50 countries of the world. Students, 16 to 18 years old, live with a family in a community abroad and attend school for a year, semester or summer. Young adults, 18 and over, work as a volunteer in a community service organization or business abroad while learning skills, a new language and culture. Teachers live with a host family in another country and teach in a local school. Since 1947 more than 300,000 individuals have had an AFS exchange experience.

International Partnership for Service-Learning (IPSL)
www.ipsl.org

The International Partnership for Service-Learning, founded in 1982, is a not-for-profit educational organization of colleges, universities, service agencies and related organizations united to foster and develop programs linking volunteer service and academic study for credit. Program locations include the Czech Republic, Ecuador (Guayaquil and Quito), England, France, India, Israel, Jamaica, Mexico, the Philippines, Russia, Scotland, South Africa, South Dakota (with Native Americans), and Thailand. Students earn 12- 18 college credits per semester and serve up to 15-20 hours per week. The programs are based at accredited universities and all aspects of the programs are conducted by in-country professionals. More than 4,000 students from 400 colleges and universities in the U.S. and 25 other nations have participated in IPS-L programs.

Global Volunteers
www,globalvolunteers.org

"Travel that feeds the soul." Global Volunteers is a premier "volunteer vacation" provider, offering unique service opportunities for individuals and groups of all ages and backgrounds. By working on locally initiated and directed human-development projects in 18 countries, including the United States, Global Volunteers participants build a foundation for peace through mutual understanding. One-, two- or three-week programs include: teaching English, caring for children, wilderness preservation, construction and assisting with health care. No special skills required. Now in its 20th year, Global Volunteers organizes over 150 teams year-round. Call 800-487-1074, email@globalvolunteers.org.

TRANSPORTATION

StudentUniverse.com
www.StudentUniverse.com

StudentUniverse.com is the leading seller of Student Airfares on the web. Verified students can find fares from more than 400 points in North America to hundreds of cities in Europe and around the world. Student Airfares are generally significantly lower than published fares, and allow for much more flexibility in terms of length of stay (up to a year), stopovers, "open jaw" returns from another city, one-ways, liberal change policies, and the ability to purchase close to departure. In addition to Student Airfares, StudentUniverse.com also sells rail passes, hostel bookings, travel insurance, and tour packages — every product backpackers need to get where they are going.

Digihitch.com
www.digihitch.com

digihitch.com is a hitchhiking and road sub-culture portal, with stories, tips, photos, forums and useful resources for budget/ adventure travelers. Includes a special European section and rideboard.

AllEuropeRail.com
www.alleuroperail.com

We know Europe better! Dedicated to making every travelers trip to Europe unforgettable, All Europe Rail, official European Rail Distributors and Travel Agents, offers a complete line of European travel products including Eurail passes, airline tickets, cars, hotels, tours and more! So don't think twice, contact us and let us help you plan a European backpacking adventure you will never forget! info@alleuroperail.com - 1-866 RAIL-TIX

Busabout Europe
www.busabout.com

Busabout is the hop-on hop-off travel network for the free-spirited independent traveler. Travel to any of the cities, towns or villages on Busabout's 50 city network or use the cheap add-on ferry connections to another 35 destinations. Relax aboard the air-conditioned coach, watch a video, listen to a guide give you the low down on the city, and get dropped off at the door of your hostel. Passes start from $329 for a two-week pass. Purchase passes through STA Travel, Flight Centre, and Travel CUTS.

HOSTELS

Hostels.com
www.hostels.com

Hostels.com lists almost 7,000 hostels worldwide and over 4,000 with online booking. The most comprehensive listing of hostels on the web, the site allows users to find out all about a hostel before booking it. You'll find pictures, descriptions and reviews by guests who have actually stayed there so that you can be sure that you really do want to stay there before you confirm your booking.

Hostelworld.com
www.hostelworld.com

Hostelworld.com provides confirmed reservations at over 3,000 hostels, budget hotels, campsites and guesthouses worldwide. All can be booked online in a matter of minutes and all reservations are guaranteed. As well as Hostelworld.com, you will also find a list of over 200 continent, country and city specific sites. No membership is required to book – all you need is a valid credit card to pay a 10% deposit and a small booking fee.

Trav.com
www.trav.com

Trav.com provides online reservations for all forms of budget accommodation including over 5000 hostels, cheap hotels, holiday apartments, campsites and bed and breakfasts.

What's your story?

Contribute your story for the next publication:

- *Western Europe From a Backpack*
- *Eastern Europe From a Backpack*
- *Italy From a Backpack*
- *Spain From a Backpack*
- *France From a Backpack*
- *Asia From a Backpack*
- *Africa From a Backpack*
- *South America From a Backpack*
- *Australia/New Zealand From a Backpack*

We're looking for first-person must-tell stories … the one story you continue to share with friends. Send us your best backpacking stories from anywhere in the world. If you have a great story from India, China, Italy, Australia, Zimbabwe, Iceland, Chile, or any other country – we're interested in publishing it!

Length: Stories average 1,000-2,000 words. While we will accept stories up to 3,000 words, shorter stories have a better chance of being accepted.

How to submit: Send your story by MS Word attachment to **submit@europebackpack.com** with the following information (on the attachment): name, story title, story location, address, phone, primary e-mail, secondary e-mail, and College or University (if applicable).

Snail mail: Pearson Venture Group, P.O. Box 70525, Seattle, WA 98127-0525

Rights: We're interested in non-exclusive rights. The author retains the copyright and may reprint the story elsewhere.

For the latest information, visit us online:

www.EuropeBackpack.com